Date Due

Music Comes to America

Books by David Ewen

THE UNFINISHED SYMPHONY

FROM BACH TO STRAVINSKY

WINE, WOMEN AND WALTZ

THE MAN WITH THE BATON

COMPOSERS OF TODAY

HEBREW MUSIC

COMPOSERS OF YESTERDAY

TWENTIETH CENTURY COMPOSERS

MEN AND WOMEN WHO MAKE MUSIC (*Revised in 1946*)

PIONEERS IN MUSIC

LIVING MUSICIANS

THE BOOK OF MODERN COMPOSERS

DICTATORS OF THE BATON

THE STORY OF GEORGE GERSHWIN

MUSIC FOR THE MILLIONS

MEN OF POPULAR MUSIC

TALES FROM THE VIENNA WOODS

LISTEN TO THE MOCKING WORDS

HAYDN: A GOOD LIFE

In collaboration with Dr. Frederic Ewen

MUSICAL VIENNA

Music Comes to America

===

DAVID EWEN, 1907-

ALLEN, TOWNE & HEATH, INC.

New York : 1947

First Printing

PRINTED IN THE UNITED STATES OF AMERICA

For Hennie—
AND THE PAST TEN YEARS

Some of the material in this book appeared originally as articles in *The American Mercury, The Baltimore Sun, Etude, Common Ground, Coronet, Decision, Tomorrow,* and *Theatre Arts Monthly.* For permission to reprint this material here—in an amplified and extended form—the author wishes to express his gratitude to these publications.

Contents

PART I: YESTERDAY

PART II: TODAY

PART I : Yesterday

———

"I PITY AMERICANS BECAUSE
THEY HAVE NO LIGHT, NO
SONG IN THEIR LIVES. THEY
ARE BUT CHILDREN IN EVERY-
THING PERTAINING TO ART."

—Chaliapin
1908

CHAPTER ONE

When America
Was Musically Young

T HE ERA following the Civil War was one of great fulfillment and still greater promise. It was an age of expansion. New cities arose, industrialization spread, population increased, speculation became rampant, fortunes were
made almost overnight. These and other symptoms pointed to
the fact that a great country was undergoing growing pains.
America was sprawling out in new directions—into the Far
West, for example, which was now being built up and popu-
lated. A country, seeing growth and development in every phase
of its activity, required more breathing space.

But what of musical activity in America? Was this period of
expansion and development, so rich in promise of every kind,
bringing with it a new age for the musical life of the country as
well?

It was well known that famous European musicians came to
this country to give concerts during the nineteenth century and
returned to Europe with both well-filled purses and strange tales
of American naïveté in music. There could be no denying that
America, in music above everything else, was innocent; she was
awkward and ingenuous and misinformed as only the very

3

young and uneducated can be. She was sublimely oblivious of any standards of artistic excellence. What concerned her most in music seemed to be the obvious, the meretricious, the sensational. A recognition of values had not yet begun to enter into her musical calculations.

Up to the closing decades of the nineteenth century, Americans regarded concerts as but another form of popular entertainment in the class, say, of the minstrel show, the prize fight, and the circus. As a matter of fact, there were many towns in the South and Midwest which believed that an announced concert would be just a novel variety of the minstrel show. It was the grumble of many who came to attend the orchestral concerts of Theodore Thomas (when that brave pioneer first explored regions formerly untouched by musical civilization) that the evening fell flat because there had been no end men and no jokes. They further lamented that the men of the orchestra had even been too lazy to blacken their faces. When Anton Rubinstein visited Memphis, Tennessee, for a recital he, who was generally considered the greatest pianist of the time, was stopped backstage by a helpful stage assistant who advised him to hurry to blacken his face in time for his "show."

It was uniquely appropriate that, when Jenny Lind concertized in America in 1850 (she was the first great singer to tour this country extensively), she should have been under the managerial wing of Phineas Taylor Barnum. It was not for a moment considered bad taste for Barnum to exploit a great artist with the methods used for his circus attractions. He aroused the curiosity of the American public in Jenny Lind's personality by spreading strange and fabulous tales about her virtue and angelic goodness. He inspired awed comments by escorting her from the boat to her hotel in regal splendor: spirited white horses drew her sumptuous carriage. In the evenings he arranged for local singing societies, or firemen bands, to serenade her beneath her window. His flair for igniting the imagination and the enthusiasm of the public for his stellar attraction soon yielded incredible results. Jenny Lind became a vogue, a passion, a disease. Clothing, food, café houses were named after her. Her photographs sold millions of copies. Young women imitated her hair dress and her clothing. Musical numbers were written to praise her charms. And the box office showed commensurate returns. Halls were overcrowded whenever she sang. For her first concert, the tickets were auctioned off at unprecedented prices, the first of which was bought by the New York hatter, Genin, for $225. The crowds came, not to hear a great artist, but to see with their own eyes an apotheosized personality.

Music at the time appealed to American audiences for the very reasons that circuses did. It exploited eccentric personalities. It introduced breath-taking extramusical features. It flaunted unexpected tricks. When it did none of these things, music held no fascination for most of the audiences of the time. Teresa Carreño was publicized throughout the country as "the greatest woman pianist in the world" in much the same manner as the "bearded lady" or the "fattest woman in the world"—not as an artist, but rather as a freak of nature. An infant prodigy of the time, who inspired no end of wonder, was a "Master Marsh" who, at the age of four, was able to play on two drums at one time. Hatton, a pianist highly favored in the middle of the nineteenth century, would appear on the concert stage with a string of sleigh bells fastened to his right leg. When he reached the proper moment in a composition describing a sleigh ride, he would shake his leg; then an assistant on the stage would use an instrument which imitated the cracking of a whip. "And this thing," reported *Dwight's Journal of Music* (December 18, 1852), "aroused a storm of applause which had no end until it was repeated several times *da capo.*"

Volovski, a Polish pianist, toured America with advertisements in which he "guaranteed" to play four hundred notes in one measure; and the singer, De Begnis, offered the attraction of singing six hundred words and three hundred bars of music in four minutes. Leopold de Meyer announced that he could perform on the piano with fists and elbows, even with a cane. Ole Bull, Norway's greatest violinist, expoited the fact that he could play "miraculous" double-stops on a "flattened fiddle-bridge." Some, like the pianist Henri Herz, even tried to lure audiences to the concert hall by announcing some such irrelevant attraction as the fact that his auditorium would be lighted by a thousand candles! The famous bandleader, Patrick S. Gilmore (Sousa's celebrated forerunner), thrilled his public by performing musical compositions that called for bells, anvils, and even actual cannon, the cannon fired by an electric button on the conductor's stand—considered at the time a marvel of engineering. At the Peace Jubilee concerts of 1869, a performance of the *Anvil Chorus* by Verdi recruited the services of fifty red-shirted firemen who contributed to the sonorities of the orchestra by striking on anvils. George William Curtis wrote that in 1862 the musical tastes of the time "reached an apogee" with *The Battle of Prague,* a cacophonous composition for tin pans written many years earlier. This composition, arranged for piano, was a war horse of many amateur pianists.

No wonder, then, that in such a bizarre setting the eccentric French-English conductor, Jullien, should have scored a sensation in 1853. He was America's musician-of-the-hour. His antics delighted America's love for the strange and the unexpected. When he conducted, he had behind him an ornately decorated velvet chair resembling a throne; into this he would sometimes sink with exhaustion at the completion of a musical number. There seemed no limit to the extravagances of his ideas. When he conducted one of his own quadrilles, he would (at a climactic moment) seize the concertmaster's violin and bow or, on other occasions, tear a piccolo from the breast pocket of his velvet jacket. Then, swaying elaborately and accompanying the ecstatic motions of his body with exaggerated grimaces of his face, he would play with the orchestra. Before he conducted music by Beethoven, he would have a pair of kid gloves brought to him ceremoniously on a gold platter. In front of the eyes of the audience, he would put on these gloves and with great dignity proceed to direct the music. For other important works he used a special jeweled baton.

He would frequently perform excellent music: movements from symphonies by Beethoven, Mozart, and even Mendelssohn. But what took America by storm was a rendition of a piece called *The Fireman's Quadrille*. The composition began serenely enough with the strings. Suddenly, from off the stage, the clang of fire bells was heard. An ingenious stage effect simulated fire. Firemen in full regulation attire rushed on the stage with fire hose, pouring actual water on the stage fire. Then, when the fire was extinguished, the firemen ceremoniously left the stage. The music, which had been proceeding undisturbed throughout the entire exhibition, now reached a feverish climax which, sometimes literally, threw the audience into a frenzy. For many years thereafter orchestras and bands throughout the country attempted to emulate Jullien's success by performing *The Fireman's Quadrille*, not quite so elaborately as Jullien, but, nevertheless, with firemen in full uniform parading up and down the stage.

Sometimes accident helped to provide American concert audi-

ences with unexpected thrills| At one of the concerts of the cele-
brated Hungarian violinist, Reményi (American audiences
were particularly partial to Reményi because of his fiddle acrobatics), he amazed his audience by apparently drawing a clear
note in crescendo from his violin at the same time that he was
going through the intricacies of a solo violin transcription of the
funeral music from Handel's *Saul*. How he could draw this pure,
clear tone uninterrupted, while his hands were involved in technical intricacies, was a mystery to fascinate a nineteenth-century audience in America. At the end of the performance the
audience deliriously acclaimed the violinist. It might be added
that this feat bewildered even Reményi himself until, going
backstage, he discovered that during the performance someone
had gone to the pipe organ and had maliciously sounded the
single sustained note throughout his entire performance.

Besides revealing an insatiable appetite for the sensational,
American music audiences also disclosed a particular weak-
ness for musical entertainment built on grandiose lines. The
bigger the musical project, the better it was appreciated. Recitals by a single artist did not go well. Americans liked variety;
they enjoyed a program that featured numerous artists. A concert of sixteen pianists on eight pianos was more likely to appeal
than a recital by a single pianist, even if the pianist happened
to be a world-famous artist. Concerts featuring a varied group
of artists, supplemented frequently by a chorus and an orchestra,
were preferred by Americans to an evening of chamber music.
Often these concerts, which enlisted the services of a variety of
artists, provided strange collaborations. At one concert, for example, Henri Vieuxtemps, Belgium's greatest violinist, appeared on the same program with a concertina artist who

delighted his public by crushing his instrument on his nose or forehead.

Americans particularly liked concerts by mammoth orchestras and Gargantuan choruses. A favored entertainment of the time would be, say, a combination of a band with a major symphony orchestra in the performance of some well-known orchestral piece. The fact that each could have given a better account of itself independently did not disturb the listeners, who were more interested in size, and in massive size, than in the quality of the performance. Thus they went in for festivals with zest —not because these festivals featured unusual choral and symphonic music but, more especially, because they utilized forces of tremendous size. There were such established festivals as those in Worcester, Oberlin, and Cincinnati which, at regular intervals (either annually or biannually), presented a cycle of grand-scale performances of symphonies and oratorios. In many western sections of the country all the musical activity would find its annual culmination in festival performances recruiting the orchestras and choruses of several different localities. Sometimes musicians would draw the limelight of attention upon themselves by arranging special festivals, as Gilmore did when he created the "Great Beethoven Centennial Jubilee" and as Theodore Thomas and Leopold Damrosch did after him. Sometimes special occasions brought forth the creation of festive musical celebrations, as the Peace Jubilee in Boston in 1869 and 1872 and the Chicago World's Fair, dedicated musically on October 22, 1892.

These festivals invariably called for unwieldy forces. At the Chicago World's Fair the fact that Theodore Thomas was to conduct "the largest orchestra ever to assemble on one stage" was the magnet used to draw in the audiences. At the Peace

Jubilee of 1869 a chorus of 10,000 voices was joined by an orchestra of 1,000. Johann Strauss II, coming to this country for the first time to assist at the Jubilee of 1872, was an attraction not only because his waltzes were known in practically every American household, but more especially because—catering to the tastes of the time—he conducted a fabulous army of singers and orchestra players. His own description of the affair is enlightening:

On the musicians' tribune there were twenty thousand singers; in front of them the members of the orchestra—and these were the people I was to conduct. A hundred assistant conductors had been placed at my disposal to control these gigantic masses, but I was only able to recognize those nearest to me, and although we had rehearsals there was no possibility of giving an artistic performance, a proper production. . . . Now just conceive of my position face to face with a public of four hundred thousand Americans. There I stood at the raised desk, high above all the others. How would the business start, how would it end? Suddenly a cannon-shot rang out, a gentle hint for us twenty thousand to begin playing *The Blue Danube*. I gave the signal, my hundred assistant conductors followed me as quickly and as well as they could and then there broke out an unholy row such as I shall never forget. As we had begun more or less simultaneously, I concentrated my whole attention on seeing that we should finish together too! Thank Heaven, I managed even that. It was all that was humanly possible. The hundred thousand mouths in the audience roared applause and I breathed a sigh of relief when I found myself in fresh air again and felt the firm ground beneath my feet.

Such festivals, developed along prodigious outlines, dramatized music for Americans through means they could best understand and appreciate: display, and the impressiveness of sheer size.

Audiences which found attraction in garish spectacles, fabulous-sized choruses and orchestras, and circus showmanship when they listened to music, could not be expected to reveal particularly discriminating tastes. Concerts in America, for the most part, could not be said to have been poised on a particularly high level of artistic attainment. There were notable exceptions, to be sure. When a Hans von Bülow essayed a cycle of Beethoven sonatas, when an Anton Rubinstein undertook a monumental cycle of concerts tracing the history of piano music, when a Boston Symphony Orchestra or a Chicago Orchestra gave a performance, when an Anton Seidl directed a Wagnerian performance at the Metropolitan—at such times there was memorable music making to please the most fastidious demands. But these performances, which reached for and achieved the highest standards, were the exception rather than the rule in nineteenth-century America. More generally, orchestral concerts (except for those by the Boston and Chicago orchestras) were forced to include dance music along with movements from the symphonies. Chamber-music organizations included light salon pieces and transcriptions of everyday favorites as companions to an occasional masterpiece. Artists—often the very great—had to compromise with their consciences and cater to popular taste.

Henri Vieuxtemps frequently included on his American recital programs such popular American pieces as *The Arkansas Traveler* and *Money Musk*. Both Wilhelmj and Anton Rubinstein performed extensively their own variations on *Yankee Doodle*. (Paderewski, too, began the composition of variations on *Yankee Doodle* during his first American tour.) Thalberg, Liszt's rival, scored his greatest successes in America with his meretricious opera fantasies which exploited his phenomenal technique; sometimes his programs in America comprised no other compositions than his transcriptions and potpourris. Wieniawski would play *The Carnival of Venice* and paraphrases of Irish ditties. Singers, even the best of them, had to build their programs around such perennial favorites as *Home, Sweet Home, Comin' Through the Rye,* and the like. Ole Bull invariably included on his program *The Mother's Prayer* and *The Carnival of Venice* or his own flashy variations on national anthems. Even a sound musician like William Mason was sometimes compelled to appeal to his audiences by the trick of playing *Old Hundredth* with one hand and *Yankee Doodle* with the other.

Misinformation went hand in hand with lack of taste. Many were the stories told by European musicians about our simplicity and ignorance! When Theodore Thomas and his orchestra visited St. Louis, one of his devoted admirers begged him to play something in a lighter vein, "say, something by Palestrina" —without realizing that he had chosen one of the most complicated choral composers of all time. When the Mendelssohn Quintet toured the country, it was frequently asked by music lovers which one of them was the famous Mr. Felix Mendelssohn. When a concert pianist informed a Midwestern music lover that he had just performed Beethoven's Sonata, Opus 2, No. 1, the latter gushed: "Oh, how wonderful! I just love opuses!"

Even so-called adjudicators of the musical art seemed hardly better informed. In Keokuk, Iowa, Theodore Thomas conducted a program including the *Tannhäuser Overture* of Wagner, the second movement from Beethoven's Fifth Symphony and Weber's *Invitation to the Dance,* the last named in an adaptation for orchestra by Hector Berlioz. The legend "adapted for orchestra by Berlioz" was printed on the program in parentheses beneath the Weber title. But the critic of Keokuk interpreted the legend as applying to all three compositions. His printed commentary the following morning is surely one of the classics of early American music criticism. "The first piece," he wrote with cool self-assurance, "was that fine trilogy which Hector Berlioz with exquisite art made from Wagner, Beethoven, and Weber. The thought of Hector Berlioz, evidently, in arranging the trilogy was to put after the passionate action of the one, the ocean-like, star-like, measureless calm of the symphony. After you have bathed in that luxury and languor long enough, there comes von Weber's *Invitation to the Dance*. Oh, there has been nothing heard in Keokuk like this trilogy."

There was only a limited audience for good music, presented with dignity and self-respect. An artist like Paderewski or Anton Rubinstein or Eugène Ysaÿe could maintain his artistic integrity in his American concerts because he could depend upon his electrifying personality to draw the audiences into the concert halls and keep them there. But less sensational artists had to struggle for an audience. Good attendance in a concert hall of moderate size was not a frequent experience for the serious artist. The Kneisel Quartet for many years consistently played in half-empty halls because they would not perform light or flashy numbers. A Denver critic emphasized the apathy of the music public to serious music when (following a concert by the Leopold Damrosch orchestra with Teresa Carreño as soloist, in 1883) he wrote bitterly: "If Mr. Damrosch had announced an opus from *Brittle Silver,* the Denver public would have thronged to hear. . . . The truth is that, having been educated up to the *Brittle Silver* standard, our Denver folk are chary of descending to the level of Beethoven."

There were always wails and lamentations voiced by Americans when musicians adhered to a comparatively high standard of artistry. Letters were sent to the newspapers by irate concertgoers complaining that Rubinstein so infrequently injected a popular note in his concerts. In Chicago, Theodore Thomas suffered abuse and criticism because he did not consider the tastes of his public in fashioning his programs. The Kneisel Quartet was incessantly reproved for making its concerts so esoteric that only a handful would care to attend.

There were audiences for opera. But it cannot be said that these audiences were much more discriminating. The golden age of opera in America, which began in the 1890's, brought together on the stage of the Metropolitan Opera House the greatest assemblage of voices in the history of operatic performances. Yet it was well known that, though New Yorkers were supposedly "opera mad," and though they made a fetish of the opera star, they did not always show discernment in their tastes.

Big names were worshiped. It was the singer, not the song, that was of consequence. "What is playing tonight at the Met?" was never the question posed by the opera lover; only, "Who is singing tonight at the Met?" The fact that, despite individual brilliant performances, opera presentations were generally slipshod (no attention was ever paid by the director to the casting of minor roles; besides, the great stars often refused to attend a single rehearsal, thereby making it virtually impossible for the conductor to achieve a coordinated performance) mattered little. What did matter was that a great star was performing; and the audience came to worship at his (or her) feet.

The Metropolitan Opera House was built, as is well known, not from artistic necessity, but because there had not been enough boxes at the old Academy of Music to pass around among the socially élite. The socialites at the Metropolitan always reacted to their opera as if it were a social, rather than a musical, function. Throughout performances at the Metropolitan there was so much conversation that, in 1891, the management was compelled to post notices in every box entreating its occupants to be silent while the music was in progress. The story goes that a society lady known particularly for her insistence on gossiping throughout an opera performance, once invited a casual acquaintance to a presentation of *Tristan*. "I should very much like to come," answered the acquaintance. "You see, I have never heard you in *Tristan*."

Opera goers were guilty of bad taste as well as bad manners. At one time the socialites insisted that the Metropolitan present the third act of Wagner's *Die Meistersinger* before the first because (so they said) "it was the only act of the opera that had real music in it," and most box holders were out of the opera house by the third act. One society lady wrote to the director of the Metropolitan in all seriousness asking that the *Celeste Aida* aria be transferred from the first act to the second because she was habitually late and missed it. Some of the more sensitive socialites also objected to dark scenes on the stage because they were depressing. They made their objections felt so strongly that the stage manager at the Metropolitan was compelled to present many somber scenes in full light. The incongruity of having Florestan in *Fidelio* exclaiming: "God, how dark it is here!" on a stage bathed in light never seemed to trouble very many.

"Ah, these Americans," European musicians would say, "they were never meant for good music." Or else they would comment sadly: "When it comes to art, they are like little children." Or, like Ferdinand Hiller, they might be apologetic. "I fear that you are sometimes too gigantic. It is a natural fault in a

young nation that likes to do vast things." Or they would be
severely critical, as Vincent d'Indy was, when he said: "Americans simply have no discrimination between good or bad." Or,
worst of all, they would become devastatingly vituperative, in
the vein of the Viennese dance king, Joseph Gung'l, who, seeing the state of musical culture in America firsthand, could only
become bitter.

CHAPTER TWO

America's Musical Pioneers

═══

B<small>UT THERE</small> was another, and happier, aspect of the age. For it was an age of musical pioneers working against discouragement and frustration to create a consciousness for good music in America. Without traditions to work for them, they labored in the thankless roles of the nation's music teachers, the builders of a nation's music institutions, the organizers of a nation's music audiences. The results were not at first clearly perceptible—and most certainly not to the visitor from abroad; they were not to become visible to the casual eye for some time to come. But, though unrecognized for the most part, these pioneers were exerting a far-reaching influence on every phase of musical life in America. In the vanguard of this band of pioneers stood Theodore Thomas, perhaps the greatest single influence in the development of the American symphony orchestra.

There had been orchestras in America before Theodore Thomas appeared on the scene. Colonial days had seen small orchestras to accompany the "ballad opera." Then there were orchestras to assist choral groups in the performance of such

17

works as *The Creation* and *Messiah*. Finally there appeared small orchestras expressly for instrumental music.

Boston might be said to have been the cradle of symphonic music in America. There, in 1810, Gottlieb Graupner gathered a few musical friends at his home to try out some Haydn symphonies; thus a Philharmonic Society was born. Ten years later an orchestra was organized in Philadelphia, that of the Musical Fund Society, which at its initial concert (April 24, 1821) gave the first American performance of a Beethoven symphony (the First, in C major). So that this symphony would be a bit less formidable to the audience, it was interrupted after each movement to permit the rendition of light vocal and solo numbers. In 1823 still another orchestra came into being in Boston—that of the Academy of Music founded by Lowell Mason and James George Webb, destined to play a rich role in the early musical life of that city. Meanwhile several different orchestras had come and gone in New York. It has been recorded that the first performance of a Haydn symphony in New York inspired the enraged audience to bombard the orchestra men with eggs and vegetables as they noisily demanded the substitution of *Yankee Doodle* or something equally appealing to their musical tastes. Orchestral music had so little appeal that, in New York, one summer series had to resort to the bribe of free ice cream to attract audiences.

Such orchestral music as there was, was not much to speak of. For one thing, it was rare to find a fully equipped orchestra. The Euterpe Orchestra in New York, for example, functioned without a bassoon because there simply was no bassoonist in New York. As one visiting German musician wrote in a communication to the Mainz music journal *Caecilia,* American orchestras, in the early part of the nineteenth century, were "bad, as bad as it is possible to imagine, and incomplete. Sometimes they have two clarinets, which is a great deal; sometimes there is only one first instrument. Of bassoons, oboes, trumpets, and kettledrums one never sees a sight. Oboes are totally unknown in this country. Only one oboist exists in North America and he is said to live in Baltimore." The original orchestration of every composer, therefore, was strangely reshuffled to conceal the absence of essential instruments in the performing orchestra.

Besides this, orchestral concerts were never carefully rehearsed; they were a weird amalgamation of the accurate with the inaccurate. The wishes of the composer were rarely adhered to; no violation was considered too serious to be tolerated. There is on record, for example, a New York performance of Beethoven's *Eroica* Symphony by an "orchestra" numbering seven instruments!

A complete, important, artistically satisfying symphony orchestra in America did not become a reality until the Philharmonic Society was founded in New York. Though the date of the founding of the New York Philharmonic is given as 1842, it actually took place some years earlier. In the summer of 1836 two American musicians were traveling to Europe aboard the packet boat *St. James*. One of these was Ureli Corelli Hill, then thirty-four years old, on his way to Cassel to study the violin with Spohr. The other was Anthony Reiff, Sr., en route to Germany to visit his grandfather. Hill was a violinist who had previously held numerous orchestral posts and who, as conductor of the New York Sacred Music Society, had given in 1831 the first complete New York performance of Handel's *Messiah*. He was, as Krehbiel pointed out, of the stuff of which true pioneers are made: "Yankee 'push,' energy, enthusiasm, industry, pluck, self-reliance and endurance were all present in the composition of Hill's character. . . . He could plan and could organize. Obstacles held no terror for him; he thought that patience and industry would surmount them. . . . He was continually looking for new fields to conquer." Anthony Reiff, Sr., was a well-known New York musician, a tenor with the St. Patrick's Cathedral choir, and a professor of music at the Blind Institute. He was a high-minded musician, idealistic and visionary.

During the seventeen-day journey these two musicians found much to talk of. One of their pet topics was the sorry state of orchestral music in America. It was during this trip that the idea of the Philharmonic first germinated—and it germinated not only with Hill (generally credited with being the father of this orchestra) but also with Reiff (who has never received the recognition he deserves in this direction). They decided that when Hill's studies ended in Germany they would meet in New York and make tangible plans for forming an orchestra. They both had many musical friends and much influence in New York. Together they combined the perseverance, energy, and high idealism which were essential to the launching of such a formidable undertaking. Concerning the orchestra they had in mind, they were clear on two specific points: It would be a large and complete orchestra, numbering more than fifty members, the size necessary to do full justice to the symphonic repertory. It would also concern itself only with the best in music, without attempting to cater to plebeian tastes. It would, once and for all, dispel the general belief held by so many American musicians that an entire concert devoted exclusively to good orchestral music would never find an audience in America.

Obviously, this talk about an orchestra, which helped to pass away the tedious hours of the voyage, was not forgotten by Hill. Two years later he was back in America, and in the fall of 1839 he got in touch with Reiff in New York and reminded him of their plans. With several other New York musicians, they further discussed the project at Windust's tavern, *Shakespeare,* in downtown New York. Another meeting was held at Hill's home, when a committee was drawn up. At a later meeting, Hill was appointed president and Reiff, vice president.

It took more than two years for the orchestra to outgrow embryonic plans and to develop into a living organism. No doubt these were years of heartache and despair for both Hill and Reiff who, time and again, must have seen their plans suddenly crumble to dust. Now it seemed impossible to get suitable reed players; now a sizable representation of the orchestra wanted to withdraw from the venture because it was, after all, impracticable. But, fortunately, Hill had tenacity and stubbornness; Reiff, enthusiasm and vision. With such a collaboration it was impossible to know permanent defeat.

At last, in April, 1842, a final meeting was called at the Apollo Rooms at 410 Broadway to draw up the concrete plans for forming "a society of professional musicians residing in the city, having for its object the advancement of instrumental music, and the performance of a number of concerts each year, to be of a higher order than anything that has been given in the city." Not even the most optimistic of the musicians who drew up these plans had hopes of immediate success: at best, these musicians knew, the public for good symphonic music in New York was a restricted one. And they probably would have expected the millennium sooner than they would have expected their frail offspring ever to achieve the mature age of a century!

It is amusing to notice that when the first rehearsal took place at the Apollo Rooms the owner of the hall had such little faith in the permanency of the orchestra that he demanded his rental fee *before* each rehearsal. The men were compelled to contribute twenty-five cents each as soon as they entered the rooms, to pay for the rental of the auditorium.

At last the first concert—on the evening of December 7, 1842, one of three performances planned for that first season! Three different conductors officiated over a program that included the Beethoven Fifth Symphony.[1] During the first ten years of the orchestra's existence, each concert was directed sometimes by two, often by three different conductors. For the sake of economy, those of the musicians who did not own dress clothes were permitted to wear frock coat, cravat, and dark trousers. Also for the sake of economy, the ushers were members of the orchestra, "selected by the governors because of their appearance and address." Wearing white gloves, each holding a long slender rod as symbol of his office, they escorted the subscribers to their places on the long pew benches. Then, hurriedly, they ascended the stage to their allotted places. All the musicians (except the cellists) performed standing.

For the next sixteen years, the Philharmonic Society presented four concerts a season. The orchestra was organized on a cooperative basis in which each musician contributed during the first season $25 into the general treasury and thereafter shared the profits, musicians and conductors sharing equally. The first season yielded $1,854 in receipts, bringing to each musician a profit of $25. The highest financial mark of this period was reached in the fifteenth season when the orchestra's income of $4,810 made it possible to give $143 to each man.

Meanwhile, America was to become more intimately acquainted with orchestral music through the tours of two European orchestras. In 1848 the Germania Orchestra of twenty-four musicians arrived for an extensive tour. Their plans were almost aborted when, after their first twenty concerts in New

[1] This was *not* the first American performance of the Beethoven Fifth Symphony, despite the contention of commemorative articles on the Philharmonic during its centenary season. The American première of this symphony took place on February 10, 1841, at the Boston Academy of Music.

York and Brooklyn, the meager attendance almost compelled
the orchestra to disband for lack of funds. The generosity of the
New York Philharmonic and that of several other local musicians, who arranged a benefit concert on behalf of the visiting
orchestra, made it possible for the tour to continue. The orchestra limped on to Philadelphia where, at one of the concerts,
the total box-office receipts were $9.50. But, come what may,
the Germania Orchestra was determined to continue its march.
In Baltimore and Washington it met a comparatively responsive
public. Finally, in Boston, the long-dreamed-of miracle took
place: the house was crowded, and it greeted the performance
of the orchestra with enthusiasm. From then on, the orchestra
was more or less successful; and it brought music to localities
which had never before heard an orchestra.

As was customary with most orchestras at that time, the Germania presented good music with the bad, popular with the
serious, profound with the sensational. It injected a popular
note with waltzes, polkas, and quadrilles; but it also performed
the symphonies of Haydn, Mozart, and Beethoven—many of
them being heard for the first time in this country. It was quite
prepared to keep in step with the times by including on its programs a novelty called *The Railroad Gallop*, in which, during
the actual performance of the music, a toy locomotive was made
to run in a circle on the stage, puffing smoke. But whether it
played good music or bad, its influence was significant. When
the orchestra finally disbanded, its service to this country had
been performed with distinction. It had provided the first important contact that many American cities had had with orchestral music.

Even disbanded, the Germania Orchestra was to promote
the interests of good music in America. Many of its members
settled here permanently and became part and parcel of our

musical activity, enriching our musical culture with their
pioneer labors. These men included Carl Bergmann (later to be
a conductor of the New York Philharmonic), Carl Zerrahn (soon
to become one of the major musical figures in Boston), William
Schultze (subsequently to join the Mendelssohn Quintet, and
after that to become professor of music at Syracuse University),
Carl Lentz and Henry Ahner (destined to become important
conductors in Philadelphia and Chicago, respectively).

The second orchestra to tour America came in 1853 under
the leadership of the eccentric and unpredictable Jullien.
Jullien, for all his nonsense, brought a standard of performance
to America which it had not previously known. He combined
with his charlatanism a fine musical sense, as well as a splendid
capacity for directing an orchestra which brought from his
organization a fire and zest and integration of performance that
proved a new musical experience for the ears of American music
lovers. This showmanship and fine musicianship were responsible for creating a more intense interest in good orchestral
music.

And in doing this he prepared the way for Theodore Thomas.

Temperamentally Theodore Thomas was uniquely equipped
for the task he had set for himself—that of educating a young
and uninformed country to a good musical life. He was the idealist who could never lose sight of the goal he had set for himself.
Yet with his idealism was blended a sound practical sense that
could make temporary concessions and yield to momentary
expedience. Had his artistic integrity been inflexible, the times
would have crucified him. But he was fortunately made of
resilient fiber, able to bend with the time and the place; still he
was of sufficient firmness in texture to remain unbroken.

There were times when he could be intransigent. When he

played music from *Tristan* for the first time in America to a singularly apathetic audience, he said defiantly: "I will keep on playing it until they *do* like it!" When asked why he insisted upon playing so many works which, because of their complexity, were distasteful to his audiences, he would answer with simplicity: "If there is but one person in the audience who takes pleasure in my music, then I have fulfilled my mission." And yet, born teacher that he was, he knew well that nothing could be accomplished if he were not willing to cater at least partially to his public. He used to say that you cannot possibly educate music audiences if they do not, in the first place, come to your concerts. If dance or salon music brought the audiences, well, he would play such trifles—but between individual movements of symphonies. If Americans liked showmanship and novelty, he would provide that—as when, in performing a polka in the open-air Terrace Garden in New York, he had two flutists concealed in the trees perform the work. But at the same time he would not forget his mission. He would not forget that if he was ready to descend a few steps toward the level of his audiences they must be made to rise a few steps toward his own.

His flexibility, his patience, his sincerity, and his passionate love for music, all these made him the ideal teacher for which America at the time was in such sad need. These—and his ever-present conviction that he simply could not fail, his ever-unshakable faith in the ultimate intelligence and taste of the American music lover. "I have gone without food," he said, "and I have walked when I could not afford to ride. I have played when my hands were cold. But I will succeed, for I shall never give up my belief that at last the people will come to me, and my concerts will be crowded. I have undying faith in the latent musical appreciation of the American people."

Theodore Thomas arrived in New York from Germany on a

hot July day in 1845 (he was ten years old at the time) with
little more baggage than the clothes he wore on his back and the
violin he held tightly under his arm. Before he had been very
long in America, that violin was to earn for its owner his keep.
Theodore played wherever there was a coin to be earned: in
saloons and theaters, at weddings or funerals. Then he undertook a concert tour of the South. It was largely a one-man affair.
Theodore was his own manager. He would draw his own posters
and handbills, which he personally distributed. He would stand
at the door to collect the fee for admission. Then, changing his
clothing hurriedly from that of a doorman to that of a concert
artist, he would finish the job by giving his concert.

After that, other engagements kept him and his violin busy.
When Jullien brought his orchestra to America, Thomas was
given a post as first violinist. This was his first contact with
good orchestral music, and the adventure exhilarated him and
changed the entire course of his life. From this time on he was
to turn more and more sharply to good music, for both himself
and his audiences. With William Mason he organized chamber-
music concerts in New York, a venture which fought desperately
against the apathy of the times to good music. He was appointed
concertmaster of the orchestra at the New York Academy of
Music. There, in 1858, he made his debut with the baton. The
indisposition of the regular conductor brought Thomas at the
dramatic last moment to the conductor's platform for a performance of *La Juive*. He had never before seen the score of the
opera, and yet he conducted with such competence and authority that he was soon afterward appointed permanent conductor.

Once he felt the baton in his fingers, he knew that the violin
would never again satisfy him. Besides, he realized that with the
baton he could be a force for spreading the love of good music

throughout America, much more effectively than he could with his violin. "I decided," he said, "to devote my energies to the cultivation of public taste in music. What the country needed most of all to make it musical was a good orchestra. The New York Philharmonic with a body of sixty players and five yearly subscription concerts was the only organized orchestra which presented orchestral literature in this large country."

In 1864 Thomas called a meeting of several leading New York musicians for the purpose of organizing a new orchestra. The result was several series of concerts in New York during the next few years—both at the concert halls in the winter and in the public parks during the summer—in which Thomas conducted programs of relatively light music. He was interested in building audiences for his concerts; education would come later.

By 1869 he had organized his orchestra on a permanent basis, so that the men might devote themselves exclusively to their work in the orchestra. Achieving this, he was able to bring to realization a long-cherished vision. He would travel with his orchestra throughout the country, to cities and towns which had never before heard a symphony concert. He would bring good music where good music was a foreign product. Thus began the famous "Thomas Road" which stretched from one end of the country to the other—paved with good music.

Varied was the response to this first strange contact with good music! In one city a leading citizen congratulated Thomas on his phenomenal success in making the first violinists turn the pages of their music simultaneously. In another city the papers commented that "the concert last night was the greatest orchestral circus the city has ever seen." In New Orleans one of the numbers on Thomas's program—Schumann's *Träumerei* —so caught the fancy of the public that it became a "hit"; people hummed it in the streets and whistled its strains in calling one another. In Utah it was suggested to Thomas that he include wedding marches on his programs, since that city was partial to that form of music. In one western town, a cowboy entertained himself, during a performance of Beethoven's Fifth Symphony, by chewing tobacco and aiming his spit at the bald spot of a bass player. In another town the floor was cleared after the concert because it was thought that the orchestra would play dance music as well.

Thomas had to introduce discipline among his audiences, who, in contact with orchestral music for the first time, simply did not know how to behave. At one of his concerts a young man was scratching matches in an attempt to light a cigar during the playing of a movement from Beethoven's Eighth Symphony. Quietly, Thomas gave the signal to his orchestra to stop playing, put his baton down gently on his stand, and turning around said to the young man softly: "Please do not mind *us*, sir. We can all wait till you have lighted your cigar." He would make it a practice to stop the music he was conducting, even in the middle of a phrase, if he was disturbed by whispering voices. On one occasion he interrupted a performance of some Mendelssohn music with a long and thunderous drum roll; then he turned around to fix his burning eyes on the offenders. At one time, when the music was suddenly stopped by Thomas in midstream, the shrill voice of a lady seated in a front row could clearly be heard piercing the sudden silence: "And I find it tastes *so* much better fried in butter!"

Thomas had to compel his audiences to listen to good music —particularly to good music by modern composers. He brushed aside criticism, antagonism, opposition, in his determination to bring his audiences into contact with the best in music. Once in New York there was such bitter opposition to his frequent performances of complex new musical works that the audience noisily interfered with a presentation of Liszt's *Mephisto Waltz.* Savagely, Thomas took a watch out of his pocket and announced that he would wait exactly five minutes for all objectors to this music to leave the hall; after that time he would perform the music regardless of the attitude of the audience. A death-like silence followed, in which the Liszt music was listened to respectfully.

For almost twenty years Thomas traveled with his orchestra, persistent in his efforts to propagandize the cause of good music. He refused to recognize the meaning of discouragement; his patience was infinite. Eventually, as he himself noted with real satisfaction, "people all over the country were beginning to acquire a definite taste for good music," even though "they had not yet learned to be discriminating." Discrimination, he felt, would come in time; the important thing was that people had been trained to come to concerts and to listen to good music attentively.

His achievements were many and varied, vibrantly affecting the musical life of the country. The visits of his orchestra inspired many cities to establish symphonic groups of their own. In St. Louis, Cincinnati, Pittsburgh, and other cities, local musicians were encouraged (by the response given to Thomas's concerts) to organize orchestral ventures of their own in their respective communities.

In New York, Thomas's assumption of the conductorial post of the New York Philharmonic for intermittent periods between 1877 and 1891 succeeded in rescuing the orchestra from its financial insecurity. Before he came to conduct the Philharmonic, the receipts were sometimes as low as $841 for a season, and the quality of the performances was sometimes as low as the income. Under him, both programs and box office saw a return to health. The average draw of a season when Thomas conducted was $15,000, while his programs brought new vitality and distinction to the musical proceedings.

It may be said that it was largely as a result of his work that America's first subsidized orchestras came into existence. For many years Thomas had visited Boston and enjoyed there a great following. Thus he set the stage for the emergence of a major Boston orchestra by creating new and greater audiences capable of supporting such a venture. The Boston banker, Civil War veteran, and music lover, Henry Lee Higginson (who had studied music in Vienna and had listened to the concerts of the glorious Vienna Philharmonic), provided a guarantee fund of one million dollars with which to finance an orchestra in Boston conforming to the highest European standards. In 1881, therefore, the first subsidized American orchestra came into being. It was the first orchestra in America that was not compelled to depend for its existence upon the volatile moods of audiences; it was also the first orchestra able to provide a living wage to its musicians, making it possible for them to devote themselves to the work of the orchestra almost exclusively. The annual budget of the new orchestra was to be $100,000. The budgets of other symphony orchestras in America were strikingly lower—the New York Symphony, for example, had only $17,000!

But Thomas was even more directly responsible for the birth of the second of America's subsidized orchestras. In 1891 a group of influential Chicago businessmen, headed by Charles Norman Fay and Marshall Field, urged Thomas (who had visited the city with his orchestra over a period of two decades) to organize a symphony orchestra in their city. They were prepared to give such an orchestra sound and permanent financial backing and to relinquish to Thomas the artistic control of the organization. Chicago had had orchestras before this time. Another valiant pioneer, Hans Balatka, had been conducting orchestral concerts over a period of many years, and he was the first to introduce many Beethoven symphonies in that city. But a permanently subsidized orchestra, assured of its existence regardless of the public response, was, of course, unknown. This was the dream which the Chicago financiers were ready to bring to reality if Thomas consented to come.

The offer was too good to be refused. Thomas imported sixty-nine of his own men to Chicago and added to this number thirty Chicago musicians. The first concert of the new Chicago Orchestra took place at the Auditorium on October 7, 1891, with Beethoven's Fifth Symphony as the major work on the program.

For the remainder of his life, Thomas served as conductor of the Chicago Orchestra, establishing an artistic program that could be equaled only by the Boston Symphony. From the very first, he strove for the highest standards. At his second concert, he presented major works by Bach, Gluck, Schumann, Tchaikovsky, and Wagner. On the third program appeared two symphonies. The fourth concert consisted of the Schubert C major Symphony and excerpts from the Wagner music dramas. Thomas felt that the day when he had to pamper an audience was over.

There was dissatisfaction among the audiences that came to his concerts. The programs, they felt, were too severe. As one Chicago critic commented acidly: "If it be desirable to educate the 'masses' to a liking for any certain style of music, sound policy dictates that some effective means be adopted for bringing the 'masses' aforesaid within the reach of the educative influences and that the uniform and exclusive offering of what they will not tolerate is hardly to be reckoned among effective means. Mr. Thomas and his advisers seem to think otherwise, and if the Orchestral Association members are willing for their own gratification to pay the cost of what has been given them, nobody else has the right to object."

The first season showed a deficit of $53,000, as Chicago audiences refused to respond to the type of concert offered them by Thomas. But the backers did not grumble. Quietly they paid the deficit, and refused to interfere with Thomas's plans. The second season showed another $50,000 deficit. Eventually, Thomas wore down the resistance of his public. He made only slight compromises such as reducing the number of symphonies played each year and substituting some shorter numbers. But, except for this concession, he adhered to his mission. The works of modern composers—many of them new to Chicago—together with the best classical literature, persistently found a place on his programs. His concerts began to appeal more and more strongly, until the deficits were sharply reduced. By the end of the sixth season the sponsors of the orchestra had to provide only $27,000.

One other achievement of major proportions belonged to Theodore Thomas. He founded and established the Cincinnati Music Festival, the most significant musical event in the country during the closing decades of the nineteenth century. Finding splendid choruses in Cincinnati during his periodic visits to that city, he decided to combine all the musical facilities into a mammoth musical venture. In May, 1873, he directed the first of these festivals. This proved so successful that a second festival was presented two years later. By 1878 the festival had achieved such importance that a special, handsome auditorium was built in which to house it properly. After the third festival, the concerts showed a net profit of $32,000. Thomas continued conducting the festivals in Cincinnati up to the time of his death, and he was responsible for the eloquent realization of its lofty aims.

And in all his concerts everywhere—in Chicago, in Cincinnati, in New York, and on tour (for he even continued his travels with the Chicago Orchestra, always breaking new ground)—he introduced musical masterpieces which were then unknown to Americans, but which were already classics in Europe—music traversing the entire expanse of musical history from Bach to the American composer, music which, but for him, might have waited indefinitely for a hearing. The suites of Bach; the piano concertos of Beethoven; symphonies by Brahms, Bruckner, Haydn, Mozart, Schubert, Sibelius; tone poems by Liszt and Richard Strauss; various works by Berlioz, Dvořák, César Franck, Rimsky-Korsakoff, Schumann, and Smetana. . . .

It may be that—as some of his friends have written—Thomas might have become a great violinist, one of the greatest, if he had never exchanged his violin for a baton. It may also be, as his contemporaries have said, that he was a great conductor— magnetic when he stood in front of his men and audiences; sincere, self-effacing, scholarly, and motivated only by the highest artistic interests when he approached a musical work for performance. But his name lives not because of his attainments as an interpreter. There have been many great musical interpreters in America, but only one Theodore Thomas. His name lives because he was an unyielding force for good in American music, because in more ways than one he left a permanent impression on America's musical life.

The New York Times admirably summed up his influence when, on his death in 1905, it ran the following editorial as an obituary:

It is hard to estimate the debt that this country owes to Theodore Thomas. It is the debt of a pupil to a teacher; it is the debt of a people led out of the wilderness to the prophet who has shown them a sight of the promised land. . . . To an amazing persistency in the face of repeated discouragement and piled-up difficulties he joined the fine and catholic taste, and most of all, the willingness to make his propaganda gradually, that were precisely the qualities necessary for his success. . . . The older generation of music-lovers learned to know their classics through Mr. Thomas' temperament and methods.

There were others besides Theodore Thomas to work on behalf of the American orchestra. Many of these have passed into oblivion, their names found only in well-documented histories. But they worked quietly and energetically to create a musical life about them, leaving their good work as an indestructible monument.

Carl Bergmann, a predecessor of Thomas by a few years and for many years the conductor of the New York Philharmonic— often referred to as the *first* important American conductor— worked with painstaking devotion to elevate the tastes of his audiences. He had been concertmaster of the visiting Germania Orchestra, and for two years had conducted the celebrated Handel and Haydn Society in Boston. When the Germania Orchestra disbanded in 1854, he came to New York and for one season directed the Männergesangverein Arion. A year later he joined the New York Philharmonic as conductor, sharing the platform with Theodor Eisfeld for ten years, and for ten years more occupying it alone. His long tenure of the post might suggest that he was popular—which, to be truthful, was not the case. He was too scrupulous and honest a musician to resort to cheap devices for pleasing an audience. He was too vigorous and uncompromising a champion of the music of Wagner and Liszt—two composers who were generally disliked. The New York music public never quite took to him. Even the press annihilated him for his experiments. When in 1856, he introduced the *Tannhäuser* Overture on the Philharmonic programs, the critic of *The New York Times* was tempted by his prejudice to make an unfortunate prophecy:

It seems to us extremely improbable that he [Wagner] will excite any enthusiasm as a composer, notwithstanding the fact that selections from his *Lohengrin* have been received with favor. They were undoubtedly curious—as selections from an opera composed entirely from recitative must be—and some novel orchestral effects may have given them piquancy. Except as curiosities, we cannot perceive how these selections could be endurable. The entire opera of *Lohengrin,* from beginning to end, does not contain a dozen bars of melody. It is the wildest kind of rambling utterly destitute of form or sequency.

The audiences, and the box-office receipts, remained small during the twenty years of Bergmann's office as conductor. More than once it seemed certain that the orchestra, which had staggered through one season, would not survive the next. In 1878 Bergmann was displaced. He took his defeat badly. He knew that he had done his job well—or, at least, as well as it could have been done at the time; by 1876, Wagner and Liszt were warmly accepted by New York music audiences—largely because of his insistent performances. He knew that during his long career he had always been true to himself and to his art. To find himself suddenly discarded after twenty devoted years was a blow that crushed him. He sought solace in drink, became a saloon habitué, and permitted his disintegration to take place without sign of struggle. Death came with merciful swiftness in the very same year.

Carl Zerrahn in Boston and Hans Balatka in Chicago, both contemporaries of Theodore Thomas, dominated the musical life of their respective cities, taking failure with success, but always stubborn in their efforts to create a higher standard of musical appreciation. Emerging as a musical figure of importance in Boston in the early 1850's, Zerrahn was conductor of the Handel and Haydn Society for forty years; for thirty years he was principal conductor of the Worcester Festival; and for seventeen years he conducted the Harvard Symphony Concerts. A self-effacing musician, he concerned himself only with the highest mission of his art. Zerrahn was one of the principal figures to create a musical culture in Boston—thereby setting the stage for the birth of the Boston Symphony Orchestra. He lived long enough to see his city become one of the greatest centers of music-making in the country.

Balatka was to Chicago what Zerrahn was to Boston. We have already pointed out that the Beethoven symphonies were introduced to Chicago through his efforts. As a matter of fact, he kept orchestral music of all kinds alive over a period of many years, beginning with 1860, directing one organization after another, until his lifework was crowned with the formation of a permanent, magnificent orchestral institution in Chicago—the Chicago Orchestra—which could carry on his labors.

And there was Leopold Damrosch.

He came to New York from Germany in 1871, already the mature musician. In Germany he had been a personal friend of Liszt and Wagner. He had concertized as violinist with Hans von Bülow and Karl Tausig, and had founded and, for nine years, directed the Breslau Symphony Orchestra. His friends urged him to come to the New World where, they said, there was a need for him. It required courage to set forth into a new and foreign land which, as frequently described by rumor, was musically barbarous; to desert a civilized musical world in which he had already won an honored place. But the soft-spoken and gentle musician had the courage—and the imagination. He took his family under his wing, crossed the ocean, and settled in New York City. On May 6, 1871, he made his American début in New York in the triple role of violinist, conductor, and composer.

At first he conducted a male chorus, the well-known Arion Society, which had been directly responsible for bringing him to this country. At the same time, he supplemented a rather meager income by teaching, playing the violin, accepting whatever musical assignments fell his way. But Damrosch was not a man to be confined to permanent obscurity. He made friends, powerful friends. In 1874 he organized his own choral group, the Oratorio Society of New York, which his energy, idealism, and spirit fashioned into one of the leading musical organizations in New York.

Soon a genuine artistic rivalry arose between him and Theodore Thomas: the one first rising to recognition, the other already firmly established as the leading musical figure in the country. It was a rivalry to delight New York, to lend drama to the musical activity of the city, to provide spice to the conversations in the drawing rooms, to arouse feuds and dissension, to fill columns of space in the magazines and newspapers.

They were opposites both in appearance and in temperament. Thomas was tall, erect of carriage, always bearing himself with great dignity and poise. He was sometimes described as cold because by nature he was quiet, reserved, undemonstrative. He had a sound practical sense which guided him in everything he did. He never lived long in a world of dreams. In his daily behavior he was matter-of-fact, rarely given to excessive enthusiasms, always calculating and controlled.

Damrosch, on the other hand, was more the visionary. He was short in build, warmhearted, gregarious. He liked the society of people and responded to them sensitively. He liked to talk volubly, oozing out his likes in a geyser eruption. He permitted his imagination free rein. By nature a romanticist, his head was often in the clouds. He could dream bold dreams, unhampered by sound practical considerations.

Each had his adherents; each, his adversaries. Each tried to counteract the success of the other with some major artistic coup. And from this spirited and sometimes bitter competition arose genuine musical benefits which were to nourish the musical life of the country.

If Thomas had an orchestra of his own—well, Damrosch would have one too. Damrosch had been conductor of the New York Philharmonic for one season (that of 1876–1877), when Bergmann was displaced; at that time, Damrosch gave the first American performance of the third act of *Siegfried.* He was eased out of this post by forces working to bring Thomas permanently to the head of the Philharmonic. Consequently, those who were with Damrosch arranged the necessary finances with which he might establish an orchestra of his own. Following the formation of the Oratorio Society, Damrosch organized the Symphony Society for the purpose of giving several subscription concerts a season in New York.

If Thomas had toured the country, so would Damrosch. In 1883 Damrosch supplemented the achievements of Thomas by taking orchestral music to out-of-the-way communities and lesser cities of the country. If Thomas introduced many new and daring works, Damrosch would do so too. Characteristic of their rivalry was the manner in which Damrosch, under Thomas's very nose, usurped the American première of Brahms's First Symphony (which had originally been assigned by the composer to Thomas) by surreptitiously acquiring the score and secretly arranging its performance before the date scheduled by his competitor. But besides the Brahms symphony and the third act of *Siegfried,* Damrosch was responsible also for the

American premières of the first act of *Die Walküre* and Berlioz's *Damnation of Faust*.

If Thomas could direct monumental festivals in Cincinnati, Damrosch could do so in New York. In 1881 Damrosch inaugurated the first music festival to be held in New York, when he directed an orchestra of three hundred musicians and a chorus of 1,200 at the Seventh Regiment Armory in a week of great choral and orchestral music. (One year later, Thomas—in a countermove—was to direct an even more elaborate festival in New York at the very same auditorium!)

But in one respect particularly was Damrosch to go far beyond Thomas. As the first German conductor at the Metropolitan Opera House, Damrosch was instrumental in bringing the American music public more intimately into contact with the music dramas of Richard Wagner; and, by doing so, he laid the permanent foundation for Wagner's popularity in this country.

The apathy of audiences to fine music was felt in branches of American concert life other than orchestral music. Americans, we have already suggested, did not like one-man recitals. Yet American musicians like William Mason (who, in 1857, gave one of the first serious piano recitals in the country) and Louis Gottschalk (the first American concert pianist to be acclaimed in Europe) were ready to swim against the tide. In this, Louis Gottschalk was more successful than Mason, not because he was the greater artist, but because he had the capacity to thrill his audiences with his personal charm. He was cut on the pattern of the later "matinee idol." Suave and handsome, he was elegant in his attire down to the white gloves which he wore even on the stage. He would remove his gloves a moment before his concert and regally throw them into the audience, where the women would fight for the possession of this sacred memento.

But Gottschalk was the exception in his ability to attract audiences to his concerts, possibly because few others would emulate his manner and method. Those who dispensed with theatricalism played to virtually empty houses. One concert manager was compelled to resort to the ruse of hiring empty carriages to make an appearance an hour or so before the time of a piano recital in New York with the hope that this parade might attract the curiosity of passersby sufficiently to inspire some of them to enter the hall!

But there were men in the field of recital music who fought against the general public indifference and who labored to make recitals more popular. One of the unsung heroes in the late nineteenth century was William Steinway, fourth son of the founder of the famous piano-manufacturing firm and president of the house of Steinway after 1876. He was a true philanthropist whose generosity enriched the concert music of America. He brought to this country the greatest pianists in Europe in ever-increasing numbers. If they were failures at the box offices, he paid the deficits out of his own pocket. Yet he never entertained the thought of profiting financially from their successes. To worthy pianists he provided the use of Steinway Hall free of charge, even supplied the programs. The great pianists, coming for concerts to this strange new world, found him an ever sympathetic and warm friend, one to whom they could turn whenever an emergency presented itself.

The artists whom William Steinway helped to bring to this country in droves for piano concerts helped to create and educate recital audiences. They made possible the great recitals later to mark the close of the nineteenth century: particularly those by such masters as Busoni, Anton Rubinstein, and Ignace Jan Paderewski (Paderewski, as a matter of fact, was first brought to this country by Steinway through a guaranty of $30,000 for eighty concerts). How backward America was considered where concerts were concerned was emphasized as late as 1872 when Anton Rubinstein's manager was aghast at the suggestion of the artist that he give a *solo* recital, without benefit of assisting artists or orchestra. A solo recital, cried the manager, might go very well in Europe where audiences were sophisticated, but it was a hopeless attraction for Americans. Yet Rubinstein's recital on January 13, 1873, in New York, drew a large audience and encouraged such more ambitious artistic ventures as Rubinstein's series of seven historical recitals and Busoni's series of concerts devoted to all the Beethoven piano sonatas.

Americans did not particularly like chamber music. The response to the early and rather primitive efforts of such ensembles as were organized by Eisfeld, Dannreuther, Mason and Thomas, and Sam Franko could freeze the heart. Often the attendance at these concerts was limited to no more than a dozen or twenty music lovers. In his hope to induce people to attend his chamber-music concerts, William Mason would stand at Union Square in New York and personally distribute advertising handbills for his performances. Every effort by sincere artists to present great chamber music fell, for the most part, on reluctant, even antagonistic ears. The critic of the *Daily Express* soundly rebuked William Mason and Theodore Thomas for not making their chamber-music concerts more popular:

They select the programs of their concerts, it would seem, almost entirely with reference to their own development and culture. . . . In that, we think, Mr. Mason presents too much of the material of his own advanced culture. . . . He seems to lose sight of the fact that it is chiefly for the performer, and not so much for all this aspiration in music, that the majority of people go to the matinee.

When, in 1885, the Mendelssohn Quintet gave a concert of music by Beethoven, Schubert, Mozart, and Raff in Erie, Pennsylvania, the local critic voiced the resentment of the audience when he wrote:

The members of the Quintet are artists of first rank and they play perfectly. *But what they played!* These musicians may call us terrible heretics from a musical standpoint. But we confess freely and openly that the so-called "classical music" with its crazy interweaving of tones and its poverty of touching melodies, leaves us cold. We would, if we could, exchange Beethoven's, Mozart's and all the collected symphonies and sonatas of Mendelssohn for a single pretty Strauss waltz, or a charming song from *Boccaccio* or the *Fledermaus*.

These early chamber-music groups were never destined to see success crown their efforts. But they can be said to have paved the way for the success in America of other and greater chamber-music ensembles.

To one phase of concert activity was America comparatively responsive, and in this phase it was rich—choral music. The early pioneers had brought with them to the New World their love for singing. Choral singing formed the foundation of American musical culture. In colonial days the church had been the center of cultural and spiritual life. To improve congregational singing, churchmen organized singing schools which, in many instances, produced choral units capable of giving public performances of an ambitious repertoire. It was to be expected, therefore, that the oldest musical organizations in America would be choral societies. The Moravians, who settled Bethlehem, Pennsylvania, had regular *Singstunde* as early as 1742; in 1744 these Moravians founded the Collegium Musicum, possibly the oldest musical organization in America. In 1786 the Stoughton Musical Society was organized through the influence of William Billings. And in 1815 the German immigrant, Gottlieb Graupner, organized the historic and celebrated Handel and Haydn Society in Boston, which was responsible for the performance of many choral masterpieces. Later immigrants to America were also contributors to this choral activity. The Germans who settled in Cincinnati and Milwaukee formed a *Musikverein* in the latter city and a *Saengerfest* in the former. The Swedes organized, in 1882, a choral society in Lindsborg, Kansas, which was responsible for extraordinary performances of Handel's *Messiah* and Bach's *Passion According to St. Matthew*. Somewhat later, the immigrant Norwegians organized the significant St. Olaf Choir in Northfield, Minnesota.

These, and numerous other choral organizations scattered throughout the country, prepared the ground for our musical emergence, educated our first music audiences, and set the stage for our early concert life. In many communities in America the sole contact with music was through the performances of local choral groups. Thus America heard Haydn and Bach and Handel even before it had learned to visit the concert hall.

The growth of musical consciousness in America was as dependent upon the spread of musical education as upon the development of concert life. Music education, too, owed a formidable debt to the labor of pioneers. It was a long road that stretched from America's first music teacher—a certain Miss Ball, "lately from London," who, in 1730, advertised lessons in "singing, playing on the spinet, dancing and needlework"—to so fully equipped a conservatory as that of the Chicago Musical College, which opened in 1867. It was a road paved, mile by mile, with the toil of musicians who had vision, faith, courage.

The growth of music education in America was impeded for

a long time by a snobbishness which decreed that only in Europe could adequate musical training be acquired. Those who had money or talent refused to consider an American education, esteeming it far inferior to that which could be acquired in Europe. Besides, sound practical judgment dictated the need for European study: the American concert public simply would not turn an attentive ear to an artist who did not have the stamp of approval from some recognized European conservatory. But this situation was only one of several reasons for the lack of serious music study in America. More regrettable still, American families did not look with favor on music as a career—for, truth to tell, music was *no* career in those days, only self-assumed martyrdom!—and they went to any length to discourage it. Finally, music was generally considered too effeminate a pastime to be cultivated by men, who avoided it fastidiously rather than have their masculinity questioned.

Despite restrictions and limitations, music study in America progressed after a fashion—furthered by valiant musicians. Perhaps the most notable of these was Lowell Mason, the father of the pianist, William. Lowell Mason was responsible for introducing music study into the Boston public schools (thereby setting an example for schools throughout the country) and was the greatest single influence in encouraging the growth of music study throughout America.

Born in Medfield, Massachusetts, in 1792, he was largely self-taught in music, spending the years of his youth and adolescence in dabbling with musical instruments. Early in life he published a volume of hymns. Soon afterward he settled in Boston to take "general charge of music in the churches there." It was in the course of this work that he initiated a project that must endear him forever to American hearts. Early in 1831, searching for a patriotic hymn to be sung at the Independence Day service at Park Street Church, he suggested to his friend Samuel Francis Smith that he write a poem that could be sung to the air of *God Save the King.* Young Smith (he had been graduated from Harvard in the famous class of 1829) thereupon wrote the lines beginning "My country, 'tis of thee"—which, to the tune we now call *America,* was first sung on July 4, 1831.

It was Mason's cherished idea to bring some knowledge of the musical art to school children. The opposition to his project was fierce, but Mason could close his ears to discouragement. He inaugurated special music classes for children as a sort of laboratory experiment; then he proved the efficacy of his experiment by giving concerts in which the children performed. This went a long way in convincing the diehards of Boston that music deserved to be included with the "Three R's" in the curriculum. When they were finally convinced, Mason unselfishly offered to become the official school music teacher without remuneration. This was in 1837. One year later, his indispensability was proved when he was given a regular stipend for his work. After this, Mason became superintendent of music of the Boston public schools and was now able to put his full educational program into performance.

Realizing that the standard of music teaching throughout the country was on a low level (many so-called teachers knew little more than the elements of the art), and recognizing that these teachers needed direction and advice, Mason decided upon an annual convention of music teachers at which they could be given guidance in their work and at which problems common to all teachers might be discussed and solved. The first of these conventions was held in 1834 and attracted twelve teachers. By 1849 the convention included a thousand teachers from every part of the East. His success in this direction encouraged Mason to travel extensively into other parts of the country, arranging similar conventions. In this way he built an army of music teachers throughout America ready and able to train young pupils. The full fruition of his labors came in 1876 with the formation of the Music Teachers' National Association, which once each year held a national convention.

Music study spread into the public schools of other cities besides Boston. It also came to the universities. Oberlin College provided music instruction as early as 1837 (it was the earliest example of music courses in an American school of higher learning). This was soon imitated by other schools and universities. Conservatories arose in communities formerly dependent on local teachers for all musical culture. These offered an organized program of music education in all its facets. Between 1865 and 1885 there were founded major conservatories throughout the length and breadth of the country. In 1867 came the Chicago Musical College, the Cincinnati Conservatory, the New England Conservatory of Music. In 1868 Baltimore opened the Peabody Conservatory. Philadelphia, St. Louis, Detroit, in turn, financed conservatories of their own. And, in 1885, one of the great music institutions of the country was founded by an indefatigable music lover and educator, Jeanette Thurber. It was the National Conservatory in New York, which was soon to be staffed by a faculty of unsurpassed brilliance, comprising Anton Seidl, Safonoff, Huneker, Paur, and Frank Van der Stucken, all under the directorial guidance of Bohemia's great composer, Anton Dvořák.

These conservatories were not yet to be the producers of genius. For many years to come, the European institutions were to appropriate all American students who showed the strongest indication of native gifts. But our conservatories were creating respectable musicians—fertile soil which was eventually to yield richer harvest. Not only were they to feed American musical organizations with fresh and well-prepared material, but they were to supply recruits, in ever-increasing numbers, to the music audiences of America. And in doing this, they played perhaps the major role in America's musical destiny.

CHAPTER THREE

Opera in America

═══

O PERA COULD be expected to appeal more strongly to the musical tastes of nineteenth-century America than did orchestral or chamber music. Opera was a spectacle to dazzle the eye as well as the ear. It was both a stimulant and an opiate for the senses. It had glamour and display such as delighted an audience which found pleasure in spectacles.

Yet even opera required the vision and perseverance of pioneer spirits before it could establish itself permanently in this country.

The earliest recorded opera performances in America were those of the English ballad operas, such as *Flora* or *Hob-in-the-Well,* presented in Charleston in 1735. Fifteen years later, *The Beggar's Opera* was heard in New York. French opera (by Grétry, Rousseau, and Monsigny) made its first appearance in New Orleans in 1791 with a refugee group of singers and was later heard in New York, Philadelphia, and Baltimore. Then came the first performances of Italian opera in the Italian style and language, when the Spaniard, Manuel del Popolo Vicente Garcia, came to New York and inaugurated an Italian repertoire of eleven operas with Rossini's *The Barber of Seville* at the

Park Theatre on November 26, 1825. Garcia's daughter, Maria
Felicita, was the Rosina in that opening performance; later she
was to become a world-famous prima donna under her married
name of Mme. Malibran.

Though Garcia's stay in America was brief (he remained only
one season), he can be counted the first of the pioneers to work
for opera in America. The repertoire he presented was by no
means extraordinary. Only four different composers were represented: Rossini, Mozart, Zingarelli, and Garcia himself. But he
whetted the appetite of New York for opera. And he encouraged
other impresarios to continue where he left off.

For many years thereafter opera was to remain virtually the
exclusive and expensive property of New York. When other
cities heard opera—Chicago and San Francisco were to hear
their first opera performances as late as 1850 and 1853 respectively—it was only through the visits of opera companies from
New York on tour.

Mozart's librettist, Lorenzo da Ponte—now at the patriarchal
age of eighty-three—was to carry the opera torch from where
Garcia left it. Da Ponte, poet-adventurer, had had a rich and
varied life up to the time of Garcia's visit to America—a life that
had carried him across the face of Europe, then to America. His
was a strange and fabulous career. It had taken him from his
Jewish origins straight into the arms of the Catholic Church,
and from the Church to a life of dissipation that included indiscriminate love-making and gambling. Poet (he wrote the
librettos for Mozart's *The Marriage of Figaro* and *Don
Giovanni*) and impresario, teacher and merchant, his checkered
career had ultimately involved him in debts from which he was
forced to flee by coming to America in 1805. Here he entered
business (as a merchant of tobacco and liquor) with disastrous
results. Then he became a teacher of Italian literature and

language in New York—long enough to save some money and
once again to venture into the whirlpool of business. And once
again he met disaster. Undaunted, he turned to writing and to
filling the post of professor of Italian literature at Columbia
College. He succeeded in sufficiently restoring his prestige to be
able to move in the best New York social circles.

When Garcia came to New York with Italian opera, Da Ponte
at once approached him (it is sometimes said that Da Ponte
inspired Garcia to come to America, but this is doubtful) and at
once associated himself with the venture as its adviser. This association with opera—Da Ponte's last major venture—was to inspire
him with a new ideal, that of creating opera on a firm basis in
America. In 1832 he joined with Montressor in establishing
opera at the Richmond Hill Theatre in New York. The venture
collapsed after thirty-five presentations. Then Da Ponte influenced persons of high station in New York to finance a still more
ambitious operatic undertaking. They built a handsome theater
in New York, at Church and Leonard Streets, expressly for
opera—the first theater in America possessing a tier devoted
exclusively to boxes. There a season of Italian opera was
inaugurated on November 18, 1833. The new theater—it was
called the Italian Opera House—attracted large audiences; the
first season of forty performances had to be supplemented by
twenty-eight additional presentations. But when the box-office
returns were counted, and the expenses paid, it was found that
the venture, for all its apparent appeal, had suffered a deficit
of almost $30,000. After a second season the Italian Opera
House decided that it had had enough.

Others arose to court success with the opera. The prosperous
restaurant owner, Ferdinand Palmo, financed opera performances in 1844 in an old theater, formerly Stoppai's Arcade
Baths, in the rather disreputable quarter of Chambers Street.

Though Palmo promised the best available singers and "thirty-two professors" in the orchestra; even though he went so far in considering his public's comfort and safety as to arrange for a special car to run after each performance from the opera house to Forty-Second Street with "police protection"—his undertaking was soon involved in bankruptcy. One year after the opening performance, the musicians started a general strike for their pay, in the midst of a performance. The sheriff confiscated all the box-office cash. Palmo's opera house thus came to an ignoble end. Good Palmo himself even lost his restaurant and was compelled to pay for his operatic escapade by turning cook, then by depending upon the charity of his friends.

It was generally felt by the leading figures of New York society that Palmo's misfortunes had been brought about, not through the failure of Italian opera to make an appeal, but rather because it had been housed in the deplorable setting of an old building in an unsavory neighborhood. They tried to prove this point more forcefully by building a new theater of spacious dimensions—the last word in luxurious trappings—for opera. In this way the Astor Place Opera House, "one of the most attractive theaters ever erected," as one manager of the time described it, was built and was promised a five-year guarantee by financial leaders. In 1847 the Astor Place Opera House presented its first season with operas by Bellini, Donizetti, Mercadante, and Verdi. It was financially unsuccessful. For the second season a new manager appeared; after him came still another. Then—signs of growing disintegration—the direction of the opera house passed into the hands of Niblo, the café owner, whose Gardens were the most celebrated popular theater-restaurant in the city. Niblo, guided by sound business judgment acquired after many years of entertaining audiences, decided to rehabilitate the sad fortunes of the Astor Place

Opera Hause by dispensing with this opera nonsense and substituting the attraction of Signor Donetti's trained dogs and
monkeys. As one of the managers of the Astor Place Opera
House, Max Maretzek, later lamented in his autobiography:

> Their [Donetti's dogs' and monkeys'] dramatic performances were
> offered to the refined and intelligent proprietors and patrons of this
> classic and exclusive place of amusement. Naturally they protested.
> It was in vain. Then they sued out an injunction against this exhibi-
> tion on the ground that in Niblo's lease of the premises only respect-
> able performances were permitted to be given in the opera house.
> On the "hearing to show cause" for the injunction, Mr. Niblo called
> up Donetti or some of his friends, who testified that his aforesaid
> dogs and monkeys had, in their younger days, appeared before princes
> and princesses and kings and queens. Moreover, witnesses were called
> who declared under oath that the previously mentioned dogs and
> monkeys behaved behind the scenes more quietly and respectably
> than many Italian singers. . . . As might be supposed the injunction
> was dissolved. . . . The house lost all its prestige in the eyes of the
> community. . . . Its death-blow had been given it as a place for
> theatrical amusement by the astute Mr. William Niblo.

The death gasps of the Astor Place Opera House were soon
followed by the birth pains of the first of America's great opera
institutions—the Academy of Music. The auditorium was three
times the size of its predecessor. Its artistic aspirations were
equally expansive. It opened on the evening of October 2, 1854,
with an admirable performance of *Norma*. That opening performance set the tone for the remainder of the season.

Managers came and went. Each season, for many years,
found a different directorial hand guiding the opera house.
Finally, in 1878, Colonel James Henry Mapleson took over and
retained control for eight consecutive seasons. But American
opera history was in the making—particularly during the Mapleson regime. The extensiveness and the quality of the repertoire

were unmatched by any heard up to that time in America. One
after another, great singers were introduced to America on the
stage of the Academy. With their performances they created
opera tradition. The incomparable Adelina Patti, mistress of
bel canto, made her official opera début—as Lucia—at the Academy in 1859. Some years later she was to become one of the most
brilliant of Mapleson's attractions. Other great singers also
contributed lustrous chapters to the brilliant history of the
Academy: among them were Italo Campanini, Pauline Lucca,
Minnie Hauk, Etelka Gerster, Emma Nevada, Clara Louise
Kellogg, Victor Maurel. . . .

At the Academy, glamour finally came to American opera
performances—not only the glamour of sensational prima donnas
and Italian tenors, but also that of brilliant audiences. The
boxes were sold at fabulous prices; as much as $30,000 was
offered and turned down for a box one season. Even at these
prices it was impossible for many families (particularly the
nouveaux riches) to acquire them. Sold-out houses became
the rule, as opera's magic world of illusion, and the spell of the
glittering star system, began to bewitch the New York music
lover.

The glamour of the Academy owed perhaps as much to the
manager, Colonel Mapleson, as to a Patti, a Hauk, or a Campanini. Mapleson was the impresario in the grand manner and
style. He spent money fabulously and was always in debt—but
in debt in the grand manner. He deified his singers: he was
known to have fallen on his knees to kiss the hand of a prima
donna. Audiences who came to his opera house soon took their
cue from him and apotheosized these stars themselves. He
smeared the ointment of flattery on his singers. This often proved
to be a magic panacea for their disturbed temperaments, their
jealousies, their artistic dissatisfactions. A great singer would

enter his sanctum with hate in her heart but, succumbing to the Colonel's charm, would leave at peace with the world. Often his praise and gallantry were substitutes for a check—for, though there were sold-out houses, Mapleson's insistence on a grand scale of opera performance at the Academy, and his utter indifference to the size of his expenditures, frequently made of his life a hard struggle to meet the next bill. His singers were often cajoled by his charm and courtly manner to sing when they, and he, knew that at that moment there was simply no money in the bank to pay for the performance. At one time, unable to pay Patti six thousand dollars due her, Colonel Mapleson was able to induce her to sing at a special benefit performance, the purpose of which was to raise the money he owed her!

As long as the Academy of Music was the only opera house in New York it was possible for Mapleson to keep the operatic ball rolling. He could pay one creditor, while placating another with promises. He could keep his stars faithful to him, and his audience faithful to his stars. The income at the box office was excellent, and—while not allocated too judiciously—was at least capable of maintaining peace and satisfaction in the ranks. But when a major competitor arose, Mapleson recognized the handwriting on the wall. It would always be a struggle to keep one major opera house alive in New York. To divide the audiences between two houses was to flirt with disaster.

Many of the rich families in New York—those of William K. Vanderbilt, William H. Tillinghast, and others—were made impatient by the difficulty of securing boxes at the Academy of Music. They decided to sponsor an opera house of their own, farther uptown. They, too, wished to be part of the opera glamour, to see and be seen from choice locations in the opera house. They wished to attain that final *cachet* of social prestige that was conferred by the ownership of a box at the opera.

Thus the Metropolitan Opera House arose at Thirty-Ninth Street and Broadway. On the evening of October 22, 1883, the favorite opera of New Yorkers, *Faust,* was presented, with Italo Campanini (proselytized from the Mapleson ranks) as Faust and the celebrated Christine Nilsson as Marguerite, a role she had created in Paris when the opera was given its world première. The opera began a half-hour late, giving the audience an opportunity to study the interior of their new opera house: the gas-lit chandelier, the mural decorations of Lathrop and Maynard, the interior decorations of Tradwill, and, above all else, the two tiers of boxes which boasted as sumptuous a display of jewels, furs, and gowns as was to be seen in New York.

Mapleson, too, opened his season on the evening of October 22. Then arose an operatic war in New York between the two houses. Mapleson had on his side tradition, background, and the sensational Adelina Patti. Abbey (the first manager to lease the Metropolitan) had as his attractions a new opera house, new scenery, new costumes (the truth was that Mapleson's stage effects were often shabby), and the distinguished singing of such artists as Nilsson, Campanini, and young Marcella Sembrich. Both houses offered repertoires that included the accepted favorites with an occasional novelty.

As so often happens in warfare, neither side emerged victorious. The attendance at the Academy fell off so sharply that even on the nights when Patti sang there was not a full house. Attendance at the Metropolitan was no better. Whatever consolation Colonel Mapleson could find in the appalling deficit facing him at the end of the season came only from the fact that the deficit at the Metropolitan was even greater: $600,000. Abbey, as a matter of fact, suffered such severe financial reverses with the first season that the Metropolitan insisted upon running a benefit for him to relieve his embarrassing financial position.

Wisely, the Metropolitan took stock of itself after the first season. It decided that its only hope of success would be by arousing the jaded operatic appetites of New Yorkers. It would try something radically new. It would depart quite sharply from its repertoire—previously devoted exclusively to the standard French and Italian favorites—and present instead a season of German operas. There had been spasmodic efforts during the two previous decades to promote German opera in New York, sometimes by mushroom organizations, but none of them had taken root. The most important of these organizations had been the Stadt Theater, catering to the German population of the city. It was here, under the baton of Carl Bergmann, that Wagner had been introduced to America: *Tannhäuser* in 1859, *Lohengrin* in 1871.

Perhaps if this policy were adopted by a major opera house, the German repertoire had a chance of attracting wider attention? So questioned Leopold Damrosch, and he broached a plan to the Metropolitan with his customary outflow of enthusiasm. He would undertake the artistic direction of a German season at the Metropolitan. The director, thinking of his failure of the previous season, listened with interest. He finally decided to follow Damrosch's ideas. The star system would be dispensed with. Instead, the emphasis would be placed on well-assembled casts and well-integrated performances. But the performances would be of such less well-known operas as Beethoven's *Fidelio*, Wagner's *Tannhäuser* and *Die Walküre*, and Weber's *Der Freischütz*. Leopold Damrosch would be principal conductor.

Novelty brought health to the box office. Colonel Mapleson might jeer at the new policy of the Metropolitan by derisively referring to its presentations as "sauerkraut opera." But the second season doubled the receipts of the first, even though the prices of admission were radically cut. The deficit was reduced to a negligible $40,000. The Metropolitan, therefore, decided to continue even more boldly upon its experiment for the following season.

From this decision, the Metropolitan was not to be swerved, even when Leopold Damrosch, the high priest of this German venture, was stricken with pneumonia. On the evening of February 11, 1885, Leopold's son, Walter, was hurriedly called upon to substitute for his father in a performance of *Tannhäuser*. Four days later, Leopold Damrosch was dead. Impressive funeral services were held for him within the Metropolitan Opera House, which was draped in black. The entire *corps* of the opera house sat on the stage. The directors of the Metropolitan adopted a resolution declaring that Leopold Damrosch had inaugurated a new era in American music, and that his loss was irreparable.

Leopold Damrosch *had* inaugurated a new era in American music, not only as the founder of the New York Symphony and the Oratorio Society, but most of all for his missionary labors on behalf of Richard Wagner. This new era was to be unfolded with ever-increasing richness of activity by Leopold's son, Walter. Young Walter was then twenty-three years old. Though he had virtually no experience as a conductor (save for a brief but none too important assignment in New Jersey), he bravely took over his father's duties with the Symphony and the Oratorio societies. The Metropolitan also called upon him to assume his father's baton in the German repertoire.

Walter Damrosch was determined to carry on the patient labors of his father on behalf of the Wagnerian music drama, and he did this with the devotion and zeal of his father. He enlisted the services of one of the foremost Wagnerian conductors of Europe to assist him—Anton Seidl, Wagner's own favorite conductor. He also combed Germany for its most

promising Wagnerian singers. When the process of combing
was over, the Metropolitan boasted as distinguished a cast of
German singers as could be found anywhere: Lilli Lehmann,
Albert Stritt, Emil Fischer, Max Alvary. During the four-month
season, nine operas were performed, of which Wagner's *Rienzi*
and *Die Meistersinger* and Karl Goldmark's *The Queen of
Sheba* were new to the repertoire. The season closed with a
generous profit.

The success of the Metropolitan spelled doom for the
Academy of Music. Patti had left Mapleson. Her passing inspired Mapleson to announce (somewhat pathetically) that for
his 1885–1886 season he was no longer interested in stars but
only in well-assembled casts. But the opera audiences no longer
came to Union Square. Instead they made their way uptown
to the building on Broadway, which Mapleson had once so
inelegantly called "the yellow brewery." After 1886 Mapleson
withdrew, a defeated man.

Another Italian company tried to lure audiences into the
Academy of Music, but without success. Then came an American company headed by Theodore Thomas. (If his rival,
Leopold Damrosch, had made such a success of conducting
operas, why not he?) Damrosch had triumphed at the Metropolitan because he had strummed on an unfamiliar string: the
German repertoire. Thomas, too, would venture on a new path:
he would encourage the American musician. "It has been
deemed not only desirable, but it has been felt just that a broadly
American spirit should animate the struggles of the movement,"
the American Opera Company announced in its prospectus.
"The plan upon which it is based, and its execution, is so thoroughly American that its most bitter opponents will scarcely
decry it as being tainted by foreign appeal." This new opera
company hoped not only to produce well-known operas in

English with American casts, but more especially to produce native operas from the pens of the foremost American composers. The company urged composers to avoid imitation of European models and to evolve a style and structure with an original design and conception. But even more strongly did it prevail upon American composers to use native material as texts for their operas.

Unfortunately, propaganda alone could not produce American operas or gifted composers or stellar all-American casts. For lack of genuine musical talent, the efforts of the American Opera Company proved futile. In 1886–1887 it was reorganized under the name of National Opera Company, at which time it abandoned the Academy of Music to become a touring company. Then, for lack of sympathetic response, it expired. The Academy, too, closed its doors to opera permanently. The operatic field in New York was now in the exclusive possession of the Metropolitan Opera House.

The German vogue at the Metropolitan was to continue for an additional five seasons. It was to provide New York with Wagnerian performances of incomparable excellence, performances which—one must confess—New York was not yet prepared to appreciate fully. The exacting and scrupulous Anton Seidl, who was steeped in Wagnerian traditions, fastidiously maintained the highest artistic standards of performance, in which he was magnificently supported by casts of superlative artists. Young Walter Damrosch was a conscientious and devoted assistant to Seidl. Under the best possible auspices, New York operagoers were able to hear for the first time *Tristan und Isolde, Das Rheingold, Siegfried,* and *Götterdämmerung.*

But the German repertoire had interested the New York opera public not because of its intrinsic musical importance but rather because it had provided the shock of novelty. After seven

years, the novelty lost its pristine appeal. The box owners were
bored to death by Wagner, and much of the general public
yearned for the return of the melodious Italian aria. When the
direction of the Metropolitan was assumed collaboratively by
Abbey and Grau in 1890–1891, a revolution against the German
repertoire was achieved. Only two Wagner music dramas were
performed; and one of these, *Die Meistersinger,* was presented
(true to the spirit of the moment) in the Italian language under
the name of *I Maestri Cantori!*

To restore the prestige of Italian and French opera, Abbey
and Grau shrewdly assembled the greatest available singers, a
few of these being presented in America for the first time.
Emma Eames, Nordica, the De Reszke brothers, Melba, and
Calvé came in rapid succession. They were to form the nucleus
of the incomparable all-star casts which were soon to create an
epoch in operatic presentations, an epoch of incomparable
splendor, officially inaugurated when Maurice Grau took over
the exclusive direction of the Metropolitan in 1897–1898.

Meanwhile, Wagner had a stouthearted protagonist in the
son of Leopold Damrosch. Even though he was no longer associated with the Metropolitan after 1891, Walter Damrosch
was determined to continue the fight for the holy cause. In 1894
he arranged a special charity concert at Carnegie Hall in which
he presented *Götterdämmerung* in concert form. The success
of this performance revealed to him that enthusiasm for Wagner
was not altogether dead, that, given encouragement, it could
be rearoused to life. Convinced that the mission of restoring
Wagner to general popularity was of major musical consequence, Damrosch (who met only deaf ears when he presented
his plan to the directors of the Metropolitan) sold his home on
Fifty-fifth Street and financed an opera company of his own,
dedicated to the Wagnerian music drama. He was gambling

for high stakes, but he won. The first season of Wagner presentations netted him a profit of $53,000. Better still, it proved
to Damrosch that there was a definite public for Wagner.

But, as Andrew Carnegie was astute enough to realize when
he advised Damrosch against undertaking a second season,
American audiences were succumbing not so much to the spell
of Wagner as to the fascination of novelty. He said to Damrosch:
"Such success as you have had rarely repeats itself. You rightly
divined the desire of the public for the return of the Wagner
opera, but this current has drawn into it many people who have
come for curiosity alone, and to whom Wagner is still a closed
book. Many of these will not come a second time." How wise
was his judgment was proved when during the second season
the Damrosch project lost $43,000 in five months. Only when
Damrosch later combined his Wagner presentations with the
French and Italian repertoire (enlisting the services of such
glamorous prima donnas as Calvé and Melba) was he able to
keep his venture alive and functioning.

Nevertheless, his efforts on behalf of Wagner were by no
means wasted. It was largely as a result of his work at this time
that the Wagnerian music dramas were soon returned to the
repertoire of the Metropolitan Opera House after several seasons of absence. In this he was abetted by the persistent efforts
of Jean de Reszke. Irony of ironies! Jean de Reszke, who had
achieved considerable note in Europe in the French and Italian
repertoire, had originally been imported to New York by the
Metropolitan Opera House to defeat the Wagner vogue. Yet
it was Jean de Reszke who proved to be one of the major forces
at the Metropolitan to restore the Wagner music dramas to the
stage!

The name of Walter Damrosch will continue to appear in

the pages that follow. The shadow of his career spreads across
a half-century of music-making in America, but never more
noticeably than in the earlier years of his career when he proved
himself a worthy successor to such passionate missionaries as
Theodore Thomas and Leopold Damrosch. This might therefore
be the appropriate moment at which to speak parenthetically of
one whose personality dominated the early musical scene of
this country.

Like his distinguished predecessors, Walter was determined
to communicate his passionate love of great music to Americans
everywhere. He was never exclusively concerned with the am-
bition of becoming a great interpreter for an esoteric circle of
discriminating listeners. He wanted to speak, through his performances of masterpieces, to the entire country, to the very
young as well as to the mature, to the unschooled and uncul-
tured as well as to the sophisticated. He appointed himself
ambassador of good will for music to late nineteenth- and early
twentieth-century America. He was as proud of the applause of
tobacco-chewing cowboys and farm hands in the West as of the
cultured musical cliques of the large cities—prouder, possibly,
if the truth were known.

He was never a great conductor. Seidl, his associate at the
Metropolitan, looked disparagingly upon his work. Damrosch's
artistic conscience was, perhaps, not too demanding. He was
probably too easygoing. If his orchestra had to make a train,
he would play a symphony at a faster tempo. If his many and
extensive travels made rehearsals difficult, he would dispense
with rehearsals. It is very likely—no, it is even certain—that if
he were a great conductor of the stature of Mahler and Seidl,
passionately concerned with every phase and nuance of each
work he conducted, never permitting himself to relax his
stringent artistic standards regardless of where he was or before

whom, he could never have been the powerful force in the growth of music consciousness in this country. As it was, he could be patient in the face of difficulties, tolerant of ignorance, sympathetic to curiosity and inquisitiveness. There was more than one way to serve the art of music. Damrosch served it in his own way, but he served it no less passionately than did the great interpreters of Europe. And his own way of serving music was to bring it directly to the masses, which had had little or no contact with it before this—to bring it to them again and again, in every possible shape and form, until they took to it.

He had made his debut on an American concert platform in a rather inauspicious manner. He was six years old when his father, rehearsing Schubert's *Der häusliche Krieg* with the Arion Men's Chorus, decided to economize by recruiting his son to crash the cymbals. For hours, the father patiently trained his son in his part. At the concert, however, the boy became so nervous that, when Dr. Leopold gave him the signal, his hands froze stiff, and he simply could not move. The performance had to continue without the benefit of young Walter's cymbals.

That early experience, however, did not dampen Walter's determination to become a professional musician like his father. He studied in America, then went to Europe for further training. Back in New York again, he assisted his father in preparing the rehearsals of the New York Symphony, the Oratorio Society, and, finally, the Wagnerian dramas at the Metropolitan. Work with his father was a valuable apprenticeship. Though he had had virtually no experience as a professional conductor—barring a few appearances with a New Jersey orchestra—he was able to inherit his father's various musical posts in New York and to fill them with musicianly competence and self-respect.

CHAPTER FOUR

Music in 1901

―――

Throughout the country, the new year of 1901 was being ushered in with ceremony. There was much to celebrate. The old century was dead, and with it an old era. America, a world power following the successful culmination of the Spanish conflict, had never before felt so confident, so conscious of her strength, her potentialities, her resourcefulness. She had permanently shaken herself free of the financial depression which had clung to her so tenaciously throughout the first, and most of the second, administrations of Grover Cleveland. As though in compensation, the fat years had followed the lean. The year 1901 promised to be the fattest of the present crop.

There was more than one horn of plenty feeding the country. In the West, the successful application of science to agriculture had brought fecundity. In the South, new industries were arising, creating bigger factories, more jobs. In the cities, there was the spirit of enterprise in the air. Big business was beginning to grow fat through the swallowing of smaller ones. The Sherman Antitrust Law was in temporary discard.

Fabulous wealth was, so it was felt, within the reach of the

64

ambitious and the enterprising. And gold—good Alaskan gold, only recently disembedded—was plentiful throughout the country. There was some social unrest, to be sure, dissatisfaction among factory workers and miners, who saw only graft and corruption following in the wake of big business. But even a large part of this element was to be placated with the succession to the presidency of a man with social conscience, one not afraid to use a big legal stick against the rising industrial powers—Theodore Roosevelt.

It was the new age arising with the new century—the age of speed and machines, of steel and industry, of enterprise and big business. The telephone had already established itself as a necessity. Electricity was bringing a more comfortable life to the many. The first trolley car and the first subway had made their appearance in Boston in 1898, and in New York in 1900. The automobile was coming into popularity. Cities, becoming crowded and noisy, were pushing skyward; the skyscraper was beginning to create a new-world architecture. (Soon, in 1902, New York would marvel at the Flatiron Building. Then would come the Singer Building, the Municipal Building, and finally the Woolworth Building, a 785-foot modern miracle.)

The majority of Americans knew that 1900 had been very good to them, and that 1901 held forth still better promises.

America was becoming concerned with herself as never before, more self-satisfied, less inclined to look across the ocean for models to imitate. American novelists like Booth Tarkington, Jack London, Edith Wharton, and Frank Norris were turning to the American scene for their themes. They now found a large and responsive audience: a novel like *The Crisis* was able to boast of a sale of 300,000 copies. Newspapers began to flourish more than ever; muckraking was becoming a popular theme for newspaper exploitation. Large-circulation magazines

(*The Saturday Evening Post, McClure's, Collier's, Munsey's, Cosmopolitan*) were discovering the hidden potentialities of nationwide advertising.

It was a great new world, the brave world of twentieth-century America, which was in the making. Most of those who drank welcome to the New Year of 1901 felt that it was, for the most part, a good world, and a world in which each of them was perhaps destined to play an important role.

To the casual observer, the new century in America, which saw such development, did not promise a noticeable change for the musical culture of the country. It was true that the invention of the automobile brought the concert life of the great city nearer to the smaller community. Also, industrial growth, the rise of the modern city, and gain in per capita wealth meant there was more money for music, as for everything else; meant bigger and better concerts, more and more resplendent opera performances. In greater numbers than ever, the musical great of Europe came to perform in America, attracted by the large sums that Americans were ready to offer as bait. The concert activity in New York in 1901 was as brilliant in its exploitation of celebrities as that which could be found in many European capitals. But money could not buy tradition and taste and background. In 1901, as in the preceding decades, Americans were still for the most part as innocent as children in their tastes. They had not yet acquired a sharpness of musical perceptiveness or an awareness of finer musical values.

For all their outward cultivation of certain forms of music (the concerts of the great European concert artists and the opera were both well attended), Americans did not credit music with a role of any flattering importance, nor esteem the musician as a particularly respected member of the community.

The adoration for the prima donna or for the long-haired European pianist was by no means an indication of the status of the musician in American life. Mention has already been made of the fact that the American family did not encourage music as a career. More than that, it did not particularly respect the musician. Olga Samaroff in her autobiography tells of an incident which occurred in the early 1900's that admirably illustrates the condescension with which the musician (even the hallowed great) was often regarded. Samaroff and Eugène Ysaÿe were invited to perform at a private social function in Chicago. The musicians were conducted to their rest rooms through a special back stairway, then fed in a private dining room, and finally conducted to their improvised concert platform which had been carefully roped off to prevent them from mingling socially with the guests. In short, they were treated like pariahs. The utmost care had been taken to see that the atmosphere in which the brilliant gathering moved should not be polluted by the presence of these musicians.

Even greater snobbery was to be detected in the attitude of Americans to musicians of their own country. For the American musician lacked even the appeal of the exotic. America had a stifling feeling of inferiority where music was concerned. This feeling of inferiority convinced most Americans that, though they might learn to appreciate great music, they could not hope to produce it themselves. Because they lacked critical perception, they preferred to depend upon European judgment for their preferences. The American musician, therefore, was compelled to acquire European prestige (usually bought at a price) and to Europeanize his name before he dared to court American favor. As the leading concert manager in the early 1900's told a young American pianist named Hickenlooper (before she disguised her identity under the assumed foreign name of Olga

Samaroff): "If you played like Liszt and Rubinstein rolled into one, I could do nothing for you without European notices."

American orchestras generally consisted of European musicians because the European musician's status was so much higher in the eyes of audiences than his American confrere's. It was to fight against just such a prejudice that, in 1894, Sam Franko founded in New York the American Symphony Orchestra, composed exclusively of American musicians. His attempt was to prove that a good orchestra did not have to go to Europe for its materials; unfortunately, the life of Franko's orchestra was too brief to give any conviction to his argument.

In the opera house there had been in the past, and there were now in 1901, Americans enjoying stardom. But these stars had previously established their reputations in Europe. For the American singer who aspired to make his mark in this country there was but little hope, regardless of his talent. One of the American members of the Metropolitan Opera House cast italicized this when he sent in his resignation to Maurice Grau with the following lament: "I am finally convinced that an American is handicapped in grand opera merely from the fact that he *is* an American. In reality, I was practically buried for two years. One time after another circumstances arose which made it evident that persons from abroad were in a better position to gain the best places." The American public was ready to buy its music culture; but it was too timid, too uncertain of itself, to foster a culture of its own.

For much the same reason, the American composer was without honor. Though adventurous musicians like Theodore Thomas, Walter Damrosch, and Franz Van der Stucken tried, from time to time, to introduce American works on their programs, these works met either with outright hostility or else with general boredom. It required courage to play American

music when audiences were unreceptive. Because of a general
lack of such courage, American music did not know frequent
performances.

Previous attempts had been made from time to time by farsighted musicians to encourage American music. When Ole
Bull became manager of the Astor Place Opera House in 1855
he offered a prize of $1,000 for the "best original grand opera by
an American composer, and upon a strictly American subject."
His all-too-brief tenure of his post—two weeks in all—made it
impossible for the ideal to be realized. Yet, when an American
opera did receive performance—the first American opera to
emerge in a major opera house was W. H. Fry's *Leonora* at the
Academy of Music in 1858—public indifference brought an
early death to the work. Later, when Theodore Thomas organized the American Opera Company in 1886, one of his aims, as
we have seen, was the presentation of operas by Americans, but
this goal, too, was never realized—principally for lack of genuine creative talent. The American public simply would not
accept a native product with the same respect and inquisitiveness with which it approached European creations. Ignace Jan
Paderewski recognized the sad plight of the American composer
when, in 1900, he established a trust fund of $10,000 with which
to offer a prize of $1,000, once every three years, to a worthy
native-born composer. The first recipient of this prize was
Horatio Parker in 1901, with a cantata, *A Star Song*.

The American composer in 1901 knew that his music might
never achieve the life of actual performance unless it were to be
picked up by some enterprising European organization—Horatio Parker's oratorio, *St. Christopher*, which failed to make
any impression when performed by Walter Damrosch in New
York in 1897, achieved substantial success at the Norwich and
Bristol festivals in England soon afterward. The composer also

knew that even if, by some miracle, his work received an
American performance, it would never be adequately appreciated by the general public. Such a situation was not likely to
encourage creative fecundity. The wonder of it is that the
period *did* produce such reputable composers as MacDowell,
John Knowles Paine, Chadwick, and Horatio Parker!

This hostility of Americans toward Americans was accen-
tuated in 1901 in a much publicized libel suit brought by
Victor Herbert against the periodical, *Musical Courier*. Victor
Herbert was not an American, but he had long since established
his home permanently in this country (having arrived in 1886
to become a cellist in the orchestra of the Metropolitan Opera
House) and had become a part of its musical life by virtue
both of his contribution as composer of serious music and
operettas, and of his work as conductor of symphonic music
with the Pittsburgh Symphony Orchestra. In its issue of July
17, 1901, the editor of *Musical Courier*, Marc A. Blumenberg,
launched a vitriolic attack on Herbert. Why, unprovoked, he
should have gone out of his way to shower abuse on Herbert
is not readily explicable, since personal feelings do not seem to
have entered into the controversy. Actually, it was probably
simply another reflection of American eagerness to annihilate
musicians of their nationality. In any case, Blumenberg mocked
at the fact that a composer of light operettas should presume to
become the conductor of an ambitious symphony orchestra
—ignoring the fact that, by the standards of the day, Herbert
was actually an admirable conductor, and that his taste and
resourcefulness were forces in educating his public to good
orchestral music. Warming up to his subject, Blumenberg
vented his heaviest wrath on Herbert's music by saying that
"everything Herbert wrote is copied; there is not one original

strain in anything he has done, and all his copies are from sources that are comic or serio-comic."

Herbert accepted the challenge of Blumenberg's verbal glove-across-the-cheek. He brought suit for $50,000 against the magazine. Herbert's lawyer fought the case on the grounds that Blumenberg's denunciations constituted not "criticism" but libel. The defense attempted to prove its case by showing similarities (sometimes far-fetched, other times quite striking) between melodies of Herbert and those of other composers. Then it completely vitiated its cause by consciously distorting a theme by Beethoven in order to make it agree more noticeably with an excerpt from a Herbert operetta. When Walter Damrosch took the stand in defense of Herbert and said that it was fantastic to accuse him of outright plagiarism, the case of the defense crumbled. The court awarded Herbert damages amounting to $15,000, which, following an appeal, were cut down to about $5,000. In any case, Herbert was completely vindicated, and his vindication was in a sense a victory for the much-abused American composer as well.

Money was being spent generously on music. Yet American orchestras waged a perpetual—frequently an unsuccessful—struggle for sheer existence. By 1901 there were thirteen major orchestras in the country. Of this number, only two (those in Boston and Chicago) were subsidized. Elsewhere, even in affluent New York, orchestras were barely able to keep alive. Benefactors arose in cities like St. Louis, Cincinnati, Pittsburgh, and Los Angeles to finance orchestral ventures. But always it was the same story. Though these orchestras attempted to pander to public taste through popular programs, the response of the audiences still was too apathetic to ensure prolonged existence. In St. Louis, for example, an orchestra had been founded in 1881, went through a few perilous years, then passed unlamented; in 1896 a St. Louis musician, Karl Schneider, had tried to restore an orchestra to the city and for a while kept it alive with his own funds. But, by 1901, the orchestra had lapsed into somnolence. In Cincinnati and in Los Angeles, orchestras that had been founded in 1895 and 1897 respectively had equally unstable foundations. In Brooklyn the celebrated Philharmonic Society had passed out of existence in 1891 after three and a half decades, when its conductor, Theodore Thomas, transferred his activity to Chicago. And in New York, towards the close of the century, Walter Damrosch's Symphony Society temporarily discontinued its season of concerts because there was not a sufficient audience for them.

Economic instability led to unfortunate conditions. The case of the New York Philharmonic might serve as an example of conditions existing throughout the country—the exceptions being, of course, the two great orchestras of Boston and Chicago. At the turn of the century, the Philharmonic (still a cooperative venture) gave only six concerts a season. These showed a deficit. The orchestra was in no position to afford a living wage to the musicians. If the musicians had another engagement on the day of rehearsal, or even on the evening of a concert, they would fail to show up, sometimes without even the courtesy of an explanation. The frantic conductor was often compelled, at the last moment, to make drastic changes. There were other abuses as well. Walter Damrosch, writing about the New York Philharmonic of 1901, said:*

I found to my amazement that of the hundred players at the concerts less than fifty were actual members of the organization, the rest being engaged from the outside, often changed from one concert to the next. Some of the members were old men who should no longer

* *My Musical Life* (New York: Charles Scribner's Sons, 1923).

have played in the orchestra at all. Most of the wind instruments were outsiders and therefore could not be properly controlled regarding attendance or rehearsals.

The American orchestra simply could not provide the musician with a livelihood. Even so distinguished a musician as Leopold Damrosch, conductor of two major musical organizations, had had to earn his living, in the last decades of the preceding century, by giving lessons on the violin and in composition, and by appearing as a violin soloist at public functions. What then could be the hope or expectation of the lesser musician? Or the musician working in a community less prosperous than New York? What Theodore Thomas wrote in 1881 was still applicable in 1901: "New York is the only city in America in which the orchestral player can make a living, and even here he must give lessons or play at balls and parties, thereby losing or injuring the finer qualities of an orchestral player."

What was true of orchestras was likewise true in other fields of musical endeavor. Concerts did not draw well unless they were given by a highly publicized and glamorous European virtuoso. Those who did not come to America preceded by a fanfare of publicity could not expect to attract attention, for American audiences were not yet sufficiently perceptive to recognize true talent for themselves.

Yet to penetrate beneath surfaces was to acquire at least a measure of hope for America's musical salvation. Actually, under close inspection, a quickening of musical life might have been detected—even in 1901. That there were thirteen major orchestras functioning at all was in itself a bold step forward, proof that the work of a Theodore Thomas had not been wasted; for when Thomas first had come on the American scene the only permanent orchestra was the New York Philharmonic. More significant still was the fact that two of these orchestras deserved to rank with the great of the world. In Boston, the symphony orchestra had known the disciplinary regime of Wilhelm Gericke from 1884 to 1889. Gericke was not only an astute interpreter but also a consummate drillmaster. His technical mastery produced an integrated and responsive orchestral group. When Artur Nikisch succeeded Gericke in 1889, Nikisch was so delighted by the virtuosity of the orchestra that he cried: "All I have to do is to poetize!" The four years of Nikisch's direction created a standard for Boston which was unique in the country, equal to that achieved at the time by the historic orchestras of Germany and Austria.

Unfortunately, the Boston audiences did not fully appreciate the fastidious work of Nikisch. Though at first they were excited by his magnetizing personality, their ardor cooled with each consecutive season. There followed clashes between the conductor and the directors of the orchestra over the programs. In despair, Nikisch offered $5,000 to be released from his contract. He went in 1893; but he had imposed upon the orchestra the permanent impression of his artistic nature. Emil Paur, another interpreter of penetrating insight, followed him during the next five years. In 1898, Gericke was once again the conductor in Boston (he was to remain at his post till 1906). His scrupulous demands and high ideals were to permit no relaxation of the high standards achieved by Nikisch and Paur.

The Boston Symphony Orchestra, by adherence to the finest in orchestral music, was the criterion by which every orchestra in America measured itself. It provided the necessary encouragement to conductors in other parts of the country to attempt the emulation of European standards. It inspired envy; and envy brought healthy imitation. When, in Chicago, the orchestra committee came to Theodore Thomas timidly and suggested that he popularize the programs in order to placate his public, Thomas was able to say: "Would you want Chicago's orchestra to be less important than that of Boston? In Boston, you know, they don't have to have popular programs." The committee reconsidered its request and discreetly withdrew.

The Chicago Orchestra was a worthy rival to that of Boston. Slowly overcoming criticism and opposition during the past decade, Theodore Thomas had been able to increase the attendance at his concerts without particularly pandering to popular taste. As a matter of fact, after the brief period in which he had made some minor concessions in his programs, he reached for new horizons as he felt the ground under him grow increasingly secure. In 1901 Thomas launched a cycle of Beethoven's music in which, for the first time in Chicago, all the Beethoven symphonies were presented in chronological order. The success of this undertaking inspired an even more ambitious one the following season: a historical cycle of six concerts tracing the evolution of orchestral music from Giovanni Gabrieli to Tchaikovsky. How decisively Thomas won his battle for great orchestral music in Chicago became eloquently apparent in 1904 when a public subscription was asked to build a new concert hall expressly for the use of the orchestra, and there were found eight thousand music lovers ready to contribute $75,000.

But another and a younger Theodore Thomas—in the person of Walter Damrosch—was on the musical scene to carry on missionary labors for music. In 1901 Damrosch was possibly the major musical figure in the country and its most significant and dynamic force. His travels throughout the country with the New York Symphony continued the work of Thomas in educating Americans to symphonic music. As early as 1885 Damrosch had toured with his orchestra, in subsequent years penetrating ever farther south and west, reaching more and more toward people who had previously never heard a concert. He was the genial and lovable intermediary between the masterpieces of music and the nonmusical public. It can only be guessed how greatly he was responsible for converting different parts of the country to the musical gospel he was preaching.

As a conductor, Damrosch also fought the battle for the deserving composer. How he struggled to bring Wagner recognition has already been touched upon, and how he continued this work with his own opera company (once again in extensive tours) when he could no longer work at the Metropolitan. And he had combined his baton efforts with those of the spoken word. Even in those years he won new admirers for Wagner through his charming lectures at the piano. Other composers neglected by the orchestras of the time found him their spokesman. He was the first American to perform Tchaikovsky's *Pathétique* Symphony; Brahms's Fourth; Elgar's First; and compositions by Saint-Saëns and Liszt, and (in later years) by Ravel, Enesco, Delius, Sibelius, Stravinsky, and Honegger.

He inaugurated Sunday concerts (symphony concerts on Sundays had been unknown before then), educational concerts for young people, children's concerts—always alert and eager to create new and larger audiences for great music. In New York he had been responsible for the erection, in 1891, of a magnificent new temple of music—Carnegie Hall—thereby, in all probability, inspiring other cities to build concert auditoriums of their own. He was the vigorous proponent of American music not only by consistently performing the works of American composers (whereas so many other conductors remained apathetic) but also by composing American music himself.

There were other signs that musical activity was increasing.

The rise of conservatories throughout the country, and the introduction of music study into schools and colleges, had swelled the number of active musicians. It was estimated that, in 1901, there were more than 90,000 professional musicians. This represented an increase of 300 per cent over 1880, while during this same period the population of the country had not even doubled. Old Lowell Mason would have glowed at the sight of such a figure!

Growing appreciation of music brought about new great festivals in different parts of the country. In the autumn of 1893 a series of festival concerts had been held in Ann Arbor, Michigan, under the direction of Emil Mollenhauer, in which the principal work was Verdi's *Requiem*. This festival was so successful that it was decided to establish it on a permanent basis, with Dr. Albert A. Stanley (professor of music at the University of Michigan) as director; and the Ann Arbor Festival was born. In 1900, in Bethlehem, Pennsylvania (the musical traditions of which, as we have seen, went back as far as 1742 to the *Singstunde* of the Moravian settlers), a Bach Choir was formed, growing out of several previous performances of the *Passion According to St. Matthew*. This choir recruited men and women from a forty-mile radius who, driven only by their love for music-making, came to Bethlehem to sing under Director John Frederick Wolle. On the groundwork of their enthusiasm and industry the annual Bach Festival in Bethlehem was built.

Musical activity of a varied nature was further demonstrating signs of life. In Boston there had arisen a string quartet comprising the first-desk men of the Boston Symphony Orchestra. This quartet (named after its leader, Franz Kneisel) was creating an altogether new standard for chamber-music performance in America. In 1900 Sam Franko inaugurated a series of

concerts of old, esoteric music which was to bring a decidedly
new flavor and richness to the musical repertoire heard each
season. Children's concerts—to educate the American orchestra
audiences of the next decade—had been inaugurated by Walter Damrosch's brother, Frank, in 1898 and further adopted by
Walter in New York, introducing an altogether new note in
music education.

The richest phase of American musical activity in 1901, however, was to be found in opera, still restricted for the most part
to New York, but flourishing in that city. The year 1901 brought
with it the "golden age of opera" performances. Three years
earlier, Maurice Grau had undertaken the exclusive direction
of the Metropolitan Opera House, and with him the epoch of
"great casts" was launched. "I can't read a note of music," Grau
would often say, while stroking his closely cropped beard. He
even confessed that his love for music was restricted almost
exclusively to comic operas and popular orchestral selections.
But he was a born showman. Suave, elegant, much-traveled, a
polished man-of-the-world, he had an innate shrewdness that
could size up every situation accurately and could take stock of
every audience. He did not delude himself that he had some
sublime artistic mission to perform. He called himself an enter-
tainer, the purveyor of shows on the grandest possible scale.
He knew that New York music audiences liked spectacles, glamour, brilliant stars. He provided all these in lavish abundance.
Artistic details were of no importance to him. He often disre-
garded the importance of stage direction; he paid scant attention to scenery or costuming; he was not exacting in his demands
for a careful preparation of each performance. For this he was
sometimes subjected to criticism by the press. "Why, Mr. Grau,"

lamented one critic, "why don't you give us some new scenery? Why don't you handle the lights better? And why don't you give your full Metropolitan orchestra instead of filling its vacancies in a haphazard way with local talent?" And, following a performance of *Don Giovanni,* W. J. Henderson wrote: "And the costumes of the accessories! From what museum do they come? From the wardrobe room of the Metropolitan Opera House, gentle reader. There is not such another museum of antiquities in the land."

The critics might rave. But Maurice Grau could smile benignly and say: "My public doesn't come to see the chorus. It comes to hear the famous artists of the company. Why should I dress my chorus in purple and fine linen?" And he could point his finger to the box office to stress his point. Sold-out houses were the rule, with often as many as a thousand standees per performance. The great casts (the like of which were to be seen in no other opera house anywhere) offered a spectacle which few New York music lovers could resist: *Les Huguenots* with Emma Eames, Nordica, Plançon, Jean de Reszke; *Don Giovanni* with Lilli Lehmann, Sembrich, Nordica, Edouard de Reszke, Maurel, and Salignac; *Lohengrin* with the two De Reszke brothers, Nordica, and Schumann-Heink.

It was perhaps inevitable that casts of stars should invite jealousy and bitterness among the featured artists. Great singers allotted minor roles fought for the right to appear in the larger parts. Stars in the principal roles showed violent jealousy over such matters as their respective number of curtain calls or the size of type used for their names on the billboards. It required the tact and managerial genius of Maurice Grau to keep his all-star casts intact, to soothe the troubled spirits of his temperamental singers with soft-spoken words.

Perhaps the most intense rivalry was that between Melba and Nordica, probably because Melba had secret ambitions to usurp Nordica's important Wagnerian roles (even though her voice was ill suited for such parts) and Nordica was aware of these ambitions. Each time Grau featured one of these artists on an opening night performance he had to steel himself to the smoldering and passionate anger of the other, who took it as a personal affront. Grau proved his impartiality in this rivalry by assigning two opening nights to each of these stars. The story goes that at one performance in which Melba was appearing she happened to discover through the peephole in the curtain that Nordica was occupying a front-row seat. Violently she stormed to Grau, insisting that she would not appear unless Nordica were ejected from the opera house. Not until Grau had convinced Melba that this was impossible, that as a purchaser of an admission ticket Mme. Nordica had full legal right to her possession of a seat in the audience, was Melba's anger cooled to a point where she would be reasonable.

No expense deterred Grau from studding his performances with great singers. If a singer lost favor in the eyes of the public, Grau stood ready to buy out the contract, even if it had still a few years to run. If a singer suddenly rose to fame, Grau was at hand with a handsome and unsought increase in salary. No price was too high for retaining the glamour of his opera presentations. And yet, when it came to spending money for scenery, for orchestral players, for costumes, for a stage director, Grau could be incredibly parsimonious.

The music dramas of Wagner, too, profited by Grau's expansiveness in the matter of casts. Anton Seidl, the great Wagner conductor, died in 1898, but he had lived long enough to restore Wagner at least partially to the Metropolitan repertoire.

The success attending the first season of Walter Damrosch's Wagnerian company further persuaded Grau that Wagner might still appeal to audiences. In 1900, therefore, Grau invited Damrosch to conduct a season of Wagner operas at the Metropolitan, offering him such valuable assisting artists as the De Reszke brothers, Ternina, David Bispham, and Johanna Gadski.

CHAPTER FIVE

Before the
First World War

T HE ORCHESTRA situation in New York, which was in a
sorry state at the turn of the century, was to undergo
significant revision. Early in 1903, Walter Damrosch
proposed a plan by which the orchestral plight of New York
might be remedied. He offered to acquire the necessary financial backing to establish the New York Philharmonic on a permanent basis. But this backing was predicated on a thorough
reorganization in which the dead wood might be replaced by
younger men.

The offer was politely turned down by the officers of the
Philharmonic. "Reorganization," they said, "would so change
the nature of the orchestra as to seriously interfere with the
control of its affairs by its members, which has always been its
vital principle." In other (and less circumlocutory) words: The
older men refused to vote themselves out of the orchestra.

The reorganization of the Philharmonic was temporarily post-
poned. Meanwhile Damrosch set about reorganizing his own
New York Symphony Society which for a few years had been
quiescent. In 1903 a small guaranty fund was procured with
which to rehabilitate the organization. Then, temporarily aban-

doning its one-time partially subsidized program, the society evolved a cooperative arrangement in which the orchestra men and the guarantors divided the profits equally.

This arrangement made possible the resumption of concert activity by the orchestra. But the plan did not work too smoothly. The experience of a few seasons underscored what had already long been proved in Boston and Chicago: only a large subsidy, which could buy the services of the men to the exclusion of other activities, could create a truly great orchestra. In 1907, therefore, a second reorganization was found essential. This time the New York Symphony abandoned the cooperative plan and went on a subsidized basis, with funds gathered by Harry Harkness Flagler. Elaborate plans could now be drawn up to model a New York orchestra after the pattern of the Boston Symphony. The orchestra men received a regular salary for their services, the salaries being increased year by year as the guaranty fund grew. Wood-wind players—of whom there was a particular dearth in the country—were recruited by Damrosch from leading European organizations. An extended series was launched—twenty-eight concerts a season.

New York now boasted a major subsidized orchestra, joining Boston and Chicago. A second New York subsidized orchestra came into being without much further delay. The New York Philharmonic, in its attempt to attract a larger audience, decided to feature a different conductor at each of its concerts in 1904. For three seasons, eight major conductors from Europe were invited to direct the eight different concerts (and eight public rehearsals) of the Philharmonic season. These three seasons saw a parade of distinguished men of the baton: Edouard Colonne, Felix Weingartner, Henry J. Wood, Richard Strauss, Mengelberg, Max Fiedler, Kunwald, Steinbach, and Safonov being among them. But the response of the audiences was still reserved. In 1907, startled by the rehabilitation of its competitor, the New York Symphony, and recognizing this to be a threat to its very existence, the Philharmonic decided that the time had come to clean house. A small subsidy made reorganization possible, and a sixteen-concert season was launched, with the brilliant Russian, Safonov, as principal conductor. Not until 1909 was a permanent guaranty acquired for the Philharmonic.

But orchestral activity in New York did not end with the concerts of these two major orchestras. There were concerts of old music directed each season by Sam Franko, until the end of the decade, through which the more inquiring music lover could become acquainted with forgotten masters. There was a Peoples Symphony Orchestra, directed by Arens, which, beginning in 1902, gave concerts at Cooper Union with admission prices ranging from ten to fifty cents. This was an important step in bringing good music to the average person instead of waiting for the average person to come to good music. Other orchestras, founded by such reputable musicians as Victor Herbert and Arnold Volpe, gave performances at periodic intervals. And, in 1904, still another important orchestra was created —to spread the gospel of Russian musical art in America. It was the Russian Symphony Orchestra directed by Modest Altschuler. Through its stanch adherence to the best traditions of Russian music, and by its pioneer efforts to bring to America not only the best works of the younger Russian composers but also the most gifted of Russian virtuosos (Rachmaninoff, Scriabin, Mischa Elman, and Joseph Lhevinne were among the artists to make their American débuts with the Russian Symphony), Altschuler's orchestra brought considerable vitality to New York symphonic life.

Other cities in addition to New York joined Boston and Chicago as centers of orchestral music. In these cities, orchestras arose in spite of prejudices, in spite of the arguments of opponents who felt that the demand for good orchestral music was too meager to warrant the extensive expenditure involved in supporting a local symphonic organization. After all, was not fine music already brought to many large cities by the great orchestras of Boston, Chicago, and New York on their annual tours? But, in many cases, civic pride was instrumental in overcoming these arguments. Why—argued others no less heatedly —should their fair city be less important musically than Boston or Chicago? And so, orchestras arose in cities which before this had known only scattered concerts by visiting organizations. On November 1, 1902, a charter was adopted by the Philadelphia Orchestra Association which placed on a solid basis the orchestra founded a year earlier by Fritz Scheel. The new orchestra hoped to encourage "performance of first-class orchestral music in Philadelphia." A year later, a subsidy was raised by Emil Oberhoffer to support an orchestra of sixty musicians in Minneapolis. In 1905 St. Paul had its large symphony orchestra; in 1906, New Orleans; in 1908, Seattle; in 1909, San Francisco.

Obviously the spread of orchestral music indicated an increasing awareness of good music. Not all the civic pride in the world could have raised the formidable sums necessary to create symphony orchestras in those cities if there had not been at least a curiosity about and a hunger for orchestral music. Yet it should not hastily be assumed that, overnight, the musical tastes of the country had already sharpened to a point of discrimination. Where programs of the highest quality were presented (as in Boston, Chicago, and New York), crowded houses were the exception rather than the rule. It was necessary to perform music of a more popular nature, together with symphonies and concertos, if audiences were to be drawn into the concert hall.

A rather good indication of the orchestral preferences of the American audiences of this period can be derived from polls conducted among them for all-request programs. In 1905 Victor Herbert, whose programs always embraced a fair representation of the best musical literature, conducted such a poll among the Sunday afternoon audiences of his orchestra in New York. The selections chosen by that audience included: Suppé's *Poet and Peasant* Overture, the March from Raff's *Lenore* Symphony, Rubinstein's *Melody in F*, Massenet's *Neopolitan Scenes* and selections from Victor Herbert operettas. Not a single symphony was chosen; not a single classical overture; not a single work by Bach, Mozart, Haydn, Brahms, or Wagner! In St. Louis, during a similar period, audiences showed hardly any more discrimination. Liszt's *Second Hungarian Rhapsody* received the greatest number of votes, followed closely by Schumann's *Träumerei*. Other works selected were Schubert's *Military March* and Johann Strauss's *Blue Danube Waltz*. A symphony did not appear on the list until the twenty-eighth choice—Beethoven's Fifth, which received a total of forty-four out of almost two thousand votes.

As a matter of fact, such extension of musical activity as took place up to the outbreak of World War I came in spite of a comparatively unreceptive public. There were, for example, only small audiences for great chamber music. Yet important organizations arose to combat public indifference and ignorance. Among them was at least one group that could be numbered with the most distinguished ensembles of the world—the Kneisel Quartet. The Kneisel Quartet, which, as one New

York critic pointed out, was "one of the greatest forces for good in the musical history of this country," was founded in Boston by Higginson from four members of the Boston Symphony Orchestra. For several years, until the Quartet could establish itself, Higginson paid its bills. From the very first, the Kneisel Quartet made no concessions to public ignorance. At its inaugural concert, which took place in Boston in 1885, its program comprised a quartet of Volkmann, the canzonetta from Mendelssohn's E-flat Quartet, the minuet from Mozart's C Minor Quartet, and Beethoven's Quintet in C. When it began its first series of concerts in New York—this was in 1891 at the ballroom of Sherry's on Fifth Avenue—it gave the American première of the Brahms G minor Quintet, and with it played the Mozart Quartet in C major and the second movement of Tchaikovsky's D major Quartet. Obviously the Kneisels had no intention of pampering audiences, of giving spoon feedings of the classics!

In 1903, the Kneisel Quartet disassociated itself from the Boston Symphony Orchestra, and established itself in New York as an independent musical organization. From this time on, it was the greatest musical group of its kind in the country. For the next decade its concerts were heard extensively throughout the country. But, as a New York critic remarked, "the career of the Kneisel Quartet in its earliest years in New York was by no means an easy one. The taste for chamber music had not been so developed in this city as to assure sufficient support for its concerts, and after a time it was on the point of giving up its venture here. The persuasion of a few ardent music lovers induced another trial; the turning point arrived and the public, finally educated to the appreciation of what was offered it in these concerts, came to give a firm and unwavering support to Mr. Kneisel and his associates."

Away from New York, the Kneisel Quartet encountered a

most striking ignorance of chamber music, which must have
proved disheartening to four high-minded and cultured musicians. They would be asked, in streetcars what public dance
they were scheduled to perform for, and when they patiently
informed the hopeful questioner that they were a group of
concert artists who played in a small ensemble, they would meet
silent incredulity. In some places the audiences had never before heard of a combination like a string quartet: "Too bad,"
remarked one kind lady to Kneisel, "that you can't afford to have
a full orchestra instead of only four players." In others, there
was vituperative criticism because light salon numbers did not
appear on the program. Sometimes ignorance bordered on the
whimsical. In one town, an admirer approached Franz Kneisel
at the end of a concert and begged him (with a rather misplaced
display of erudition) to have the quartet play, some day, an
all-Wagner program!

In New York it was considered a mark of social distinction
to be seen at a concert by the Kneisels. There was, consequently,
a smart audience for these performances. But away from New
York (and in New York, as far as other chamber-music groups
were concerned) it seemed impossible to sell chamber music
to large audiences. Hermann Klein attempted to educate audiences to chamber music by trying the experiment of presenting
in New York only single movements from the great quartets—
with the hope that the sample might tempt the audiences to
ask for the complete work. But he had to admit defeat and
abandon the project in the face of sparsely attended concerts.

Yet—remarkable to note!—chamber-music performances developed during this period. The Kneisels were indefatigable in
their concert work. They provided a healthy diet of such music.
Besides, another great quartet came upon the scene in 1904—
undismayed by the apathy of the times. Financed by E. J. De

Coppet, the Flonzaley Quartet was born, to work with the Kneisels in spreading chamber music in America. It was at a Flonzaley concert that a woman approached the second violinist and begged to look at his instrument. "Why," she exclaimed with amazement, "it looks exactly like a first violin." During its first years of concert work in America, the Flonzaleys played in so many half-empty halls that one of their members suggested: "Why not let us try coming out on the stage on bicycles, as they do in the circus? *That,* surely, would make an impression!" But Mr. de Coppet was willing to foot the bills patiently until the Flonzaleys should receive the appreciation they deserved.

It is quite true that concert audiences had by this time outgrown the adolescent love of the circus tricks that had marked music-making of a half-century earlier. But what now brought them into the concert hall was still something quite remote from the lure of great music itself. What held appeal was usually such irrelevant attractions as Paderewski's golden crown of hair (his magnificent pianism was incidental), or Jan Kubelik's magnetizing pyrotechnics (what matter if he also was guilty of bad musicianship?), or De Pachmann's strange stage idiosyncrasies. These, and other equally exotic attractions, played an important part in shaping the musical tastes of the time. It has been generally recognized that Fritz Kreisler's first success in America, in the early part of the first decade, was derived, not from his profound interpretations of works by Bach and Beethoven, but from his transcription of Dvořák's *Humoresque,* which for several seasons he was compelled to perform at almost every appearance. Rachmaninoff's appeal to American concert audiences, during his first tour in 1909, rested most securely on the fact that he was the composer of a prelude known to every schoolgirl who played the piano; audiences wanted to hear the composer play this favorite. A great artist, concerned only with his art, and not interested in exploiting either himself or his personal peculiarities, was not likely to have great drawing power, even if he was a master in his field.

Richard Strauss, when he came in 1904 with the Wetzlar orchestra to conduct programs of his own music, was handsomely received by smart audiences, even though he did not particularly indulge in self-publicization; but Strauss was already the most celebrated and controversial figure in the music of the time and was therefore certain to arouse curiosity. Other musicians, less spectacular but no less significant, were ignored. Chaliapin, coming to the Metropolitan in 1907 fresh from triumphs at La Scala and in Paris, found no great enthusiasm for his searching art. Vincent d'Indy, probably the greatest French musician of his time, came in 1905 to direct American orchestras principally in his own works. He met apathy toward his conducting and outright antagonism toward his music. He was too shy and retiring, too absorbed with exclusively musical considerations to create a stir.

Pablo Casals, an equally reticent artist, also failed to make an impression when he came to this country in 1904—even though at the time he was generally recognized in Europe as the foremost of living cellists. His audiences were bored by the severe programs that included so many works by Bach (at his début he gave, for an encore, a Bach unaccompanied sonata). Also, his personal mannerisms were too reserved, his stage behavior too austere. His manager, in despair at the half-empty houses, begged him to adopt a more pleasant stage manner. "If you would just *smile*," pleaded the manager, "if you would just try to be a little pleasant when you come on the stage, I'm sure American audiences would like you so much better." Casals's answer was to change his manager rather than his manner. But he had to wait many years before audiences sufficiently overcome the effect of his unprepossessing personality to be able to recognize the magnificence of his performances. Many years later, in commenting on the crowded halls in which he played, Casals remarked acidly: "And I'm *still* not smiling!"

The American musician—and particularly the American composer—still suffered at the hands of public indifference. This incapacity to give the American composer his due was reflected in the "MacDowell affair," which created a stir in the press in the 1900's. Edward MacDowell was at the time in the full ripeness of his creative powers. He had already been recognized in Europe as America's leading serious composer; his best works were esteemed the products of a fine and original creative mind. And that a man of such musical stature should have been subjected to really shabby treatment by a great university throws a strong light on the indifference of the age to distinguished native composers.

This "MacDowell affair," which involved Columbia University, has been so thoroughly and dispassionately treated by John Tasker Howard in his valuable book *Our American Music* that it is unnecessary to retrace the ground in these pages. But the essential facts should be reviewed briefly, since the incident forms an integral part of the musical picture of the time.

In 1896 MacDowell accepted President Seth Low's invitation to take the chairmanship of the newly organized music department at Columbia University. The acceptance was perhaps a mistake on MacDowell's part, as Mr. Howard suggests. MacDowell was by temperament unsuited for the organizational routine of conducting a university music department; and he was not meant for the drudgery of teaching elementary classes in harmony, composition, and music history. But it cannot be charged that MacDowell did not fill the office with his customary devotion; he applied zeal and energy to his many pedagogical duties. At the same time, he was too much an individualist, too much the idealist to accept the dull *status quo* of the Columbia University music courses. He dreamed of a thorough reorganization of his department in which the study of music might become living and palpitant; he visualized a department of fine arts at Columbia in which the study of all the arts would be correlated. About twenty-five years earlier another great American musician had had a similar vision—Theodore Thomas when he was appointed director of the Cincinnati Musical College. But Thomas had been forced to resign his position in disgust when he discovered that all that was demanded of him was a formalized music school dispensing the usual stereotyped form of music education.

In 1902 Nicholas Murray Butler succeeded Seth Low as president of the university. He listened to MacDowell's ideas, but found them impracticable. And, while MacDowell was on sabbatical leave, Butler reorganized the department, not along the progressive lines suggested, but followed the accepted university standards. In such a scheme of things, where the study of music was so routinized, MacDowell felt that he could play no part. He decided to withdraw quietly and confided his intentions to Butler in a private interview. His resignation was immediately accepted.

The newspapers got wind of MacDowell's resignation and, sniffing a story, emphasized the fact that MacDowell was withdrawing because he had failed to achieve a revitalization of his department. Butler denied this emphatically, explaining (in a letter to the New York *Times*) that MacDowell had resigned only because he wished to devote more time to composition, and also that Columbia had recognized MacDowell's genius by offering him a "research scholarship."

MacDowell had no use for stuffy lies. In a letter to the New York *Post* he contradicted Butler's explanation. "President Butler has evidently misunderstood my interview with him when he affirms that my sole object in resigning from Columbia was to have more time to write: he failed to explain the circumstances which led to my resignation. . . . There is certainly individual idealism in all universities, but the general tendency of modern education is toward materialism. . . . For seven years I have put all my energy and enthusiasm in the cause of art at Columbia, and now, at last, recognizing the futility of my efforts, I have resigned the chair of music in order to resume my own belated vocation." As for the generosity of Professor Butler's offer of a "research professorship": "The research professorship offered me by the president consisted of my lending to Columbia the use of my name, with no duties, and no salary."

The trustees of Columbia University and President Butler were infuriated at MacDowell for having rushed to a newspaper with his explanation; they considered it an improper act, forgetting for the moment that President Butler had himself been guilty of it a few days earlier! As MacDowell commented in a letter to the trustees of the university: "Mr. Butler's misleading communication to the press was a far graver breach of this confidence than my using the only means in my power to correct the statement."

What specifically had brought about the rupture between MacDowell and Butler has never been completely clarified; nor is it possible, for lack of illuminating details, to say that one party was in the right, while the other was in the wrong. But a few conclusions are obvious, even from such sparse information as we have at our disposal. A more farsighted and idealistic head of a university than President Butler might have been able to take full advantage of MacDowell's capabilities

and vision to create one of the truly great centers of musical
learning in the country, if not in the world; the cry of "im-
practical" is always the last resort of the reactionary. It also
seems probable that if Butler had not been so eager to dispense
with the services of MacDowell, some compromise might have
been reached whereby the greatest creative figure in American
music might have remained at the head of the music department at Columbia. Finally, there was more than a suggestion
of shabbiness in the treatment of MacDowell by the university.
After MacDowell's resignation, Butler announced that Mac-
Dowell's assistant, McWhood, had been promoted to an adjunct
professorship, explaining that McWhood had as a matter of fact
assumed the greater share of teaching assignments in the department long before this. The implication obviously was that
MacDowell had been filling a sinecure, relegating his teaching
assignments to assistants, whereas the reverse was the truth—
namely, that MacDowell had been overzealous in assuming the
obligations of a crowded teaching schedule.

The affair left a permanent mark on MacDowell. He felt that
he had been wronged, that he had been put in a disagreeable
light, that he had no redress. It left him a sick and broken man.
He found it difficult to find the tranquillity with which to return to intensive composition. He yielded to a smothering
melancholia. By 1905 his nervous disorders had been so aggra-
vated that his mind began to wander. Finally he lost all mental
clarity and became like a child. He would sit near a window,
perpetually smiling, oblivious of his surroundings and his fate,
thumbing the pages of a fairy-tale book which seemed to bring
him a strange and inexplicable pleasure. From this he was released by death, which came on January 24, 1908.

I would not like to leave the assumption that MacDowell's
mental disintegration was caused by his treatment at the hands

of Columbia University. But that this was a contributing cause, that it helped to bring MacDowell nearer his doom, is obvious. In our own day, MacDowell would have been accorded every honor and tribute which we can bestow on a great creative figure. But the early part of the twentieth century had not much use for its own genius, and so it crushed him.

America seemed equally incapable of giving homage to genius for its own sake, rather than for its superficial trimmings. This was stressed in the case of Gustav Mahler. In a later day, nearer our own time, Mahler's savage pursuit after perfection, his stubborn refusal to make compromises with the high standards he set for himself, his irritated impatience with anything that did not relate directly to (or react to the best interests of) great music, his strength of will that made him intransigent where art was concerned—all this would have been honored. For these qualities Mahler would have been apotheosized. But during the first decade of the twentieth century these qualities proved puzzling, and he was continually misunderstood.

Mahler came to America for the first time in 1907 to conduct at the Metropolitan Opera House. On January 1, 1908, he made his bow with *Tristan und Isolde*—a performance further made memorable by the debut of Olive Fremstad. On November 30, he began three special guest performances with the New York Symphony. Soon after these performances a few women came to him with the offer to become musical director of the New York Philharmonic. They explained that they realized that the reorganization which had taken place with the orchestra two years earlier had not been successful. The standards of the orchestra were still lax. The personnel was uneven. These women

were prepared to acquire a large guaranty fund with which to
establish the Philharmonic on a stable basis. Would Mr. Mahler
consider taking over the conductor's baton?

Never sparing himself, Mahler accepted the offer, assuming
the full direction of the Philharmonic together with his assignments at the Metropolitan. It was a fatal step. For at the Metropolitan things had gone well. He had given incandescent performances of Mozart and Wagner. Though there had been a few
notes of carping criticism by some enemies, his interpretations
were welcomed for their freshness, vigor, musicianly fastidious-
ness. But at the Philharmonic, Mahler encountered dissension,
petty obstructions to the lofty artistic program he had set for himself. As Edward Burlingame Hill commented in an obituary of
Mahler: "His musicians, accustomed to easy-going ways and
less compelling ideals, fretted at his efforts at perfection. The
managers of the Society, either careless or indifferent to the
lofty artistic standards of the director, sought to baffle or nullify
his authority and his purpose."

When he came to New York he was at the height of his artistic powers. In Vienna, from 1897 to 1907, he had been responsible for one of the magnificent eras in the history of the
Court Opera—probably the greatest era of all. At the time that
Mahler had assumed the direction of the Court Opera, it had
degenerated to artistic and financial stagnancy. With his perseverance, driving energy, artistic devotion, and fanatical zeal
Mahler set for himself the task of restoring to the Vienna Opera
its former artistic prestige. He spared no one in his almost mani-
acal devotion to work and in his frenetic pursuit after perfection; least of all did he spare himself. He completely renovated
the opera company, dismissed old and tired singers, and introduced in their places new personalities. He reconstructed
the repertoire, introducing many novelties which had never be-

fore been heard in Vienna, and giving a hearing to many works
of promise. He restored discipline. He made drastic reforms in
stage direction and brought about a renovation of the scenery
and costumes. Most important of all, he insisted that many of
the old operas which had been in the repertoire many years be
restudied minutely by singers, orchestra, and chorus. As a result, operas by Wagner, Mozart, and Weber were reworked as
if they were new compositions—scene by scene, phrase by
phrase. In doing all this, Mahler transformed the Vienna Opera
into the leading musical institution in the world.

In Vienna there were those who called him hard because with
his fearless honesty he always spoke his mind with dis-
concerting candor. There were those who hated him lustily,
first because of his undisciplined tongue, then because he
was a Jew, finally because his idealism and integrity were
often misinterpreted. He was, truth to tell, not easy to get
along with. He was irritable, hypersensitive, easily aroused to
anger. But for each of his enemies there was also a devoted dis-
ciple to realize that he walked with the step of a genius. Those
who worked with him for a long time, who came face to face
with the nobility of his spirit, learned to love him. The singer,
Theodor Reichmann, of the Vienna Court Opera, at first spoke
of him as a "Jewish monkey"; but, when he had learned to know
the artist more intimately, he changed his description to "the
God Mahler." The young musicians who were inspired by him
—Bruno Walter, Otto Klemperer, Schönberg, Richard Strauss
—frequently said that, from him, they learned the true and
terrifying meaning of artistic integrity and the devotion to an
ideal.

But his enemies were powerful in Vienna. They created one
stumbling block after another to obstruct his way. He was a
Jew and a martinet, and for these reasons he was hated by in-

dolent singers and overworked orchestra men. He was a genius
who brought forth performances the like of which had not been
heard even in Vienna, and for this he was secretly envied. Vienna, which so loved to encourage the battle of personalities,
pitted him against the other great Wagnerian conductor, Hans
Richter; those who were devoted to Richter posed as anti-
Mahler. When Richter left the Vienna Opera, the Richter adherents became more vicious in their attacks upon the competitor. Finally there was even some opposition from those high in
power. Directors of the Court Opera objected to the lavish expenses which the restudied versions of his opera performances
entailed. Even the Emperor found something to grumble at:
a favorite singer of his beloved Kathi Schratt had been pen-
sioned off by Mahler because he had passed his prime.

But Mahler was not one to tolerate interference or to accept
compromises. Quietly he handed in his resignation. He did not
have to go. Even those who hated him confessed that he had
done wonderful things for the Vienna Opera. And many of
those who worshiped him wielded powerful influence. However, Mahler could not continue working in an atmosphere
charged with envy, malice, charlatanism. On October 15, 1907,
he gave his last performance in Vienna—Beethoven's *Fidelio*.
He would not reconcile himself to giving anything but his best;
and he sadly felt that his best was no longer wanted in Vienna.

He eagerly accepted the offer of the Metropolitan to come
to America. He came with great hope in his heart, even though
his health was poor. He felt that, in a country too young to have
deep-rooted prejudices as an outgrowth of set traditions, he
could bring his dreams to fruition without the interference of
cabals, quarrels, and jealousies that stood in his way in Vienna.
To Willem Mengelberg he wrote from America:

I shall spend the next few years in America. I am thoroughly delighted with the country. . . . If I were young and still had the energy
which I gave unstintingly to Vienna for ten years, perhaps it would
be possible to create here the condition which appeared to us at home
an unattainable ideal—the exclusion of every commercial consideration from matters pertaining to art—for those in authority here are
honest and their resources are unlimited.

But he was to be sadly disillusioned. Those in authority were
(as he wrote) honest and with unlimited resources. But together with these qualities he found an additional attribute—stu-
pidity. In New York, as in Vienna, Mahler was hated. His "sins"
were more than one. He refused to inject a popular note in his
programs—which prejudiced his audiences against his concerts.
He would change the instrumentation in certain symphonic
masterpieces for the sake of better tonal balance, and for this
the pundits rose up in arms against him. He refused to be a
"social lion," rarely attended any social functions of those who
ruled the musical destinies of the city, and when—on rare occasion—he *did* attend he would be silent and morose. For this
he incurred the disdain of high society.

As a result, Mahler was continually hounded on all sides. The
musicians who played under him in the Philharmonic resented
him (why did he have to drive them like slaves?). The women
who employed him were impatient with him (why did he have
to be so obstinate in the matter of programs, even to the point
of excluding Tchaikovsky's beloved music?). The critics who
reviewed his concerts annihilated him (by what right did he
tamper with the sacrosanct classics?). The public would not
take to him. Without a doubt, he was a failure as conductor of
the Philharmonic. The New York *Tribune* recognized this
when, shortly after his death, it reviewed his career: "He was

looked upon as a great artist, and possibly he was one, but he
failed to convince the people of New York of the fact and, therefore, his New York career was not a success."

This opposition shattered his health. He broke down under
the impact of continual friction. On February 21, 1911, he collapsed in New York. Less than three months later he was dead.
Those in Europe who adored him insisted that America had
crucified him.

"It is generally understood that Mahler had frequently struggled with the women managers of the New York Philharmonic,"
confessed the New York *Sun*. The New York *American* elab-
orated upon this theme:

Worried by New York women, Mahler was taken gravely ill. When
an American correspondent called on May 4, he met Mme. Mahler
who said that she attributed her husband's illness to nervous pros-
tration and its consequences caused by his unfortunate relations with
the Philharmonic Society of New York. "You cannot imagine," she
said, "what he suffered. . . . In New York, to his amazement, he had
ten women ordering him about like a puppet. He hoped, however,
by hard work and success to rid himself of his tormentors."

The extent to which Mahler was misunderstood, even by the
most competent of New York critics, became even more evident
a day after his death when H. E. Krehbiel went to press with
a vicious denunciation. "Mahler was willing wantonly to insult
the people's intelligence and taste by such things as multiply-
ing the voices in a Beethoven symphony (additional kettledrums in the *Pastorale*, for example), by cutting down the
strings and doubling the flutes in Mozart's G minor."

But (as Krehbiel should have known) such practices were
traditional and artistically justifiable. Young Ossip Gabrilowitsch pointed this out in a letter to the New York *Times*, in
which he flew to the defense of the attacked hero.

Such items in editing of the classics . . . were first introduced by no less a man than Richard Wagner himself and his practice has since been used by every prominent conductor. . . . As a conductor, Wagner was the first to double the horn parts in the Ninth Symphony. After that, Hans von Bülow added two horns in the Seventh Symphony, augmented the brass in the *Coriolanus* Overture, changed the division of strings in the third *Leonore* Overture, and introduced innumerable other changes. Most of these alterations have since become a tradition.

Then, having answered Krehbiel, Gabrilowitsch spoke eloquent words of homage to Mahler—proof that at least a few rare spirits in America at the time realized Mahler's true worth.

Mahler is to me the very incarnation of the highest ideals, artistic and human. I did not believe that such ideals could ever be realized till I met him. To have known him made life seem nobler, more worth while living. He had the kind of a limitless devotion to a high cause that only a saint has. He was the one artist I have ever known to whom personal success meant nothing. Not one atom of vanity was in his disposition. His was the child-like naïveté of true genius. . . . The attitude of placing the thing above the man—the art above the artist—was characteristic of Mahler's work. He realized that there was just one thing more important than all, more important than the audience, singers, orchestra or stage management—and that was the composer. But there was still one thing more important to him than the composer—and that was the composition. He knew that in order to give a work its full eloquence the reproducing artist must be able to recreate the composition as if it were flesh of his flesh and blood of his blood. This he did, and that is why he presented works of the standard repertory with such spontaneity, such freshness, that one seemed never to have heard them before.

At least part of Mahler's failure with the Philharmonic, and success with the Metropolitan, rested on the fact that opera appealed to audiences more strongly than did symphonic music. In the early 1900's Heinrich Conried described Americans as "opera mad." Conried knew of what he was speaking. Succeeding Maurice Grau as manager of the Metropolitan Opera House, Conried guided the destinies of opera in America from 1903 to 1908.

Conried was born for the theater. Coming to the Metropolitan Opera House by way of his excellent dramatic productions at the Irving Place Theatre, Conried combined a shrewd flair for showmanship with a certain amount of healthy ideals. He knew the value of sensation to the box office, and he could provoke it. Besides, he recognized the uses of publicity and exploitation. Whatever may have been his blunders—and they were many—he did not fail to inject dramatic interest into the opera season, and through more than one method.

Perhaps his greatest achievement was an attempt to place opera on a plane higher than the singer. For this he paid a heavy price—that of his own downfall: the times were not yet ripe for so radical an innovation. Conried felt that the integration of an entire performance was more important than the indiscriminate sprinkling of a cast with stars. Thus, he was fastidious about conductors, importing two of Europe's greatest directors —Mahler and Felix Mottl. He spent money lavishly on costumes, stage sets, and the reconstruction of the stage itself; Grau would have considered these expenses sheer waste. He was as proud of his acquisition of Carl Lautenschlaeger, stage director from Munich, as Grau had been when he signed a much-publicized prima donna.

Not that Conried was less concerned than Grau had been to make money for the Metropolitan. The Metropolitan, which had been reorganized with the arrival of Conried by a group of New York millionaires (Otto H. Kahn now makes his first appearance as a power behind the operatic throne), was essentially a business venture that had to show profits. Conried knew that the tenure of his post depended upon the financial success of the institution; besides, Conried's own income was dependent on the box-office health, since the manager drew a share of the profits.

But Conried aspired toward financial success through means other than those employed by his predecessor. Conried placed less emphasis on the star. The all-star casts of Grau were dispensed with. Conried, therefore, permitted the contracts of leading singers to expire without a protest. When a French manager offered him some of the leading French opera singers of the time, he turned a deaf ear. If the opera public wished to be electrified, Conried would do this at the same time that he brought new prestige to his opera house. He would invite the great opera composers of Europe to be present at the Metropolitan performances of their masterpieces; New York was always partial to great personalities in the flesh. He would shift public adulation from the opera singer to the composer. Conried also decided to entertain and to thrill his public with "novelties"—new operas, unfamiliar operas, which by virtue of publicity could be made events of sensational interest. There was, after all, more than one dish to arouse the palate of American music lovers. At least, so thought Conried in 1903.

Though the emphasis of the Conried regime was on the opera rather than the singer, it must not be assumed that the great star was altogether discredited. Far from it! The personality of the opera singer still shone with its former luster, and audiences were still bewitched by it. From the Grau regime, Conried had inherited Gadski, Calvé, Sembrich, Homer, Dippel, Scotti, Journet, Plançon—ample assurance that there would be great singing. Conried himself was responsible for bringing Geraldine

Farrar to New York. And it was during the Conried regime that the greatest of all opera personalities became a public idol—Enrico Caruso.

Actually, Caruso had been Grau's plum. Caruso had scored a triumph in Monte Carlo where he had been heard by Henry Dazian who advised Grau to engage the singer without delay. An agreement was reached between Grau and Caruso whereby the tenor offered to come to New York for the 1903–1904 season for forty performances at $1,000 a performance. When Grau was displaced by Conried in 1903, Caruso's manager came to the new Metropolitan director to inquire whether the agreement still stood. A compromise was reached. Caruso would sing in twenty-five performances at the formerly stipulated price. Before long, Conried—shrewd enough to recognize what a prize possession had fallen into his hands—bound up Caruso on an all-inclusive contract.

An absurd legend was circulated that Conried first became interested in Caruso after visiting Italian barber shops, bootblacks, and restaurants and learning from them that Caruso was the greatest living tenor. What is probably closer to the truth is that a recording of Caruso's performance of *Vesti la giubba* impressed Conried profoundly. At any rate, on November 23, 1903—the inauguration of Conried's first season as director of the Metropolitan—Caruso made his American debut in *Rigoletto*. It cannot be said that Caruso was an immediate success. He was not at his best, most probably because of his excessive nervousness. Before curtain time he paced up and down backstage, wringing his hands, biting savagely at his lips, using the strength of his will to suppress actual weeping. He upset everyone near him—Sembrich and Scotti who were in the cast with him, Conried who was apprehensive in his own right, and the conductor Arturo Vigna, who was also making his American debut. Most of all, Caruso was upsetting himself. His nervousness did not help him. His full stature as an artist was not immediately perceptible. The critic of the *Tribune* even spoke of his "tiresome Italian mannerisms," though there were some who spoke well of the quality of his voice.

But by the end of the first season, Caruso had gained such popularity that he was once again starred in the opening night performance of the second season (establishing a tradition at the Metropolitan which was to continue for the next sixteen years, with only one interruption). Tickets for the opening night performance were at a premium; as much as $80 was paid for a pair. The Caruso madness had begun. By the end of the second season the receipts for Caruso performances totaled $65,000—an increase over the first by more than 100 per cent. The third season saw still another substantial gain in box-office receipts: Caruso operas brought in $87,000. Caruso was now unquestionably the shining light of the Metropolitan. "The fact now is to be recorded," wrote W. J. Henderson in that year, "that the public has gone to the opera in the season just ended almost solely for the purpose of hearing Enrico Caruso sing. The public has not cared a rap what opera was sung. The invariable request proffered at the box-office has been: 'Can you let us have seats for Caruso's next performance?'"

Thereafter, during the Conried regime, Caruso's reign at the Metropolitan was not threatened. His voice brought tears to the eyes of his public—a voice incomparable for texture, range, shading; a voice powerful yet supple, exquisite in its upper range, sensuous in middle tones, extraordinarily expressive in a lower register. What Edouard de Reszke had written to Caruso in a personal letter proved no exaggerated praise. "I never heard a more beautiful voice. . . . You sang like a god. You are an actor and a sincere artist. You were able to draw from my eyes many tears. I was very much touched and this happens to me very seldom. You have heart, feeling, poetry and truth, and with these qualities you will be master of the world."

Master of the world? Well, master over musical New York at any rate. Caruso dominated every performance in which he appeared. The characters he interpreted acquired altogether new fascination for the Metropolitan public: Radames, Canio, Don José, Pinkerton, the Duke of Mantua. *La Bohème* had never quite appealed to Metropolitan audiences until Caruso appeared as Rodolfo. . . . The great Italian tenor arias never seemed to cast such a spell in the opera house as when they poured, in liquid tones, from his throat. Audiences were sometimes content to sit through an entire opera in order to hear him sing one immortal aria: say, *Una furtiva lagrima* or *O Paradiso.*

True, he sang in most of the leading opera houses of the world. But New York accepted him as its own son, its personal discovery, its individual possession. It was extravagant with its worship. Caruso became choice material for newspaper copy— his daily habits, his opinions even on matters about which he knew nothing, his love life—as his admirers hungrily consumed everything that was written about him. He was glorified by the silent motion picture (in one of these he was so bad that the film was never released!). He was fabulously paid, probably the most fabulously paid singer of all times. He could earn a hundred thousand dollars in a few weeks of opera and concert appearances. From phonograph records alone he received a royalty of at least a hundred thousand dollars a year, over a period of more than a decade. As a symptom of his great fame in America, he even became a victim of blackmailers and kidnappers.

Despite the sensation caused by Caruso, a sensation which grew with each passing season, Conried asked his audiences to interest themselves less in great casts and more in great opera. Conried was, as a matter of fact, the first Metropolitan manager to inaugurate the search for "novelty," which has since dominated the activities of the opera house. In his very first season, Conried directed the full beam of his publicity limelight not on Caruso's arrival, but on his proposed première of *Parsifal,* which was to be the first stage production of the Wagner music drama heard anywhere in the world outside of Bayreuth. Wagner might be liked or disliked in New York, but (as Conried realized with his fine theatrical instinct) *Parsifal*—composed for Bayreuth alone and exhibited nowhere else—was savory meat for an appetite craving new taste sensations.

Conried could be depended upon to exploit the première of *Parsifal* fully. He had a keen scent for publicity values. In this he was abetted by Bayreuth itself, which rushed into the American law courts to keep the performance from taking place. During the litigation Conried saw to it that the dispute was lavishly spread across the front pages of American newspapers. The announced presentation of *Parsifal* became the most publicized and hotly disputed music event in New York in many years. Not even the greatest of Grau's all-star casts could arouse such palpitant interest.

Arguments for and against the production split New York into two battle camps. There were those who sided with Cosima Wagner: on legal grounds, because she held the exclusive rights to *Parsifal* and had the privilege of prohibiting its performance out of Bayreuth if she so desired; on religious grounds, because they felt it sacrilegious to present a devout subject on a public stage; on sentimental grounds, because the master had written the work for Bayreuth and there it belonged. Others, however, were with Conried when he argued that *Parsifal* had, after all, been given a New York performance in 1890 without

interference (in a concert version, it was true; but a performance
nevertheless); also, that it was the artistic duty of Cosima to
permit a masterpiece of such dimensions to be witnessed by the
world at large.

The battle was bitter. It grew more vitriolic as it was prolonged. Letters poured into the newspapers in which the general
public expressed its opinion, pro and con. Sermons were
preached in the pulpit throughout the country. Bayreuth had
issued a warning that anyone participating in the performance
would be boycotted in all future Wagnerian performances at
the shrine; Felix Mottl, as a matter of fact (imported expressly
to conduct the music drama in New York), announced flatly
that he would have nothing whatsoever to do with the venture.
Some, looking upon Conried's attempted performance as an
outright theft, bitterly renamed the drama *The Rape of Parsifal.*

All this succeeded in stirring the curiosity of all in the pro-
vocative opera. When, therefore, Conried won his legal fight
and announced that the performance would definitely take
place, the sale of tickets reached prodigious proportions, even
though the prices of admission had been practically doubled.
Out-of-town orders were so numerous that most of them had
to be turned down. Special *Parsifal* excursion trains were run to
bring out-of-town music lovers to the performance. A few
minutes before five o'clock, on the afternoon of December 24,
1903, a group of trumpeters (Conried always had a touch for
good theater) advanced to the main entrance of the Metropolitan and blew several motives from *Parsifal* to announce the
arrival of curtain time. Such was the eagerness of the public to
witness this publicized spectacle that—wonderful to say!—it
came on time. Until midnight, an excited audience witnessed
the first American production of *Parsifal* conducted by Alfred

Hertz. The cast included Ternina, Louise Homer, Journet, and Van Rooy.

For the rest of that season, *Parsifal* remained the most exciting opera in the Metropolitan repertoire. It played to sold-out houses. In place of the originally scheduled five performances there were eleven, bringing almost $200,000 in receipts. Meanwhile performances were also eagerly attended in major cities throughout the country, brought there by wandering companies, such as the Savage production (in English) and one by the Walter Damrosch company. Drama lectures on *Parsifal* were conducted with stereopticon slides; a variety of shows with the legend of *Parsifal* as their subject were hurriedly contrived.

But America eventually had too much of *Parsifal*. After all, the audiences had thronged the opera house to hear the work mainly because of curiosity over a highly publicized novelty. These audiences were too immature to recognize in it a masterpiece of profound and searching beauty. When the novelty wore off, there remained only the long monologues, the static action, the lack of singable melodies to provoke boredom. In New York interest in *Parsifal* died down to such an extent that by 1905 it was exhibited at the normal scale of admission prices, while in 1906 tickets could be procured virtually free for the asking. There were many who now derisively spoke of the *Parsifal* performances as "Metropolitan prayer meetings."

Conried continued to inject novelty into his repertoire. He brought America its première of *Hänsel and Gretel* and, as an added feature, he invited Humperdinck, the composer, to be in the audience. In the same manner, Puccini was in personal attendance at performances of his *Madame Butterfly* and *Manon Lescaut*. Besides these operas, Conried brought lavish productions of Goldmark's *The Queen of Sheba*, and *Die Fledermaus*

and *The Gypsy Baron* of Johann Strauss. But not until 1907
did he succeed in creating a tempest such as had attended the
première of *Parsifal*. This new tempest was created by *Salome*,
an opera by the *enfant terrible* of modern music, Richard
Strauss. *Salome* was performed for the first time in America on
January 22, 1907 (two years after its world première in
Dresden), with Alfred Hertz conducting a cast including Olive
Fremstad, Journet, Van Rooy, and Dippel.

Conried thrived on publicity and controversy. For these purposes he hoped to bring Strauss himself to America to conduct
his own opera. Negotiations for this fell through, but there was
no dearth of publicity. As a matter of fact, Conried received
more of this than he had bargained for. The Oscar Wilde play,
with its sensual theme, and the musical score, with its suggestions of lasciviousness, outraged the morals of the time. Conried
was not too farsighted when he arranged a special dress rehearsal for an invited audience to take place on Sunday morning. Many came straight from church services, and the shock of
contrast was more than most of them could stomach. They left
the opera house denouncing the "lewd" spectacle.

After the first performance, a righteous-minded citizenry
descended on Conried with fury for permitting such a display
of obscenity on his stage. The clergy rose up in battle. The
critics, too, joined in this universal chorus of outraged feelings.
Krehbiel wrote that "the stench of Oscar Wilde's play had filled
the nostrils of humanity," while still another writer spoke of the
opera as a "decadent and pestiferous work." One critic vented
his spleen as follows: "As to the mind and morals, they were
diseased. Not to emphasize disgust, their state was one of de-
composition far advanced. As to the music, it fits. It makes
worse that to which nothing but music could give added
degradation." A few musicians (like Emil Paur) tried to defend

the Strauss music, but their voices were drowned by the furor of the opposition.

Before the second performance could be put on the stage, Conried received a curt note from the directors of the Metropolitan informing him that they considered "the performance of *Salome* objectionable, and detrimental to the best interests of the Metropolitan Opera House," and protesting "against any repetition of the opera."

There was nothing for Conried to do but withdraw *Salome* after one performance.

The season of 1907–1908 was Conried's last. A concatenation of circumstances, of which the *Salome* fiasco was only one, brought about his downfall. More important by far was the serious competition being offered by a new opera company at the Manhattan Opera House, sponsored by the wealthy cigar manufacturer, Oscar Hammerstein. When he originally built the Manhattan Opera House, Hammerstein had announced that it would be the home of operatic productions in the English language. But long before the house was completed he announced a change of plan, inspired undoubtedly by the fact that he discerned that Conried's star was sinking. He would present great operas in their original languages, and with the world's greatest singers. When he promised to restore to New York the De Reszke brothers (so long absent), New York opera lovers began to buzz with excitement. Actually, he never succeeded in bringing the De Reszkes back to America. But in their place he presented a great array of operatic celebrities— Melba, Nordica, Tetrazzini, Schumann-Heink, Zenatello, Cavalieri, John McCormack, Bonci, Dalmorès, and Renaud, with the fine and indefatigable Cleofonte Campanini as artistic director. The emphasis would be on French operas (which had been sadly neglected by the Metropolitan). Like

Conried, Hammerstein would introduce novelties to excite attention—novelties like *Pelléas et Mélisande, Elektra, Louise, Tales of Hoffmann*—but never at the price of sacrificing a great cast. It cost Hammerstein a fortune. Somebody once asked him why he had gone into opera. "Is there any money in it?" "Of course!" answered Hammerstein. "*My* money is in it."

Bellini's *Norma* opened the new opera house on the evening of December 3, 1906. Thereafter, the Manhattan Opera House offered serious competition to the Metropolitan, luring away its audiences, many among whom craved the fascination of great singing stars. If on November 25, 1907, Hammerstein introduced to America Debussy's highly controversial *Pelléas et Mélisande,* he could offer with it the equally magnetizing attraction of the sensational Mary Garden, who was making her American début at the same time.

The success of the Manhattan Opera House created friction between the severely troubled directors of the Metropolitan and Conried. The directors could not forget that Hammerstein had acquired the sensational Tetrazzini under Conried's very nose, and that many of the French singers originally offered to (and rejected by) Conried had been strikingly successful at the Manhattan. When the 1907–1908 season at the Metropolitan showed a deficit, it became obvious that Conried was through. The pretext for his withdrawal was his ill health. But it was generally accepted that he had left because the Metropolitan needed new managerial blood desperately if it were to survive its temporary anemia. The dangerous competition of the Manhattan Opera House was proving fatal.

In 1908 the Metropolitan was once again reorganized. For the first time, a sharp departure from a long-established custom was decided upon. Henceforth the manager of the opera house would no longer have a share in the profits. He would draw a salary. The element of gamble was to be removed from the manager's activities, thereby permitting him to devote his energies exclusively to the production of operas without fear of personal involvement in financial losses.

Under the new arrangement a manager was recruited from La Scala in Milan, Guilio Gatti-Casazza. At the time little was known of him in New York, except that he had enjoyed great success at La Scala. It was generally believed that he had been brought to America only because the Metropolitan was eager to acquire the prize possession of La Scala—the firebrand conductor Arturo Toscanini, and (at least, so it was rumored) Toscanini had refused to come unless the manager of La Scala came with him. In any case, the opening of the Metropolitan season of 1908–1909 found young Toscanini on the conductor's platform and Gatti-Casazza sharing the manager's office with Andreas Dippel, who had been assigned to take charge of the German repertoire. And with them a new era for the Metropolitan began.

Meanwhile, operatic activity was extending its sphere beyond New York, where, except for the tours of the Metropolitan and of special companies, it had been confined almost exclusively up to now. In 1908 Oscar Hammerstein built a special opera house in Philadelphia where, several nights a week, he brought his New York company. In 1909 opera came to Baltimore, also through the Hammerstein company. When the Hammerstein company disbanded, forces from its ranks formed the nucleus for the Chicago Grand Opera, organized in 1910 with Andreas Dippel as manager and Campanini as principal conductor— destined to become one of America's great opera organizations.

More opera came to Boston during the first decade. In 1908 the cornerstone was laid for the Boston Opera House, which was to be directed by Henry Russell. It was to have the best-equipped stage in the world and was to speak the last word in lighting and scenic fixtures. On November 8, 1909, the opera house opened with a magnificent performance of *La Gioconda,* said to have been one of the best performances of the opera to have been heard in America. Henry Russell proceeded to keep his opera house artistically alive. He brought Felix Weingartner to conduct the Wagner music dramas—Weingartner making his American operatic debut with *Tristan* in 1912. ("The orchestra sang a marvelous song," wrote Philip Hale ecstatically of that performance.) Russell vitalized the repertoire by adopting Conried's plan of novelties, his principal novelty being Debussy's *Pelléas.*

Russell was sufficiently perceptive to realize that nothing succeeds in the American opera house like sensation. When his projected performance of *Pelléas* failed to attract attention, he decided to borrow a leaf from Conried's managerial book and resort to sensational methods. He announced to the press that Maurice Maeterlinck, who never permitted himself to be interviewed, would come to America for the performance of the opera that had been based on his play. Russell offered a prize of $1,000 to any journalist who could succeed in interviewing the playwright on his arrival. He might just as easily have offered a million dollars, for Maeterlinck had no intention of coming to America, and Russell knew it. In any case, Russell's offer created nation-wide interest. Every boat was carefully watched for Maeterlinck's arrival. Every man with a beard or strange get-up was carefully scrutinized for a possible disguise. By the time *Pelléas* reached performance, the fever of interest in Maeterlinck had reached such a pitch that the house was a sell-out; people came because they, too, wanted to participate in this game of finding Maeterlinck.

Such tactics may create an interest in one performance, but unfortunately they cannot guarantee lasting success to an opera. After the second presentation, *Pelléas* was incapable of attracting an audience, and it passed quietly out of the repertoire.

The *Pelléas* affair was but one of the many indications of the naïveté of the American opera public, of its inability to recognize solid musical merit, and of its childlike appetite for publicized sensations. It was for the most part an uneducated public, delighted by superficial glitter, unable to distinguish between good and bad, between right and wrong. When Chaliapin sadly spoke of the opera public as "mere children" when it comes to music, his characterization was accurate. The extension of the operatic sphere did not bring with it—at least not at once—greater sophistication. In 1904, when Walter Damrosch took a performance of *Parsifal* to Oklahoma, he was amazed to see the local manager go up to the stage immediately after the conclusion of the serene and spiritual prelude. "I would like to announce," the manager said casually, "that Stewart's Oyster Saloon will be open after the concert." Then, with his momentous announcement delivered, he gave the signal to Damrosch to continue. At the Boston Opera House, many demanded their money back after witnessing the second performance of *Pelléas et Mélisande* because they had expected a double feature like *Pagliacci* and *Cavalleria Rusticana*. In El Paso, in the 1900's, a visiting opera company presented *The Barber of Seville* with some minor deletions. A musician in the audience casually remarked to his neighbor that certain cuts had been made. In a few moments, his pronouncement spread throughout the theater like contagion. A riot developed among the outraged members of the audience who felt that they had been cheated. The sheriff was called; Texas gunmen surrounded the bewildered impresario; and the commotion subsided only when the impresario announced that he would immediately refund the price of admission.

In New York, opera audiences were perhaps less ingenuous, but hardly more critical. The collapse of *Parsifal* was proof that great opera in itself was no magnet. The scandal of *Salome* emphasized the inability of its audience to penetrate beyond mere superficials. Besides this, there were other evidences that the tastes of the public were still unformed. A notable example of this was a performance of *Pagliacci* at the Metropolitan, in which the tenor Albert Reiss sang. Caruso, who was in the wings, urged Reiss, on the spur of the moment, to let him sing the off-stage serenade. No one in the house seemed to recognize the substitution; though if it had been known that the idolized Enrico was singing, his performance would have created a furor.

Conried was gone. But the shadow of Conried stretched across the Gatti-Casazza regime. For, like his predecessor, Gatti-Casazza refused to deify the singer, preferring to use the attraction of opera novelties with which to draw the audiences into the opera house.

The new manager did not conceal the fact that he was first and foremost interested in the box office. The advice Verdi once gave him had long since become one of the guiding principles of his career as impresario. "Remember," Verdi had said when Gatti-Casazza became director of La Scala, "that this theater is intended to be full, not empty." Gatti-Casazza never forgot. At the Metropolitan, as in La Scala, he was determined to keep the auditorium full.

By 1910 his co-manager, Andreas Dippel, was dismissed, leaving Gatti-Casazza in full control of the Metropolitan. But even more important than this for Gatti-Casazza was the fact that in 1910 the Manhattan Opera House—after having given 463 performances of forty-nine different operas—suddenly closed its door permanently. What caused Hammerstein to withdraw from his opera war with the Metropolitan was at the time a deeply guarded mystery. Since then, however, it has been revealed that a contractual arrangement was made between Hammerstein and the directors of the Metropolitan by which, for the cash sum of over a million dollars, Hammerstein agreed to withdraw from the opera scene in New York for a period of ten years. In 1913 Hammerstein tried to evade his contract, and made plans for opera performances at the Lexington Theatre. But the Metropolitan rushed to the courts and restrained him.

From the moment that the potent competitor of Thirty-Fourth Street was gone, the Metropolitan knew unprecedented prosperity. For this prosperity, Gatti-Casazza was to a large degree responsible. Inscrutable, reticent, detesting publicity for himself, secretive about anything pertaining to his personal life, he was the sphinx-like power behind the artistic destinies of the Metropolitan. His warm Italian blood being unaccustomed to the hardship of New York winters, he would sit in his small steam-heated office, usually dressed in a buttoned coat, muffler, and hat, directing his opera house with a firm hand. Always was he ready to deflect the limelight from himself to his enterprises. Sensitively he gauged the desires of his audiences and catered to them; yet at the same time the ideals of a great opera institution were not altogether discarded. If the audiences liked Italian operas, the Italian repertoire would form the major share of the opera season. But Gatti-Casazza did not forsake Wagner (for whose cause he had fought so stubbornly in Milan), nor Debussy, nor Richard Strauss, nor the famous French masters. Nor even the much-neglected American composer. It was because of Gatti-Casazza that an American opera was performed at the Metropolitan Opera House for the first time—Converse's *The Pipes of Desire*, in 1910. It was also due to Gatti-Casazza that the directors of the Metropolitan offered a prize of $10,000 for an original opera by an American composer, won in 1912 by Horatio Parker with *Mona*. But operas that were not liked were soon discarded by Gatti-Casazza, regardless of their artistic merit. He was determined to make opera in New York a solvent business. That he succeeded in doing this—and at the same time keeping the Metropolitan in the front rank of the opera institutions of the world—spoke eloquently for his gifts as impresario.

The prima donna fell from her mighty seat. Gatti-Casazza simply would not pamper his stars. If (like Emma Eames) they preferred not to work with him in *his* way, he let them go, regardless of their fame. He was interested in *good* opera, but good opera that brought profits into the box office; no star, however great, would deflect him from this purpose. His never-ceasing parade of novelties brightened each season's activities, and was good business as well: world premières of such operas as Giordano's *Madame Sans-Gêne*, Granados's *Goyescas*, Puccini's *The Girl of the Golden West*, Humperdinck's *Königskinder*, as well as a formidable list of other premières and revivals.

The dynasty of the prima donna was succeeded by that of the conductor. Until 1911, Mahler was there, to devote herculean energy and devotion and genius to the performance of Mozart, Wagner, and Smetana. And with Mahler there was the guiding genius of La Scala—Arturo Toscanini. There was no question that the artistic control was in Toscanini's hands and that he brooked no nonsense from temperamental prima donnas. "Madame," he said firmly to one prima donna who insisted that *she* was the star, "stars are found only in heaven." When another "star" insisted on holding a note longer than the score demanded, he rudely interrupted her with the orchestral close. He worked his singers and orchestra men to exhaustion in his savage pursuit of the ideal performance. He was superhumanly concerned with the slightest details (supported by a memory which had photographically caught the minutest markings of the printed page). He could be brutal and vulgar in the face of sloppy singing or shiftless playing. He was concerned with only one mission: the realization of the opera as the composer had conceived it. He pursued that mission with an inflexible will. Most of the singers hated him because he was a despot. They came to Gatti-Casazza with lamentations of how he abused them. "What can I do?" softly asked Gatti-Casazza, with a shrug of his shoulders. "He abuses *me*, too."

But one thing was certain, even to those who were least patient with Toscanini's violent tempers, despotic commands, and brusque behavior. When his rehearsals were over, and he sat in his conductor's chair directing the actual performance, the music of Wagner or Gluck or Verdi emerged from under his baton as if reborn, fresh in every phase and line as if it had just been composed. Even in those days, the critics exhausted their supply of superlatives in speaking of his performances. One New York critic wrote soon after Toscanini's arrival:

Perhaps "intense" describes the most characteristic trait of Toscanini's conducting. The same electrifying current of magnetism throbbed through it, though there was also an undercurrent of poetic feeling, beautifully reserved and delicate at times, and again rising to the surface with torrential force. There was passion, now suppressed, now leaping into flame, but always controlled by a great will and mind. There was profound understanding of the musical and literary significance of the drama. There was extraordinary mastery of detail, and an all-compelling grasp of the broadly dramatic outlines.

With Gatti-Casazza in the manager's office (one eye on the artistic program, the other on the box office); with Mahler and Toscanini in the conductor's stand; with men like Joseph Urban and Giulio Setti in charge of scenery and chorus, respectively; with a company of singers including Caruso, Fremstad, Homer, Scotti, Farrar, Alda—opera in America flourished during the first years of the Gatti-Casazza regime. But deterioration was at hand. Mahler died in 1911. Four years later, in a fit of temper, Toscanini withdrew and returned to Italy because (so, at least, runs the most credible version) he could not obtain at the Metropolitan the conditions necessary for the complete projection of his art. A young and talented conductor was recruited from Mannheim to fill Toscanini's place—Artur Bodanzky. But even then Toscanini was irreplaceable. After he left, the glowing, smoldering performances which he had directed with such patience and painstaking care belonged to the past—things to cherish in the memory, but never to experience again at the Metropolitan. Then came the American entry into the war, and with it a mutilation of the repertoire. For the next fifteen years, the Metropolitan Opera House went into artistic decline, even though Gatti-Casazza's shrewdness made it possible for this decline not to be reflected immediately in the box office.

PART II: Today

———

"THE REMARKABLE EFFORTS OF AMERICAN, AND ESPECIALLY NEW YORK, SOCIETY TO RAISE THE STANDARD OF MUSICAL LIFE HAS NOT BEEN IN VAIN. THEY HAVE USED EVERY MEANS IN THEIR POWER AND HAVE NOT SPARED MONEY IN THEIR EFFORT TO SURPASS EUROPE IN THIS RESPECT. THEY HAVE SUCCEEDED. NO MAN WILL DARE DISPUTE THE FACT."

—Rachmaninoff
1930

CHAPTER SIX

Music and
the First World War

O UR REPUDIATION of German music and musicians during
the First World War has been frequently explained as a
symptom of war hysteria. That, at best, is only half the
explanation. I strongly believe that an attitude toward great
music such as we displayed in 1917 can arise only if a nation
has not yet developed its musical tastes fully, if its musical consciousness is not altogether awakened, if music has not yet
become an essential part of its cultural life. I feel, therefore, that
our violent antagonism toward any music even remotely associated with Germany reflected not so much our hysteria as our
musical immaturity at that time.

We have merely to glance at the musical activities of the
European allies at this period to realize that we were almost
unique in our passionate and savage repudiation of German
music. London could listen to a performance of *Tristan und
Isolde* during an air raid and could sponsor a monumental Bach-
Beethoven festival. Paris could conduct a festival devoted to the
works of Robert Schumann. Maurice Ravel, serving his country
as a volunteer truck driver in the automobile division of the
French Army, refused to subscribe to any movement to expel

the music of modern German composers from French musical
life. But America was determined to be holier than the saint.
We were at war with Germany. We could, consequently, have
no traffic with anything German. Not even the great German
music which was a negation of everything for which Imperial
Germany stood: Beethoven, for example, the greatest democrat
in music! For great music, I insist, did not yet mean so much
to America in 1917 that it could not be swept away with the big
broom of prejudice.

The Metropolitan Opera House was performing an American
opera, Reginald de Koven's *The Canterbury Pilgrims,* when the
word arrived that President Wilson had asked Congress to de-
clare war on Germany. Artur Bodanzky, who was conducting
the opera, immediately struck up *The Star-Spangled Banner.* In
a box sat the American Ambassador to Germany, James W.
Gerard, who led the audience in cheers for the President.

These outward manifestations of patriotism were soon to be
translated into prejudicial actions which played havoc with
musical life in America. For the remainder of that spring, this
tendency was held in check. The Wagnerian repertoire at the
Metropolitan remained untouched; the Good Friday performance of *Parsifal* was received respectfully. German musicians
were unmolested. But, by fall, the storm, so long controlled,
burst.

In October the New York Board of Education ruled that German operas were not to be discussed in the classroom or in
special lectures. At the same time, the Museum of Natural
History forbade a lecture on *Parsifal.* Somewhat before this, the
Philadelphia Orchestra (sensing the sentiment of the audience)
began translating into English all German titles of musical
works.

These were the first shots fired against German music. Others were soon heard. In November, Gatti-Casazza announced that during the new season there would be no German operas in the repertoire, nor any other works that "could cause the least offense to the most patriotic Americans." In January the New York Philharmonic promised that it would not perform the music of living Germans. Walter Damrosch made a similar promise, but at the same time begged American music lovers not to extend their ban to the works of the German masters.

In the face of a perceptibly growing opposition to German music, Mrs. Ossip Gabrilowitsch and Mme. Olga Samaroff-Stokowski made a special trip to the White House to discuss the question of a boycott of German music. They brought back with them from Washington statements from President Wilson and Colonel House to the effect that extending the war to dead composers was altogether unnecessary.

But in the rising storm of prejudice, the weak voice of sanity was not clearly heard, or, if heard, was not listened to. In Pittsburgh *all* German music was definitely banished from all concert programs; several other cities followed suit. By the fall of 1918 there was such violent opposition to German music of any kind that when the gifted French conductor André Messager visited this country with the Paris Conservatory Orchestra and included on his program the Beethoven *Eroica* Symphony he was deluged by letters of protest. ("How did you answer these protests?" Messager was asked. "Why," he answered firmly, "in the only way an artist *can* answer them. At my very first concert I performed the *Eroica*.")

Opposition to German music soon found victims in the flesh. Innocent men were regarded with suspicion, watched as if they were criminals, spied upon by government agents, in some cases actually victimized. "This particular campaign," wrote Gabrilowitsch angrily at the time, "emanates chiefly from people of

German extraction who are advertising their Americanism in the noisiest possible way at the expense of good music—and good morals." In any case, Leopold Stokowski, Ossip Gabrilowitsch, and Leopold Godowsky (mark! none of whom were German by nationality) were among those continually held suspect and shadowed by secret-service men. Gabrilowitsch's concerts, as a matter of fact, were boycotted by certain groups. Nikolai Sokoloff might have been engaged as a conductor of the New York Philharmonic at this time if a rumor had not been circulated that he was pro-German, thereby making him an untouchable. Frieda Hempel was barred from making several public appearances, despite the fact that she had frequently protested her allegiance to this country and had often sung the American national anthem.

In most of these cases, possibly in all, the persecution was not deserved; the indefatigable watch of secret-service men yielded nothing whatsoever to implicate these suspects. With Fritz Kreisler, or course, there was at least some justification for persecution by patriotic societies—since Kreisler, after all, had served as a captain in the Austrian Army from 1914 to 1915, when he was wounded and granted a leave of absence. In November, 1917, the director of public safety in Pittsburgh demanded that the local police cancel the concert license for a Kreisler concert. This being successful, other Kreisler concerts in towns in New Jersey, Pennsylvania, Ohio, and West Virginia were also canceled. Absurd stories were circulated to discredit Kreisler completely: one of the most vicious was that which placed Kreisler in command at a battle in which American soldiers had been massacred—an incident that simply could not have taken place since at the supposed date of the battle Kreisler was known to have been in America. All this, however, convinced Kreisler that discretion was the better part of valor.

He withdrew from all concert activity, lived in complete retirement in Maine during the remainder of the war, and spared himself a much more cruel fate than that he had already experienced.

A fate, for example, such as Karl Muck knew.

The *cause célèbre* of the First World War was, of course, that of Karl Muck. Even today much misinformation and misunderstanding persists about it. As late as 1940, the pianist-conductor Rudolph Ganz went to print with a fierce attack on Muck's conduct during the war. Yet when all the evidence is studied impartially, if personal animus is put aside, it becomes evident that (as I have written elsewhere) it was not Muck but this country that emerged from the incident with discredit.

Karl Muck first came to the United States in 1905, invited by Major Higginson to become conductor of the Boston Symphony Orchestra. In the years that followed (Muck conducted the Boston Orchestra from 1906 to 1908, and again from 1912 to 1918), Muck revealed himself to be one of the great musical interpreters of the time. He combined penetrating scholarship, integrity, and self-effacement with a dynamic personal magnetism that is the inborn quality of all true leaders. He had, to an extraordinary degree, the capacity to sense the hidden demands of a musical score and to give them life. Under his fastidious direction, the great Boston Orchestra reached peaks of artistic attainment it had not known even under Nikisch. Long before 1917 H. T. Parker had summed up Muck's qualities:

Muck has in astute balance the sense of both large things and small, of whole design, and of incidental detail, of the vitalizing trunk as well as the branches or the leafage of the symphony. . . . He has also the melodic divination that is an essential attribute of a conductor. He feels no less the richness of expanding song, and he persuades his men to like divination and feeling. His tonal and rhythmic and modulatory shading is of an exquisite sensibility. . . . His men play in his own image and with a euphony of tone that is half of them and half of him, and with a melting, a sparkling or swelling beauty of voice that is most of themselves.

When America entered the war, Muck was placed in a difficult position. He was known to have been a friend of the Kaiser, from whom he had received honors and appointments. He had, as early as 1915, been quoted as having said that, as a German, his sympathies in the war lay with his country. These facts had already tempted some to suggest darkly, even before America declared war, that Muck was a paid agent of the German government, sent here to spread propaganda for the German cause. These rumors were magnified when America's entry into the war converted Muck from a neutral alien into an enemy alien. It should be emphasized at once that as soon as America entered the war. Muck went to Higginson with his resignation, which Higginson stubbornly refused to accept. Higginson insisted that he was unable to procure another conductor of Muck's stature, and that he would disband the orchestra rather than be a witness to its deterioration. He begged Muck to reconsider his decision, emphasizing that in times of war it was a greater duty than ever for a great artist to continue his work oblivious to outside destructive forces. In the face of these arguments, and because of his devoted friendship with Higginson, Muck promised to remain at his post.

He had to pay a heavy price for his decision. Rumors breed strange tales. Some of those about Muck, whispered in 1917, gained general credence, absurd though they sound to us today. They said that Muck had a secret telephone receiver hidden in the cellar of his Boston home. One neighbor insisted that, in telephoning her butcher, she clearly heard the voice of Muck discussing with some German a shipment of dynamite with which to blow up the Longfellow house and Faneuil Hall (though why a German agent should squander dynamite for this purpose was never explained). Another story had it that Muck had a hidden wireless set in his Maine cottage by which he got into contact with German submarines and gave them instructions. Some said that they saw beams of light from Muck's window—signals to distant submarines. One or two could recognize the humor implicit in these wild accusations. A Boston lady was seriously asked if she ever saw such lights signaling from Muck's window. When she said that she had, she was further asked what she had done about it. "Why," she replied softly, "I answered them!"

But most Americans saw nothing laughable about the rumors. They branded Karl Muck as a spy and demanded some action against him. A curious story is told about the time Muck conducted the third *Leonore* Overture of Beethoven in Cambridge, when he adhered to the general practice of having the trumpet passage performed offstage. One patriotic woman, who did not know that this trumpet music was part of the composition, later described how "the clarion call of our young soldiers drilling outside confused the traitor Muck to such an extent that he stopped the orchestra more than once and looked as though he were about to faint."

It needed but one small incident to integrate the opposition against Muck. The incident proved to be Muck's supposed refusal to perform *The Star-Spangled Banner* at a concert in Providence. Today we know that Muck never refused to perform the anthem. Actually it was Major Higginson who stoutly maintained that the American anthem had no place on a program of serious symphonic music. The whole affair was magnified by a Rhode Island editor who was out to get Muck. At any rate before Muck even heard of the incident it had become a national issue. It remained a national issue, even though Muck soon included the anthem on his programs.

From this time on, events moved swiftly. In my book *The Man With the Baton* I have described the steps that led to the final tragedy of Muck's imprisonment:

On November 7, a mass meeting was called in Baltimore (after a concert, scheduled there by the Boston Symphony Orchestra, had been officially forbidden by the Police Commissioner), to denounce Karl Muck as an enemy of the American people. Governor Warfield of Maryland, stabbing his fist towards the galleries, cried out that no true American could remain satisfied until Muck had been "mobbed" to death; and he succeeded so admirably in arousing the fever of the audience that a gray-haired lady in the gallery forgot her dignity sufficiently to exclaim towards the speaker, "Let's kill the bastard!" Shortly thereafter, the *Providence Journal* openly accused Muck in its editorials of acting as a paid agent of the German government. And ladies' societies consecrated to patriotism announced that henceforth a general boycott of the concerts of the Boston Symphony Orchestra would be in effect, and that anyone daring to enter Symphony Hall in Boston would be branded a traitor to his country.

Tangible action against Muck was demanded more and more loudly. Mrs. William Jay, speaking for a large group of patriotic citizens, wrote a letter of protest to Major Higginson:

As a result of the intense feeling regarding a man who bears the German Emperor's decoration, and whose sympathies are most palpably opposed to the United States, the Boston concerts . . . have become a gathering place for everyone who hopes for a defeat of Allied arms. . . . In our opinion even art must stand aside so that every possible influence can be brought to bear to terminate the war with an Allied victory. To this end there seems no swifter means of emphasizing the wholeheartedness of the United States than by terminating the German influence in musical affairs.

"Dr. Muck is probably German in feeling," answered Major

Higginson, "but he has done nothing wrong. He has been eminently satisfactory to me as a conductor and as a man."

But Mrs. Jay was not satisfied:

Five representative cities—Pittsburgh, Detroit, Baltimore, Springfield, and Washington—have already refused to permit Dr. Muck's presence, thereby reflecting wishes of their citizens. Are we to pour forth our blood and nerve and brain and treasure and still hold to German musical domination? Rather a thousand times that the orchestral traditions fade from our lives than one hour be added to the war's duration by clinging to this last tentacle of the German octopus.

The antagonism to Muck became intensified. An attempt was made to suppress Muck's scheduled Carnegie Hall concert in March. When this suppression proved ineffectual, the newspapers headed their reports of this event with: "New York Bows Head in Shame as Muck Leads. Germans Applaud Their Hero Loudly."

Again quoting from my book:

By March of 1918 the antagonism to Muck had become so bitter and vitriolic that even Henry Lee Higginson was compelled to reconsider the situation. It was announced that at the end of the season Muck would, finally, relinquish his baton. But a nation once aroused was not to be so easily silenced. It was no longer satisfied with Muck's resignation but demanded revenge in a form more palpable. . . . Perspective had, by this time, become so warped that we find a Detroit newspaper referring to Muck as "the world's worst conductor."

In the last weeks of March, Karl Muck—who did not permit the venom of a mob's hate to poison his artistry—was working ten hours a day preparing Bach's *Passion According to St. Matthew* for the last concert of the season. He was expending as much scrupulous care on details and as much high inspiration as though he were working under the most ideal conditions, as though there were no war across the ocean nor an angry mob outside the concert hall, as though the only important consideration in the world was to play Bach as beautifully as possible. After one of these intense all-day rehearsals—on March 25—Muck was arrested at his home at nine o'clock in the evening for being an "enemy alien." The newspapers implied with dark inferences that there rested in their hands powerful evidence, which they could not at the time disclose, but which definitely implicated Muck as a political enemy. For a long time, this "powerful evidence" remained a secret. Finally, when the truth leaked out, it was learned that the only complaint the Government had against Muck was the fact that he had not registered as an "enemy alien" as was required by law of all Germans; and Muck had not registered because, though he was German by birth, he was actually a Swiss citizen.

Pending a sentence from Washington, D. C., Karl Muck was confined to prison, and the event aroused wide jubilation and self-congratulations from one end of the country to the other. On April 5, the decision finally arrived from Washington. Karl Muck was found guilty of espionage by the Department of Justice, and was ordered interned for the remainder of the war in Fort Oglethorpe, Georgia. Justice had finally prevailed: one of the world's foremost artists was now Prisoner 1337.

For fourteen months, Muck remained a political prisoner in Georgia. Then—silent forces having been at work—it was decided at Washington to deport him as expeditiously as possible. On August 12, 1919, Muck was hurried in secrecy and stealth aboard the *Frederick VIII.* He had arrived in America in glory, but was to depart as a criminal. His bon-voyage had a fragrant odor, indeed! "Good riddance of Dr. Karl Muck" was the flower which the editorial page of the leading musical magazine in America contributed to the bouquet. And a second prominent musical journal was no less generous: "There is no room for any Dr. Mucks at the head of the Boston Symphony Orchestra or any other musical institution."

It was some time after the armistice before prejudice against German music was to disappear. A year of peace still found, in some quarters, hostility to the music of the enemy. In December, 1919, Fritz Kreisler was scheduled to give a concert at Cornell University. The mayor of Ithaca issued a proclamation before the concert asking his citizens to boycott it. The hall, nevertheless, was full, which so enraged members of the American Legion that they cut the electric wires. For a while, Kreisler continued playing in the dark, but before long he had to discontinue his performance because a riot broke out and the police had to rush in to quell it.

The ban against Wagner was not lifted until late in 1919, when Josef Stransky restored a few excerpts from the music dramas to the programs of the New York Philharmonic. The German language returned to the concert hall at a concert given by a soprano, Alma Simpson, on October 7, 1920, when she sang Schumann's *Aufträge* and Brahms's *Wiegenlied*. Wagner music dramas returned to the repertoire of the Metropolitan in the winter of 1920, presented at the time in the English language. One season later they were again performed in their original language.

The war against German music was over.

CHAPTER SEVEN

1920

THE WAR was over. The American, somewhat disillusioned by his attempts to mix in European affairs, became more concerned than ever before with his own country. He was proud of America's sovereign economic position among the countries of the world. He was more conscious than ever of America's increasing strength: her amazing industrialization, her phenomenal growth, her prodigious expansion of mass production. America was now producing sixty billion dollars of manufactured goods, an increase of more than 500 per cent over 1901. Machines were dominating human existence—lightening the tasks at home; controlling the factory; bringing speed, abundance, pleasure.

The American glowed with well-being. A greater prosperity was at hand than ever before envisioned. It was estimated that, in 1920, there were forty thousand millionaires in the country. Several million wage-earners in the country had incomes of between two and ten thousand dollars a year. The ordinary man in the street had visions of the power and wealth to be won through dabbling in stocks and bonds. The good life was here as never before. One out of every five families owned an automobile. Thirty million attended the movies every week.

The American no longer felt a need to be apologetic about

his country. The former feeling of inferiority now made way for a rather loud-voiced and blatant self-assurance. America was the greatest country in the world, so he sang as an endless refrain. What could be done abroad could be done here twice as well. We were the rulers of the world, not only in gold, but in finance, machinery, factories, and big business. In science also we were at the head: over a million patents were filed in one year immediately following the war, about as many as the next three leading countries together could boast of. Even in the arts we were coming to the fore with gigantic strides. Literature was producing Theodore Dreiser, Sinclair Lewis, and Sherwood Anderson, who wrote of the American scene with such human insight as to inspire the admiration of even the European intelligentsia. Native poets like Vachel Lindsay, Carl Sandburg, and Edgar Lee Masters were singing an indigenous American music in verse. In drama there was Eugene O'Neill; *Beyond the Horizon,* Pulitzer Prize Winner of 1920, was worthy to stand with the great European plays of the time.

And in music—even here the American became more sure of himself, less inclined to look across the ocean for models, more confident than ever before of American potentialities and resources. This reorientation, a postwar phenomenon, was a most significant trend. Once the American no longer felt himself inferior to Europe, he could cultivate his own music in his own way and achieve unrestricted fertility.

During World War I, musical activity in America had become temporarily dislocated. After the war, however, there was restitution. It might be said that the World War was the most important single factor, up to that time, in converting America into a musical country. In Europe the terrible period of readjustment brought economic instability and political uncertainty; Europe, counting its dead and nursing its wounds, was faced first with the problem of recovering from the ravages of a four-year illness. It was in no position to devote attention to the arts. Besides, even if it had chosen to do so, it was too poor to pay its artists.

European musicians, therefore, came more frequently than ever before to practice their art in America. Many settled here permanently. Others centralized their activities in this country, whereas formerly they had concentrated them in Europe. In America, where the war had left few open sores but where, on the contrary, there was unprecedented opulence and expansion, the European musician felt that he could follow his art to the best advantage. The migration of great European musicians began in 1919 and continued uninterrupted for the next few years. America had the price to pay the piper. The great orchestras of Europe were depleted of their best material, which was greedily absorbed by American symphonic organizations. After the war the American symphony orchestras became the greatest in the world. The foremost conductors of Europe came in ever-increasing numbers to give them shape and form. In this way, orchestral music was made to flourish.

European representation thus enriched every phase of musical activity in America—not only our orchestras, but also our opera houses, our music conservatories, our smaller ensembles, and our concert activity. Europe, in short, was bled white of its musical genius; and by the same process, America was receiving a revitalizing transfusion. Out of the upheaval of World War I, a great and enriched musical life emerged in this country, bringing maturity and sophistication where formerly there had been ignorance and naïveté.

CHAPTER EIGHT

Music Performances
after the War

PREVIOUS TO 1917, American music audiences had interested themselves primarily in the opera. After the war, symphonic and chamber music began to crowd into their sphere of interest. Opera had not lost its appeal. If, for example, at the Chicago Opera there were appalling deficits, it was not because opera failed to draw audiences—which was not the case —but rather the result of the extravagance of its new director, Mme. Mary Garden. She became the first woman impresario of opera in 1919, succeeding Campanini. From then on, she spent money with a lavish hand—on sets, costumes, singers, and on sumptuously mounted premières and revivals. Under her supervision the opera house had deficits three times as large as before. Even the greatest box-office success in the world would not have been capable of supplying funds for Mary Garden's inflated budget. In 1923 the opera house underwent reorganization. Mary Garden returned to her original role, that of prima donna, and the direction passed on to Giorgio Polacco. From then on, until 1929, the opera house functioned on a more normal basis, and prospered.

Opera came to the west coast when the San Francisco Opera

was organized in 1922. Recruiting its principal stars from the corps of the Metropolitan Opera House, it presented a season of opera with continued success.

At the Metropolitan Opera House box-office prosperity continued up to the outbreak of the national economic crisis in October, 1929. Prices for single seats twice rose to new heights, and subscriptions sold better than ever. Opening nights and gala premières retained their one-time glamour. Queues and inflated prices obtained by speculators were a faithful indication that the appeal of the opera still remained high. It was quite true that the age of great singers had gone. The immortal Enrico Caruso died in 1921—his last appearance having taken place on Chrismas Eve of 1920 in *La Juive*. Geraldine Farrar retired in 1923. With them passed two of the last representatives of a noble line of singers. Occasionally a new star arose to dazzle —in the manner, say, of Maria Jeritza who sang *Vissi d'arte* in a supine position. But the age of great singing, which had once been a part of the daily operatic routine, was definitely at an end.

Because great voices no longer magnetized audiences at the Metropolitan, the direction of Gatti-Casazza—particularly during the closing years of his regime—was subjected to severe criticism. But weighing the contributions and the defects of the administration in the balance, one must say that the scales tip in favor of the former. Gatti-Casazza did his job well, by whatever standards one chooses. He wanted to make money—and he made it. Under him, opera in New York was so profitable that for many years he accumulated a handsome surplus. But this did not prevent him from introducing many unprofitable and experimental novelties and from paying more flattering attention to American composers than any other impresario before him had done. In his twenty-seven years he was responsible for

110 novelties, of which thirteen were world premières of American operas. Obviously his financial success was not bought with smugness.

It was sometimes said that he paid too much tribute to the Italian composer. From a convenient perspective one can see that this was not true. He did a service for Wagnerites for which they can never be sufficiently grateful, by inaugurating seasonal cycles of the Wagner music dramas without any deletions. He gave the Metropolitan repertoire a truly international character, such as it had never before known, by presenting brilliant premières of new works by the foremost European composers.

Most important of all, every department of the opera house was strengthened and enriched by him: the chorus, the orchestra, stage direction, the mechanical equipment. There were weak performances and some undramatic seasons. But over a span of more than twenty-five years he was able to keep the Metropolitan Opera House one of the great centers of opera-making in the world.

Gatti-Casazza resigned as director of the Metropolitan in 1935, after the existence of the opera company—seriously threatened during the early years of depression which had exhausted his surpluses—was made secure by a public subscription. His successor, Herbert Witherspoon, died of a heart attack before he could actively assume office. The direction of the Metropolitan fell to Edward Johnson—formerly a celebrated tenor at the Metropolitan and more recently Witherspoon's assistant.

With Johnson was inaugurated a new, progressive era for the Metropolitan, in which the repertoire was further freshened and performances were revitalized. The American-born singer received from Johnson unprecedented attention. Democratization set in with the 1940–1941 season when the historic diamond

horseshoe was eliminated and the boxes were put on general
sale for any and all who had the price to pay.

Prosperity returned after several lean, dark years. For this,
however, the sensational success of the Wagnerian soprano,
Kirsten Flagstad, was largely responsible. Like Caruso, Flagstad
had been inherited from the preceding administration. She had
been acquired by Gatti-Casazza and had made her début in his
closing season. Flagstad was, therefore, Gatti-Casazza's farewell
gift to his successor. No gift was ever more providential. She
may well have represented the difference between failure and
success for the new manager.

Flagstad had stepped from obscurity to adulation with one
performance, *Die Walküre,* in which she made her début on
February 2, 1935. Flagstad brought back to the stage of the
Metropolitan a great voice of the dimensions of Fremstad's.
More important still, her dynamic presence on the stage electrified those who worked with her, inspired them to new heights of
artistic achievement, and resulted in Wagnerian performances
such as had not been heard at the Metropolitan in more than
thirty years. Glamour returned to the stage; queues to the box
office. She became one of the greatest drawing cards that the
Metropolitan had known in almost twenty years. Whenever she
sang—and her stamina was such that she could sing frequently
—there were sold-out houses. Nine performances of *Tristan und
Isolde* alone netted more than $150,000. It is an eloquent com-
mentary on her popularity as Isolde that when she could not
return to the Metropolitan for the 1941–1942 season, *Tristan
und Isolde* was temporarily withdrawn from the repertoire!

The spread of orchestral music throughout the country during
the 1920's was one of the more important musical developments
of this period. It has been recorded that four-fifths of the professional orchestras functioning in 1940 had been established *since*

World War I; one-half of them after 1929. Between 1920 and 1930 about fifty new major orchestras arose in the country, an increase of more than 150 per cent over the preceding decade.

This period also saw a phenomenal rise in community orchestras—semiprofessional orchestras which enabled the music lover to perform symphonic music as well as to listen to it, and which brought great orchestral music to small towns. Between five and ten thousand of these orchestras were organized during this decade. Finally, there were many thousands of school orchestras in every part of the country.

But these figures tell only part of the story. It is of greater significance to point out that, before 1920, every important orchestra was located in a city of first magnitude; after 1920, distinguished orchestras arose in smaller cities as well. Great orchestras were no longer the exclusive monopoly of Boston, Chicago, and New York. Cities like Detroit, Philadelphia, Cleveland, Los Angeles, Pittsburgh, and Rochester suddenly became equally celebrated for their orchestral activity. With excellent European material at hand to supply the needs of American orchestras, a new standard arose—sometimes comparable, often superior, to that formerly maintained in Europe. That standard every major orchestra had to reach if it hoped to survive.

It cannot be said that, at least in the period spanning 1920–1930, great orchestral music was the exclusive attraction in the American symphony hall. The American public, still reluctant to abandon its youthful fetish for heroes, now apotheosized the orchestral conductor. Where once American audiences had patronized the opera and glorified the prima donna, so they now sponsored the symphony orchestra and deified the conductor. And just as once the public had gone to the opera house to hear the singer rather than the opera, so it now crowded the concert auditorium to watch the conductor rather than to hear the symphony. America, in short, was conductor-crazy.

In Philadelphia a sensational conductor was magnetizing his audiences with his mercurial temperament and his electrifying personality. Leopold Stokowski—blond hair, classic profile, sensitive hands, a figure to delight a tailor—was worshiped by the audiences of the Philadelphia Orchestra. He had transformed the Philadelphia Orchestra from a third-ranking symphonic group to one of the great musical organizations of the country. He did this with an inflexible iron will which ruled despotically —and ruled not only the orchestra men but the audiences as well.

He had come to Philadelphia by way of Cincinnati (where he had conducted the symphony orchestra for three years), and to Cincinnati by way of St. Bartholomew's Church in New York, where he had been an organist. In Cincinnati, whither he had gone in 1909, he had made his presence felt. He insisted on, and obtained, military discipline among his men. He inaugurated his life-long habit of making little speeches to his audiences— sometimes to explain a new work, sometimes to rebuke them sharply for their bad concert manners. Deaf to expediency, he forced new music upon them, going so far as to feature an all-American program, a remarkably heroic venture for the time. He made it clear that he would brook no opposition or interference of any kind.

He left the Cincinnati Orchestra because he said he did not get the cooperation of his men. It is possible that a more potent influence was a generous contract, calling for $600 a performance, which the Philadelphia Orchestra dangled before his eyes. At any rate, in 1912 Stokowski came to Philadelphia and remained its musical lord for more than twenty-five years. He asserted himself forcefully without delay. When he wanted to perform the Mahler Eighth Symphony—a symphony calling for two orchestras and a chorus of a thousand voices—he brushed aside the objections of the directors that the performance was too expensive. He went even further: he took this Gargantuan musical army to New York to repeat the concert. He demanded, and received, as many rehearsals as his exacting artistry required. He played the programs he thought audiences should hear, not programs that descended to the lowest level of audience intelligence. He became the apostle of the modern composer, at a time when the modern composer was impatiently dismissed by the public. He flaunted his memory by conducting without a score. (When he first did this, one kindly listener clicked her tongue in sympathy and said: "What a pity that the wonderful Mr. Stokowski hasn't learned to read a score! When he does, he'll become an even greater conductor!" He was always the center of interest—the dynamic, dominating, irresistible force behind his concerts. He was always dabbling with experiments: now dispensing with lights, now with applause; sometimes introducing new instruments into the orchestra (such as the Thereminvox); then dispensing with the traditional office of concertmaster; and changing the seating arrangement of his orchestra men. His concerts were always alive with novelty and adventure. And they attracted audiences, capacity audiences, in Philadelphia and New York.

Detroit had a magnetic conductor of its own, less dynamic perhaps than the incomparable Stokowski, but no less appealing. He was the celebrated virtuoso, the poet of the keyboard, Ossip Gabrilowitsch. Gabrilowitsch first conducted a symphony concert in New York City on New Year's Eve of 1917, when an orchestra was improvised for the occasion. A few months later he conducted the Detroit Symphony in a guest performance. At that time the audience rose to its feet to honor him (a sight rather rare west of New York). His success brought him a permanent post with the Detroit Symphony. Introspective, extremely sensitive, poetic by nature, soft-spoken and gentle, detesting display of any kind, uninterested in self-exploitation, he appealed to his audiences by qualities far different from those of a Stokowski; but his appeal was no less potent. The public came to his concerts, and they worshiped him. When he firmly announced that he would resign his post if a new and suitable auditorium were not built for the orchestra in time for the opening of the 1919 season, the funds were easily procured. Detroit would not think of losing its popular conductor.

Other cities, too, had their orchestral heroes. Cleveland formed a new orchestra in 1918 and placed at its head the bespectacled Nikolai Sokoloff, who had served an impressive apprenticeship with the San Francisco and Cincinnati orchestras. Cincinnati had the Belgian violinist, Eugène Ysaÿe—a painstaking artist and a scrupulously exacting interpreter. When Ysaÿe resigned in 1922, he was replaced by a young and energetic conductor from Hungary, Fritz Reiner, fresh from his striking successes at the Dresden Royal Opera and the Teatro Costanzi in Rome. San Francisco honored Alfred Hertz, onetime principal conductor of the Metropolitan Opera House, who had abandoned opera in 1915 for the orchestra. St. Louis called the pianist Rudolph Ganz to give a few guest performances with its major orchestra; these were so warmly received that, in 1922, he was elevated to the post of principal conductor. Los Angeles, in organizing a symphony orchestra in 1919, appointed one of its most forceful musical figures to take the baton—Walter Henry Rothwell. Minneapolis, following a season of guest conductors, gave its permanent post to the dynamic Henri Verbrugghen in 1923.

The Boston Symphony Orchestra had, for a period, fallen on lean artistic days. Karl Muck was gone—in disgrace. With him went one of the great orchestral epochs in American music. In his place came the Frenchman Henri Rabaud, a respectable musician, but by no means a Muck. Pierre Monteux, an extraordinarily well-equipped conductor, a fine and sensitive artist, succeeded Rabaud, directing the orchestra from 1920 to 1924. But Monteux worked against insuperable obstacles. The failure of a strike in the orchestra to establish a union resulted in the resignation of twenty of its important musicians, including the concertmaster. With such a depletion of forces, the orchestra for a while became a skeleton of its former self. Not even so gifted a man as Monteux could restore to this skeleton much of its flesh and muscle. But, in 1924, a new conductor came to the platform of the Boston Symphony—a leader of fiery temperament, capable of commanding and being obeyed, a penetrating interpreter, an exacting drill-master, a magnetizing force. Serge Koussevitzky, founder of the world-famous Koussevitzky Concerts in Moscow (which he had financed from personal funds), later the guiding spirit of the Concerts Koussevitzky in Paris, had personal attributes which America admired in Stokowski. He came to America an almost legendary figure: the man who had brought Western music to Russia, and Russian music to the Western world. He came, also, with dynamic personal qualities. He was not the man to pamper his orchestra or his audiences. He knew what he wanted to achieve, and he went in that direction in a straight line. He overhauled his orchestra, recruiting outstanding musicians from European and American orchestras. His iron-fisted discipline created a unified ensemble in a short period. He worked hard, and demanded that his men work hard with him. He restored to Boston something of its one-time orchestral glory. He came, he was heard, he conquered. Koussevitzky became the musical god of Boston.

In New York, even more than elsewhere, the orchestral conductor became the fashion in music after World War I. The New York Philharmonic had, for many years, known the rather uninspiring direction of Josef Stransky, who had succeeded Gustav Mahler. Stransky gave his audiences the music they liked to hear, performing it as honestly as he could. He had, perhaps, taken the wishes of Pulitzer too literally: When Pulitzer made his bequest to the Philharmonic, he asked that the programs avoid being "too severely classical," with most emphasis placed on the works of Beethoven, Wagner, and Liszt. At any rate, it cannot be said that Stransky's programs showed great imagination. For this reason, no doubt, the audiences liked his concerts. During his regime subscriptions grew from $25,000 to four times that sum. But discriminating music lovers and musicians recognized that he was little more than a conscientious drillmaster, performing rather hackneyed programs in a routine and uninspiring way. Such persons had no high opinion of his talents. Karl Muck once had said acidly: "Stransky can do nothing. And the nothing he can do least is accompanying." At a party in New York at which famous musicians were entertaining by using the instruments with which they were least familiar (Harold Bauer played the double bass; Georges Barrère, the violin) someone suggested that Stransky be called upon to act as conductor.

Eventually opposition to Stransky grew in intensity. It passed from the unprofessional musicians to the press. Richard Aldrich came out openly with fiery attacks on the conductor in the New York *Times*. On February 18, 1923, Aldrich reviewed Stransky's shortcomings, finding his conducting

. . . dominated by an element of commonplace; a lack of discernment into the deeper significance of great music; a failure to appreciate the finer values, to reach the heights and the depths; a disposition to be satisfied with the superficial and the perfunctory. There
have been times, also, of technical failure and insufficiency. Mr.
Stransky has been a hard worker, and no doubt has given the best
that is in him to the Philharmonic Society. It is no discredit to a man
that he does not lift himself by his bootstraps to a higher level than
that upon which nature put him.

Other critics soon followed Aldrich's lead. The audiences of
the Philharmonic, beginning to listen to the concerts with a
more critical ear, soon became impatient with their conductor,
particularly when they contrasted him with the magnetizing
Stokowski (who visited New York regularly with the Philadelphia Orchestra), or the driving, energetic Bodanzky (who had
formed an orchestra of his own in New York), or even the sensitive Pierre Monteux of Boston. After the war was over,
Stransky's days with the Philharmonic were numbered; it was
merely a question of finding a logical successor.

In 1921, Willem Mengelberg, the famous Dutch conductor
of the Concertgebouw Orchestra of Amsterdam, visited New
York as a guest of Bodanzky's National Symphony Orchestra.
He came to the city trailing a magnificent career; he also
came with extraordinary performances, prepared with his
scrupulous attention to every detail, in which the thrice-familiar
classics seemed reborn to a new life. His Beethoven had a
grandeur, his Tchaikovsky a poignancy, his Strauss a clarity
and force which even audiences, not yet overfastidious, could
recognize and admire. And, as a sharp contrast to Stransky's
stodgy programs, he always kept his concerts dynamic with unusual novelties of the past and present. New York audiences
accorded him the adoration they customarily reserved for the
movie star. Cheering at his concerts became a general practice.

Sometimes at the end of one of them the audience would rush to the stage and try to embrace him or to kiss his hand.

One thing the Mengelberg sensation proved: Stransky would have to go. In comparison with the drama and excitement of a Mengelberg concert, the Philharmonic evenings appeared drab. Attendance fell off sharply. The directors of the Philharmonic discussed the problem behind closed doors. Finally they reached a momentous decision. The Philharmonic would absorb the best elements of Bodanzky's competitive organization. Of this new organization the idolized Mengelberg would become artistic director. Stransky was told of this decision only after it had become a *fait accompli*. A handsome bonus, and some palliative words of tribute, were produced to soothe the wounded feelings of the discarded conductor. In 1922 Mengelberg came to the Philharmonic. For several years at any rate—or until a new and greater attraction would catch the fancy of the audience—he was a pampered attraction.

The cult of the conductor was now practiced in the symphony halls as never before. To satisfy this cult, Walter Damrosch had to bring in to head the New York Symphony Society a long and varied series of guest conductors with whom to satisfy the inexhaustible craving of New Yorkers for novelty on the conductor's platform: Albert Coates, Bruno Walter, Otto Klemperer, Enrique Arbós, Fritz Busch, Vladimir Golschmann, Eugene Goossens, Clemens Krauss, Ossip Gabrilowitsch. The Philharmonic countered with their own array of guests to supplement the activities of Mengelberg: Sir Thomas Beecham, Wilhelm Furtwaengler, Georgescu, Kleiber, Molinari, Reiner, and Toscanini.

The apotheosizing of the conductor continued until the end of the decade. Conductors were exploited, then abandoned; cheered one season, ignored the next. Mengelberg, for example, began to lose favor when, in 1925, Wilhelm Furtwaengler—of Leipzig Gewandhaus and Berlin Philharmonic fame—came to enchant his audiences with poetic readings, bringing an altogether new refinement and sensitivity to the classics. There were cheers of adulation for Furtwaengler, extravagant press notices, crowded houses—as Mengelberg was forced to take a position of secondary importance. Then Furtwaengler was ignored to a point where he had to abandon New York permanently, in a violent fit of temper—ignored because Arturo Toscanini had come to the Philharmonic and had created the greatest sensation of all.

The ten-year reign of Toscanini over the Philharmonic inspired such hero worship as American concert halls had never before experienced. The Metropolitan Opera House prima donna, in her greatest glory, never got such adulation as was accorded the wiry Italian conductor. He became a legendary figure; fabulous tales (many of them—strange to say—true) were circulated about his temperament, his memory, his ear. Toscanini could do no wrong. Tickets for every Toscanini concert were at a premium—regardless of what program he chose to conduct. The story goes that rich families who were accustomed to turn their Philharmonic subscription tickets over to their servants suddenly had to bribe them to return every ticket that was for a Toscanini concert. Enthusiasm at his performances was unchecked. Toscanini conducting Mozart, or Toscanini conducting Martucci—it mattered little to his worshiping public. What mattered was that Toscanini was on the conductor's platform.

And so, not only with Toscanini, but with such other magnetizing conductors as Stokowski and Koussevitzky, not the music performed, but the performance became the major consideration. Have you heard Toscanini's *Eroica?* Kousse-

vitzky's *Petrushka?* Stokowski's Brahms?—Thus people asked in
the corridors of the concert auditoriums. The conductor's treatment of the score became the chief interest; and, in this interest
the music itself assumed relative unimportance. Toscanini conducting Italian nonsense could pack the hall; a lesser conductor
like Monteux directing a program of great music was a minor
attraction. The newest trick of the conductor became a consideration of shattering significance: conducting without a score,
or without a baton; conducting a symphony without permitting
applause between the movements. Superficial considerations
assumed exaggerated importance: the gestures of a conductor
used to signal his demands to his men; the shape of his back (is
it true, they asked, that some conductors actually wore cor-
sets?); the beauty of his hands. Abuses even more regrettable
then arose, for some conductors, eager to attract attention and
to hold it, distorted compositions in order to present new and
personalized readings of familiar works—exaggerating dynamics
and tempo, or giving overemphasis to accompaniments.

There were many sincere musicians to lament this deification
of the conductor. Daniel Gregory Mason voiced the sentiments
of this group when he wrote a letter to the New York *Times* on
January 29, 1928:

The competition in showmanship that has gone on in New York
during recent seasons is bad for music from many points of view. It
vulgarizes the taste of audiences by making them value sensation
above beauty, exaggeration and feverish seeking for effect above the
moderation and balance that alone wear well. It demoralizes orchestras by subjecting them to many and constantly changing influences and traditions, not giving them time to perfect themselves
under any. It retards the growth of our composers by denying performances to new works, to permit of familiar war horses. It de-
bauches the conductors themselves by withholding appreciation for

their more solid inconspicuous but lasting qualities and constantly inviting them to make stars of themselves.

There was no question that this glorification of the conductor did not serve the best interests of great music, that it reflected a lack of sound judgment. But this was an ill wind that could also blow some good. The appeal of the personality of the conductor brought audiences to the concert hall in increasing numbers, and it kept them there. Though they may have come to honor the conductor, they remained to hear the music and, eventually, to appreciate it. In spite of themselves, audiences began to acquire a greater discrimination, a healthier set of values. It was not long before their hysterical adoration of the conductor gave way to an intelligent and sincere admiration for symphonic music; eventually the conductor was relegated by audiences to a position of lesser importance, below that of the composer himself.

When Toscanini and Stokowski were enjoying their great following as conductors of the New York Philharmonic and the Philadelphia Orchestra, respectively, critics sometimes suggested that, if these conductors were ever to retire, the orchestras they directed would have to close shop. There would be no audiences for the concerts of the Philharmonic or the Philadelphia Orchestra without Toscanini or Stokowski as the attraction. Such a lament did not take into account the increasing intelligence and discrimination of audiences. Toscanini and Stokowski have both withdrawn from their positions, and yet the orchestras they directed with such brilliance are continuing to function before large and appreciative audiences. More amazing still, each continues to function successfully even though no great and lustrous personality was recruited for the replacement. To the Philharmonic came John Barbirolli, at the

time virtually unknown to the majority of Philharmonic subscribers—young, energetic, comparatively inexperienced. He
came for one season, and remained for several years. In
Stokowski's place there was young Eugene Ormandy, who had
gained his conductorial training in the motion-picture theaters
and over the radio! Ormandy has made such a permanent place
for himself in Philadelphia that the passing of Stokowski is no
longer lamented.

The truth is that the fetish of the conductor began to wane
after 1930. The slow process of education had succeeded in de-
flecting the enthusiasm of the audiences from the personality of
the conductor to the music he was directing. This alone can
explain the unpredictable success with which comparatively
obscure conductors like Barbirolli and Ormandy could step into
the formidable shoes of Toscanini and Stokowski without alien-
ating audiences and causing famine at the box office. But there
were other healthy signs as well. For one thing, the stage and
personal idiosyncrasies of conductors seemed to make very little
impression now. Conductors no longer felt the necessity of conducting every concert from memory, or indulging in strange
baton acrobatics. Conductors who now were admired—men like
Rodzinski, Golschmann, Goossens, Ormandy—were reserved
and self-effacing in their performances. Equally significant is
the fact that the desire of audiences to see new personalities on
the conductor's platform has become less and less intense. The
guest-conductor vogue—which often led to an orchestra's having
half a dozen conductors in one season—was no longer the guiding policy in most places. More and more orchestras were now
content to have one conductor assume the artistic burdens of an
entire season. Besides, when an audience found a conductor it
admired, it remained faithful to him. Most of the conductors
now directing the major American orchestras have been holding

their posts for several years; they are likely to remain in the same positions for many more years to come.

That musical tastes in the country were slowly being refined and sensitized was even more noticeably demonstrated by the increasing interest in chamber music. There is no extramusical appeal in concerts of trios, quartets, and quintets—only the music itself, in its purest form. For this reason, chamber music had never before attracted any but the most esoteric audiences; and these in only a few large cities. But the sphere of chamber music broadened—slowly before World War I, perceptibly after it. The Kneisel Quartet—the first great American string quartet, which had labored for many years on virgin territory—disbanded in 1917. It had begun its distinguished career in empty halls and ended it in comparatively crowded ones. It was a major force in bringing chamber music to America. The noble successor to the Kneisel Quartet was the Flonzaley String Quartet which toured the country until 1927. It played more than 2500 concerts in about 450 cities of the country—a traveling missionary for chamber music, preaching this gospel where it had never been heard before. Its work further expanded the horizon for chamber music, building receptive audiences, making long-neglected masterpieces familiar, arousing an ever-increasing awareness of this wonderful branch of the musical art with its beautifully conceived performances.

Increasing interest in chamber music brought about the arrival of other ensembles. Before the war there were the New York Chamber Music Society, organized in 1914, the Letz Quartet, and the Elshuco Trio, the last two founded in 1917. During the decade after World War I, the ensembles sprouted with increasing fecundity: the Gordon String Quartet (1921), the Lenox String Quartet (1922), the Elman String Quartet

(1924), the Musical Art Quartet (1926), the Perolé String Quartet (1927). To these were joined the great chamber-music ensembles which (now that there were audiences for such concerts) arrived from Europe for extensive tours. The London String Quartet first came to this country in 1920 and returned for the next five seasons. They included among their many concerts monumental cycles devoted to all the Beethoven quartets. From Brussels came the Pro-Arte Quartet in 1923, bringing with them many rarely heard modern works. From Canada the Hart House Quartet arrived in 1924. The Roth Quartet came in 1928, and the Lener Quartet in 1929—both from Hungary. Their concerts included an extensive cycle by the Roths devoted to modern chamber music, and an equally comprehensive historical series by the Leners. After 1930 the Busch, Budapest, and Coolidge quartets were added to the busy concert scene.

This growth of chamber-music consciousness is perhaps one of the truly significant developments in the concert life of America following the war, for this consciousness stemmed from exclusively musical values. It might, therefore, be appropriate here to speak of a woman who has played no small role in this development. Little is known of her, little has been published about her. Her excessive modesty makes her shrink from the limelight of publicity. Yet she has been the patron saint of chamber music in America, and in her unspectacular manner has wielded far-reaching influence in developing chamber music here.

A little more than thirty years ago Elizabeth Sprague, heiress to a prominent chain of stores in Chicago, married Dr. Frederick Shurtleff Coolidge, a young physician. At the time of her marriage, Elizabeth Sprague was considered by her friends a unique and somewhat mystifying character. With millions at her fingertips, she seemed sublimely uninterested in the luxuries that wealth could bring her. Sensitive, intelligent, remarkably self-sufficient, she became absorbed in two major interests: music (she played the piano well, and even composed) and humanity. Young though she was, she was guided by the need to help fellow human beings less fortunate than she.

When she married Dr. Coolidge, a young man as idealistic as she, the pair decided to combine wealth and medical knowledge for the benefit of humanity. Dr. Coolidge established his office in the slums of Chicago, devoted his scientific knowledge to bringing medical aid to sick persons who could not afford to pay a physician's fee. To each case he brought not merely science and zeal, which made him work twelve hours a day, but also sympathy, food, medicine, money. For almost seven years the Coolidges resembled guardian angels to the needy of Chicago. Unobtrusively, they denied themselves the leisure and pleasures to which their wealth entitled them, so that an ailing humanity might be succored.

But their work was to be suddenly halted. Hard work in slums among diseased patients inflicted a severe penalty on Dr. Coolidge. Always delicate in constitution, he discovered that he had become tubercular. Mrs. Coolidge now summoned her wealth to help her own husband. They left Chicago and for the next few years they lived in sanitariums. After three years of sickness, Dr. Coolidge died.

Mrs. Coolidge groped for some escape from her sorrow. She found it in her first love: music. But the personality of Elizabeth Sprague Coolidge was too dynamic to derive satisfaction from passive escape. Having found music again, and having once again experienced the great happiness that can be drawn from art, she turned her wealth toward spreading that happiness more universally.

She had engaged the Hugo Kortschak Quartet to perform

private concerts at her home in Pittsfield, Massachusetts, when
the ideal possessed her to make wonderful chamber music
available to all music lovers. In 1917 she financed a new
chamber-music ensemble, the Elshuco Trio. In the autumn of
1918 she financed a special festival of chamber music in a small
hall, the Temple of Music, which she built expressly for that
purpose in Pittsfield. This festival, to which admission was
free, was so successful that she decided to make it an annual
event. These were the beginnings of Mrs. Coolidge's active participation in chamber music. From this time on she devoted her
resources and imagination to fostering chamber music in this
country. It can be said that she has done more for the cause
of chamber music in this country that has any other single
person. Her achievements have been so many that it would be a
formidable task to enumerate all of them. Moreover, the secrecy
with which Mrs. Coolidge has often worked makes it impossible to guess in how many pies she has had a finger.

She has financed leading chamber-music ensembles, not only
the Elshuco Trio (which has already been mentioned) but
also the William Kroll Sextet, the Coolidge Quartet, and the
South Mountain Quartet. She was responsible for bringing to
this country such ensembles as the Roth and the Pro Arte
quartets. She has personally financed annual festivals of great
chamber music in Pittsfield, Washington, Los Angeles, San
Francisco, and other leading American cities; and has brought
important cycles of Brahms, Beethoven, and the modern composers to leading universities, libraries, and other public institutions (the admission invariably being free). She has financed
nation-wide broadcasts of modern chamber music by the leading composers of our time. In 1925 she created the Elizabeth
Sprague Coolidge Foundation for the purpose of sponsoring
festivals of music at the Library of Congress and for providing

an annual prize of $1,000 for an outstanding chamber-music work. She has commissioned leading American composers to write new works, among them being Charles Martin Loeffler, Howard Hanson, Henry F. Gilbert, and Walter Piston. In her silent role of benefactress, Mrs. Coolidge has exerted an inestimably powerful influence in the spreading of great chamber music throughout the country.

Chamber music has recently found other worthy sponsors. I. A. Hirschmann, a department-store executive, proved that there was a large and responsive audience for great chamber music when he founded the New Friends of Music in New York, a nonprofit organization. Presenting late each Sunday afternoon during the winter season a chamber-music concert by some outstanding ensemble or group of artists—and featuring from time to time significant cycles devoted to the works of Beethoven, Mozart, Schubert, Brahms, and the like—the New Friends of Music has consistently played to capacity audiences at Town Hall and has been self-supporting. In recent seasons its concerts have been broadcast, sponsored by the Book-of-the-Month Club.

CHAPTER NINE

New Horizons
for Music Education

PERCEPTIBLE strides were being made in the field of music
education. Its growth had, up to the time of World War I,
been smothered by the insistence of talented music students that they seek their musical training in Europe. After that
war, musical education in America emerged to a new life. For
one thing, living in Europe was impracticable for the young
student during the turbulent years of the war and the era of readjustment. The American musician was compelled, through
the force of circumstances, to seek his teachers at home. Then,
the increasing self-assurance of the American—his awakened
pride in his country's capacities—made him less inclined to exag-
gerate the value of European instruction. The tendency to study
in America, which received a powerful impetus during the years
of the war, grew and developed further as the leading teachers
of Europe came here to ply their trade. The young violinist
eager to study with Leopold Auer, the young pianist seeking
instruction from Godowsky, or the young singer who desired to
acquire her education from Sembrich or Emilio de Gogorza no
longer had to travel several thousand miles to a foreign land.
These teachers, and many others equally distinguished, were

now to be found near at hand—in New York, Philadelphia, Chicago, or Cincinnati.

Great musical institutions arose to rival the distinguished prewar conservatories of Europe. Between 1900 and 1917 only one great music school had been created—the Institute of Musical Art, financed by a $500,000 bequest, had opened in 1905 in downtown New York with an impressive faculty (including Georg Henschel, Etelka Gerster, Franz Kneisel, and Percy Goetschius) headed by Frank Damrosch. But after 1917 no fewer than three fine music schools came into being. In 1918, George Eastman—the Kodak manufacturer—purchased the Institute of Musical Art in Rochester and created the Eastman School of Music as an affiliate of Rochester University. When, in 1924, Howard Hanson was made director, the institute became one of the most progressive music schools in the country, nursing and developing a notable group of talented young composers including David Diamond, Frederick Woltmann, Gardner Read, Burrill Phillips, Paul White, and Bernard Rogers.

The year 1924 seems to have been a momentous one for music education in America. In that year two other great schools came into existence: one in New York—the Juilliard Graduate School; the other in Philadelphia—the Curtis Institute of Music. Both, handsomely endowed, opened altogether new educational vistas for the gifted music student. The Juilliard School, created with a 15-million-dollar fund by August Juilliard, had "an artist faculty who can impart what they have learned from actual experience on concert or opera stage to students who are sufficiently well prepared to profit by what the artist teachers can give." With Ernest Hutcheson as dean, and Oscar Wagner as his assistant, an admirable faculty was gathered, including such masters of the concert world as Josef Lhevinne, Felix Salmond, Carlos Salzedo, Paul Kochanski, and James Friskin. In

1926 the Juilliard Foundation took over the Institute of Musical Art and formed one extensive educational system by joining the institute with the Juilliard Graduate School, making the former a preparatory school for the latter.

The Curtis Institute, supported by a 12½-million-dollar endowment by Mrs. Mary Louise Bok, was headed by Josef Hofmann in 1927. Its faculty then included some of the greatest artists of the day: Efrem Zimbalist (later to become the head of the school in succession to Hofmann), Carl Flesch, de Gogorza, Elisabeth Schumann, Marcella Sembrich, Felix Salmond, Carlos Salzedo, Louis Bailly, and Fritz Reiner.

A new note in music education was, some years later, to be struck by the celebrated conductor Serge Koussevitzky, when, in 1940, he organized the summer Berkshire Music Center at Tanglewood, the grounds of the famous Berkshire Symphonic Festival. The Center was the realization of a lifelong dream of Koussevitzky to create an educational setting in which pupils, teachers, and trained musicians could mingle, teach and study, and exchange ideas and experiences. The call to talented pupils for a summer course of study brought to Tanglewood, in July of 1940, three hundred gifted young men and women from every state of the Union, for a special six-weeks course in conducting, or opera singing, or instrumental performance, or composition. Many of these students were graduates of leading conservatories; these, and others, were already filling important musical posts. But they sensed that something new was being tried out in the way of music education, and they came to be part of the experiment.

During World War II, the music center temporarily suspended activity. But the first summer of peace, in 1946, saw a resumption of its program with an eminent faculty including

Copland, Lopatnikoff, Herbert Graf, Koussevitzky, Robert Shaw, and many others.

At Koussevitzky's Music Center pupils come into contact with a new style of musical education. This new style consists in instruction inside and outside the classroom. The students remain on the grounds of Tanglewood all day, practicing on their instruments or sprawling on the grass and working silently on their lessons. Usually the teachers are found on the grounds, at the service of any pupil who may be momentarily stumped by a technical or aesthetic problem. A student in composition may sit under a tree, working on a composition. Aaron Copland may pass by, look over the student's shoulder, and then and there give him some practical suggestions.

Instrumentalists form the bulk of the student body at the Center. They receive a unique training. In addition to being instructed directly by the first-desk men of the Boston Symphony Orchestra, these young instrumentalists are always watched and studied by their teachers. When the students combine in performances of chamber music (which is a regular part of the curriculum), Richard Burgin, concertmaster of the Boston Symphony, is near by to give advice and criticism. When the students assemble for orchestra work, they are under the vigilant eyes (and ears) of experienced Boston Symphony men. Comes an intricate passage for oboe or flute, and the first oboist or flutist of the Boston Symphony is there to give assistance.

Composition classes are conducted informally by Aaron Copland and Nikolai Lopatnikoff (in 1946). Opera classes are under the direction of Dr. Herbert Graf, and part of the instruction consists in the preparation of special performances in a theater built for that purpose. Vocal instruction consists not only in private coaching but also in choral work. Students are rehearsed in such choral masterpieces as the Bach B minor Mass and Beethoven's *Missa Solemnis,* and then they join the Boston Symphony Orchestra in public performances.

The conducting classes are Koussevitzky's special interest. Some forty students (some of them already conductors of established orchestras) form the class that receives practical and theoretical experience under Koussevitzky. Classroom lectures form only a small part of the curriculum. Each student conductor is expected to rehearse the Center orchestra of students at least a few times. He is given a week's notice in which to prepare a given work; then he steps to the head of the orchestra and begins his rehearsal just as if he were preparing for a public concert. Koussevitzky does not spare his students. They are not given thrice-familiar Haydn or Beethoven symphonies to prepare. Difficult modern works are mere routine for these young conductors, and they are expected to take even the most complicated scores by such modern composers as Schönberg, Copland, Hindemith, Randall Thompson, Richard Strauss in their stride. As these young conductors work with the orchestra in this complex music, Koussevitzky is at their elbows, offering criticism. Besides following this practical work in rehearsing an orchestra, these pupil conductors are expected to attend Koussevitzky's rehearsals with the Boston Symphony and to be present at all the music lectures held on the grounds and at all student performances. Koussevitzky insists that a good conductor must first have a well-balanced music culture. It is interesting to point out that Leonard Bernstein, perhaps the greatest baton discovery of our day, was a student of Koussevitzky at the Center.

I have commented in such detail on the Berkshire Music Center because it has brought new horizons to music education, because it suggests untold possibilities for the music education of tomorrow, and because it proves that America is becoming increasingly receptive to new pedagogical ideas.

In the evolution of a musical country, the emergence of several great conservatories and music schools—serving talent of a high order—is, after all, not quite so important as another educational development which came to the fore after World War I—the diffusion of music education to the masses, to students, young and old, many of whom pursue music not as preparation for a professional career but simply as a pleasurable avocation. In New York there was, in 1914, the Manhattan School of Music in the upper east side section. It rose to answer the need for a school catering primarily to those who lacked either the talent or the money required for entering a conservatory. In 1918 Harold Bauer and Pablo Casals became the first two members of its Artists' Auxiliary Board. One year after this, the school, with a faculty numbering twenty-three members, was giving an education to one hundred students in every department of music. Furthermore, the community music school gained in popularity and importance, as more and more people sought some systematic training in music. The rise of community schools similar to the one in New York ultimately resulted in the formation of the National Guild of Community Schools, which had a membership of thirteen schools in eleven different cities. These thirteen schools boasted a faculty of 385 teachers and a student body of 4,848, with an additional 1,349 students on a waiting list clamoring for admission.

In the academic schools of the country, music began to assume an ever-increasing importance. Vocal music came to the fore for the first time under the direction of Frederick H. Haywood of the Eastman School of Music, who was chairman of a national committee on vocal training. Choral music thus achieved for the first time a status of respectability in the public schools of the country. One of the major forces in this development was Dr. Archibald Thompson Davison who, in 1912, became conductor of the Harvard Glee Club. In 1919 it was announced that the Harvard Glee Club would no longer devote itself to college songs, popular ballads, and light numbers (the practice of all college glee clubs at the time) but to the choral music of the masters—Bach, Palestrina, Brahms. In a short period the Harvard Glee Club developed into an artistic body to command admiration—so much so that, in 1921, it embarked on a concert tour of Europe, performing twenty-three concerts in thirteen cities. Subsequently it achieved sufficient artistic significance to be able to collaborate with the Boston Symphony Orchestra in performances of choral masterpieces.

The Harvard Glee Club was a beacon which shed a light of direction to glee clubs throughout the country. Other organizations followed its lead, abandoning their repertoire of trite and popular music for the classics and giving fastidious and tasteful performances. Competitions spurred them on in their work. Intercollegiate glee-club contests were held throughout the country, showing year by year the remarkable growth of these musical organizations, their amazing seriousness of purpose, and their genuinely musical importance.

In *The Craftsman* (December 1915) Karl Muck had written in an American magazine:

Teach your children . . . in every school in America . . . all the beautiful music that the greatest musicians of the world have produced. Have every school one rich chorus, have children sing out all the joy and love of their young hearts. Beyond this, every school should have its orchestra. I do not believe there is a school in America that would not furnish you talent for an orchestra.

Twenty years later his wish was to reach fulfillment. After

the war, not only choral music, but orchestral music as well, developed tremendously in the schools of the country. The board of education in Oakland, California, was the first to recognize the importance of music in the curriculum. In 1916 it approved the expenditure of several thousand dollars for musical instruments to be allotted to students for orchestral work. Actually this move was too progressive for the times. It brought such vehement protests that the superintendent who was responsible for this venture was compelled to resign. Nevertheless there came into being an idea that could not be killed permanently. It was given powerful impetus by George Eastman in 1919, when he provided $15,000 to be used for the purchase of musical instruments for the public-school children of Rochester. Other cities, inspired by Eastman's example, also provided funds for a similar purpose. By 1920 school orchestras and bands were rehearsing in every part of the country. True, there had been school orchestras before the twentieth century (there had been one in Ohio as early as 1867). But as a general national movement, receiving the full support of educators, the school orchestra did not sweep the country until after World War I.

In 1921, at the National Conference of Music Supervisors held in St. Joseph, Missouri, there was a forty-piece high school orchestra sent by the small town of Parsons, Kansas. One year after this, at the same conference, a full symphony orchestra from a Richmond, Virginia, high school gave another performance. These admirable concerts encouraged the educators to inspire ventures of a similar nature in their own communities. In 1923 a committee was formed by the National Conference of Music Supervisors to arrange a contest among the orchestras of different and scattered communities. This venture grew by leaps and bounds. So many orchestras entered the contest that, before long, it was necessary to hold regional contests to select the entrants for the national one. It is estimated that, by 1930, there were more than 30,000 school orchestras functioning regularly throughout the country.

At the same time, there arose the all-state orchestra. Indiana invited all high-school orchestras of that state to send their best qualified representatives to form a state orchestral group. This proved so successful that, in 1926, Detroit followed with a similar undertaking. Before long, forty different states had sponsored their own all-state orchestras. From this it was only a short step to the all-national school orchestra. Under the direction of Joseph E. Maddy, one of the leading spirits in the development of orchestral music in the schools, the National High School Orchestra of between two hundred and three hundred members, representing school orchestras from every part of the country, came into existence. Out of the National High School Orchestra there grew one of the most notable music-education centers in the country. The need for a place where music students from every part of the country could come to rehearse and study encouraged Maddy to institute a summer camp at Interlochen, Michigan, in 1928. Each summer several hundred young people from the high schools came to live in a setting of idyllic beauty, to study music, to rehearse in choral and orchestral groups, and to give weekly concerts.

An altogether new departure in music education in the public schools was initiated in New York City through the creation of the High School of Music and Art. Dreaming of a municipal conservatory where the musically talented of the city could acquire a thorough training free, Mayor F. H. LaGuardia helped to found the first city public school in which it is recognized that the gifted musical child deserves a specialized musical training as part of his regular education. "After all," argued the Mayor, "what is so unusual in the idea of a high school with a special purpose? We have textile high schools, technical trade schools, and business high schools. Why not a music school?" The academic studies are not neglected. But the child with a bent for music can acquire a well-rounded training in every phase of musical activity. He is encouraged to be creative; every once in a while the students of the High School of Music and Art hold a concert devoted exclusively to compositions by their fellow pupils. "I believe," the Mayor said at the time, "that this is one of the best contributions which I will be able to make to the educational system of the city as long as I am Mayor of New York." He did not overstate his contribution. He pointed out a new and hitherto untraveled road for public education which, it is hoped, other cities throughout the country will also travel.

CHAPTER TEN

Music for the Millions

———

UT THE greatest force in making America a country of music lovers was unquestionably that of mechanization. A developed concert life, expanding educational resources, growing musical institutions, increasing audiences—these were, of course, significant in the evolution of a musical culture. But in the face of mechanization—which *could* bring the art of music into every household—all other influences assume secondary importance. Inevitably, the process by which an uneducated and uninformed public is trained to visit the concert hall or opera house regularly is, at best, a slow one. Over a period of fifty years there has been noticeable development in this direction. But the transformation of America into a musical country would not have been consummated in fifty or a hundred and fifty years if the machine had not entered the picture. Through the machine, the mountain came to Mohammed: music came to the average American—and into his living-room.

"Mechanical music," "canned music," "robot music," "tin-box music"—the epithets hurled at it were many and varied. Yet, in spite of sneers, the real value of this kind of thing in the cultural growth of America assumed Gargantuan proportions. Your ordinary citizen, to whom the music of Bach and Sibelius was as remote as, say, the poetry of John Donne or the paintings of Giotto, began to familiarize himself with the works of these and other masters. Music filled a larger and larger role in his everyday life.

In the beginning there was the Swiss music-box, pleasantly tinkling a single folk song or popular air in the American home. Then, in the 1900's came the mechanical player-piano, the first important mechanized musical instrument. Arthur Whiting wrote in the July, 1919, *Yale Review:*

The early model of the player had the exuberant spirits of a machine gun. The notes of Mendelssohn's *Spring Song* were shot out like bullets so that the musically timid hastened to take cover. . . . In the overwhelming solos there was no recognition of the principles which underlie playing; no important or unimportant sounds; no increase and decrease of volume. Such crudeness, however, soon gave place to machine-like imitations of light and shade, to sound emphasis of the melodic line and variations of speed.

Ultimately, this primitive piano-player developed into the Ampico, the Duo Art, the Welte Mignon—a fairly faithful reproduction of the greatest performances of concert pianists. The player-piano became a fashion and a fad in the American home. Chopin, Beethoven, and Liszt, at the hands of Paderewski, Rosenthal, or Godowsky became the evening entertainment in the nation's living-rooms. As Mr. Whiting further described these sessions:

They all stand before the . . . mechanical player which, being entirely self-possessed, has even more platform imperturbability than the applauded virtuoso, even a larger number of decorations on his chest from the hands of grateful sovereigns. . . . After a few introductory sounds which have nothing to do with music, and without relaxing the lines of its inscrutable face, the insensate artist proceeds to show its power. Its security puts all hand-playing to shame; it never hesitates; it surmounts the highest difficulties without changing a clutch. Always masterful and headlong it can, if required, utter notes faster than the human ear can follow. Bouquets of adjectives, thrown by the excited audience towards the unperspiring, unexhausted performer, fall unnoticed at its feet. Since that memorable performance, poor sister has hardly touched the keys.

The player-piano had been preceded (but was eventually displaced) by a still more important reproducing instrument: the phonograph. The latter was hardly more than a toy for adults in the closing years of the nineteenth century, producing sounds the identity of which were not always recognizable. Yet it became (almost over night) the most potent single missionary for great music in this country.

Its history must form a salient part of the musical story of America. Born in 1877, the year in which Edison first took out a patent for a reproducing machine, its growth was rapid. In 1888 Edison perfected the wax cylinder. On May 16 of the same year, Emil Berliner, inventor of the disc which was to replace the cylinder, gave a demonstration before members of the Franklin Institute of Philadelphia. By 1896 the flat disc was sufficiently developed to permit extensive reproduction of great voices. By 1900 recordings were prepared commercially. Maria Michailova was the first important singer to record commercially. Enrico Caruso was the first of the great Italian tenors reproduced on records; it was the phenomenal sale of Caruso's records which converted the recording of music into a tremendous industry. Independent companies then arose to put on the market the singing of many other outstanding singers.

Despite the fact that these great voices were often submerged under the surface noise of the needle scratch, despite the fact that it was not often easy to discern the artistry of the performer in the squeals and snorts that emerged from the horn, the public was delighted with this musical novelty, which it called a "screech box." In 1903 Columbia issued the first of its "Celebrity Discs," the list of artists including Jean de Reszke, Sembrich, Scotti and Schumann-Heink. Victor (which had been on the market for several years, reissuing European recordings) followed suit with an artists' list of its own. Recorded music was proving to be more and more practicable. Artists who only a few months earlier had been jeering at this new contraption were hurrying to put their signatures on recording contracts. Within a few years there was hardly a singer of note who was not making records: Louise Homer, Campanari, Emma Eames, Gadski, Nordica, Lilli Lehmann, Journet, Caruso, and innumerable others. The great instrumentalists also were engaged for records. First came Joachim and Sarasate; after them, Mischa Elman, Maud Powell, Kreisler, Kubelik, Paderewski, and de Pachmann.

The ornate mahogany cabinet of the Victrola now occupied something of an imperial position in the living-room of the middle-class American family. Relaxation came with the cranking of the talking machine for a program of good "canned music." The sale of serious music records reached ever-soaring heights, achieving, in 1921, the sales peak of ten million discs. The American was being educated in music *en masse*. Opera excerpts took precedence: the sextet from *Lucia* (sung by Caruso, Tetrazzini, Jacoby, Amato, Journet, and Bada, and priced at $8.00 for one side); Galli-Curci and her electrifying coloratura voice in the "Bell Song" from *Lakmé;* Titta Ruffo injecting a note of burlesque with his breath-taking incantations of *Figaro! Figaro! Figaro!;* the incomparable Enrico laughing through his tears in *Vesti la giubba.* Light concert numbers also enjoyed prodigious sales: Alma Gluck singing the *Elégie* of

Massenet with the accompaniment of her husband's violin;
John McCormack nostalgically remembering Ireland; Kreisler
playing of love's joys and sorrows with his characteristic Viennese charm; the Elman tone, opulent in the Schubert *Ave Maria*
or the Tchaikovsky *Mélodie;* the pyrotechnics of the prodigy,
Jascha Heifetz, traversing with incredible digital exploits the
music of Wieniawski and Sarasate; the great pianists sentimen-
talizing over a Chopin *Nocturne,* the Mendelssohn *Spring Song,*
or the opening movement of Beethoven's *Moonlight* Sonata.

For many years the recording apparatus was too insensitive to
reproduce authentically anything beyond a solo voice and piano
accompaniment, or the music of a single instrument: an attempt to record an orchestral accompaniment for an opera
aria, tried in 1905, failed dismally. But experiments continued.
In a few years, several groupings of instruments, and finally a
full orchestra, were capable of being transferred to the disc.
In 1917 three great orchestras joined the Columbia list of
celebrities: the Chicago Symphony conducted by Stock, the
Cincinnati Orchestra under Kunwald, and the New York Philharmonic with Josef Stransky. Victor followed the lead: in 1918,
the Boston Symphony appeared on the red label, in 1919 the
Philadelphia Orchestra under Stokowski, and, in 1921, the
orchestra of La Scala under Toscanini. At first, orchestral music
came in four-minute (or, at most, eight-minute) excerpts:
Hungarian Dances by Brahms, the second movement of
Beethoven's Fifth Symphony, the last two movements of the
Mozart E-flat major Symphony (the symphonic movements
always badly truncated), and the more familiar passages from
the Wagner music dramas.

Thus, America was learning its music piecemeal—four minutes at a time. It was being given a hurried familiarizing sip

at a strange potion before being asked to drain the entire cup. Eventually it was no longer content with a mere taste: finally, in place of encore numbers, truncated orchestral pieces, and opera arias, it demanded complete symphonies, concertos, operas, and masses.

In her autobiography, *An American Musician's Story,** Olga Samaroff-Stokowski gives an admirable description of the early years of recording from the point of view of the recording artist:

Artists usually lunched with officials of the company when they recorded in Camden. . . . Possibly the overindulgence in iced tea accounted for the nervousness which caused me to play a wrong note or two in every record I made of Mendelssohn's *Spring Song.* When I played it through for the sixth time, there was not a single mistake until the very last measure, which thereupon brought forth my despairing "damn."

"Never mind, Madam," said one of the recording experts who officiated on such occasions, "the same thing happened to Caruso the last time he was here. He was ready to cry. It just gets you sometimes."

Even without heat and too much iced tea, there was something peculiarly unnerving about the buzzer that dominated life during the process of making phonograph records. After everything had been adjusted, and all possibility of outside noises eliminated (you had to be sure your piano stool did not squeak and reasonably certain you would not have to blow your nose), there would be two peremptory buzzes which means "get ready"; they were followed by a minute suspense during which you reached an agonized conviction that you did not know a single note of the piece you were going to play; finally, a single, fateful buzz started you off as though someone gave a violent shove to a sled at the top of a steep toboggan slide. . . .

Recording was young. . . . Electric recording had not been perfected and experimentation was going on in every direction. From the start, however, the musicians and recording companies were en-

* New York: W. W. Norton & Company, Inc., 1939.

gaged in a long-drawn-out conflict. The *casus belli* was the choice of music to be recorded. The musicians wanted to record great music; the recording companies demanded popular music. . . . The opera singers had a relatively easy time, although even they were lured by the almighty dollar into sentimental renderings of songs like *The Little Gray Home in the West* which earned fortunes for all concerned. But at last many really good operatic arias came within the category of "popular music." Relatively few great instrumental compositions did.

Orchestras, string quartets, and solo instrumentalists battled with manifold difficulties. Aside from the questions of popularity, the compositions they particularly wished to record were usually too long to fit the time limit of the record. The largest record only played four minutes and fifty seconds for each side of the disc. Unless the musician was willing to make inartistic cuts, long compositions necessitated a series of records that were unpopular at the time because they were too expensive, and—according to the prevailing psychology—too "highbrow" for the general public. . . .

Very often a battle with the company on the choice of music would result in a sort of compromise. For instance, they would let me play a Rhapsody of Brahms, if I would consent to record the *Spring Song* of Mendelssohn. . . .

The acoustical problems of phonograph recording still require a special technique of performance. In the old days, however, before electric recording was developed to the point of being usable, difficulties were still greater. Singers had to be moved about while singing so as to increase or lessen the distance between them and the recording apparatus according to the volume of tone they produced. An overloud tone caused "blasting," the recording studio term for the raucous sound it produced. The acoustical funnels hanging over a piano which transmitted the sound-vibrations to the wax matrix had to be carefully placed. The difference of a hair's breadth in their position might cause certain tones to obtrude themselves with an unpleasant quality. A pianist in those days was obliged to operate within a very limited tonal gamut. A very soft tone did not record clearly, if at all. A *fortissimo* tone caused "blasting." Naturally, the restraint necessitated by these limitations interfered with freedom of musical feeling. It was as though a painter were forced to work with a palette from which some of the most important colors were removed.

When the radio became a fad, it was generally believed that the phonograph was through. Since, with the twist of a dial, the radio loud-speaker would disgorge a good variety of popular and semi-classical music, the effort of cranking a phonograph and turning records every four minutes grew to be too taxing. Finally, both phonograph and the library of records were relegated to either the cellar or the attic—and, seemingly, to obsolescence. The imperial corner in the living-room now belonged to the superheterodyne.

Yet, just when a dirge was being intoned for the passing of the phonograph, something approaching a miracle took place in the recording industry. Like the phoenix of fable, it was to rise suddenly from its own ashes, to become even more significant than it had been before. Unexpectedly, the phonograph not only came back to its one-time popularity after suffering a period of complete discard, but also achieved new heights of artistic importance.

In 1930, when virtually every other industry in America was threatened by collapse, the phonograph industry reached a new five-year high. In 1937 the Victor Company triumphantly announced that in that year its sale of serious music exceeded that of 1930 by 535 per cent. Since 1937 the graph on the sales chart has been consistently mounting. In 1939 there was a sale of fifty million records, five million being serious music—a rise of one and a half million in the serious-music field over the preceding year. In 1940 almost ten million serious-music records were sold. During and after World War II, the sale of serious-music records soared to astronomic heights, its flight restricted only by the wartime problems of production. In 1945, 156,000,-

000 records were sold; in 1946, more than 225,000,000—and this figure is still growing. It has been computed that the average record-buyer bought twenty-one discs in 1945 as compared with only nine in 1929. More than 300,000 phonograph machines were bought in 1940, bringing the total number of phonographs in use above the four-million mark. In 1946, the number of phonographs in American homes numbered between six and seven million. Ten million phonographs is a conservative estimate for postwar America.

Actually, what brought about the recrudescence of the phonograph was that very thing which, at first, had been believed to spell its ruin. The radio did not destroy the phonograph. On the contrary, it succeeded in giving it a new lease on life.

For one thing, the perfected radio brought to the science of recorded music a revolutionary method. Formerly, reproduction on records had been achieved acoustically. The performer, or performers, played into a large horn which was used to converge the sound and increase its intensity at the recorder with sufficient power to cut into a wax disc, which in turn became the matrix for the records. This method succeeded in only approximating on discs the tone qualities of the voice and solo instruments. It failed to reproduce an orchestra or chorus with any degree of clarity or sharpness of detail.

The radio, however, introduced the use of the electric microphone into recording. The sound is now uttered into a microphone (just as in the broadcasting studio) and thence transmitted to an amplifier that enormously increases its power. The output of the amplifier goes to a device called a "cutter," which is essentially a phonograph pick-up driven electrically instead of mechanically. This "cutter" drives grooves into the wax disc.

From the radio, too, the phonograph acquired an altogether

new type of loud-speaker in which the amplification is achieved through radio tubes. Electrical recording voiced through this new type of speaker finally brings a fidelity to musical recording almost lifelike in its quality. For the first time, recordings succeeded in converting symphonic and choral music cleanly, clearly, and sonorously. For the first time, the disc succeeded in catching exact shades of tone qualities from the different instruments. And, for the first time, a tonal range could be reproduced spanning the low notes of the bass and the high notes of the piccolo. The professional musician or astute music lover could no longer sneer at recorded music or refer to it as "canned." Recorded music had achieved, through its radio innovations, so human a quality that it could now afford aesthetic pleasure to even a discriminating ear.

These scientific contributions of the radio to the phonograph might have been foreseen by the scientists in the laboratory as early as 1924, the year in which recording through microphone first came into existence. What could not be prophesied at the time, however, was the phenomenal growth of musical consciousness which was to take place in the country partly as a result of the radio, and partly as a result of the early educational efforts exerted by the first phonographs. Repeated hearings of operatic, symphonic, and chamber music over the air (following, as they did, previous intimacy with opera arias and movements from symphonies, acquired from the old-time phonograph) educated an entirely new army of music lovers. It was these music lovers, even more than the musician or the student, who were responsible for the unexpected boom in the record business. The official figures of record sales are a carefully guarded secret, but the figures quoted above are generally considered accurate.

It is strongly believed by record distributors that the majority of those who buy records regularly are not professional musicians, nor even music students, but neophytes who in recent years have suddenly discovered that music is not a remote and forbidding world. Having learned that it can become a personal, human experience within the reach of everyone, they are now willing to pay high prices to make this experience a permanent one in the home. Some of these record purchasers have never been in a concert hall; their entire music experience has been gained through the radio and records.

There is a radical difference between the demand for records before 1920 and the present demand. This, in itself, is an illuminating commentary on the growth of musical intelligence in this country in recent years.

Before 1920 people who bought records generally emphasized the importance of the interpreter over the music itself. Today, it is the music and not the artist that sells the records. People demand, first of all, a specific work; then, and only then, are they interested in the performer. A recent survey among several gramophone shops in New York revealed to this writer that Kreisler or Heifetz playing a musical trifle will not sell one-tenth so well as these artists interpreting a work of major musical significance. Twenty years ago or so the best Kreisler sellers were his Viennese bonbons—*Liebesfreud, Liebesleid, Schön Rosmarin.* Today these Viennese morsels are fabulously outsold by his interpretations of the concertos of Beethoven, Brahms, and Mendelssohn.

Another important difference distinguishes the record buyers of before and after the phonograph's renascence. Formerly buyers preferred one-record excerpts of the major musical works. In 1926, however, the first album set came into being, presenting a large work in its entirety. It met with such an enthusiastic response that, henceforth, phonograph companies revised their entire recording programs to put emphasis on album sets. Today, albums of an entire symphony or concerto or string quartet or opera find a ready market—even though the complete work may cost as much as $10 or $15.

A third, and probably the most significant, difference between the record buyers of these two periods is the shift of interest from thrice-familiar classics to less familiar masterpieces. The great symphonies of Beethoven, Tchaikovsky, Brahms are, of course, consistently good sellers—so much so that the companies have found it profitable to issue each in several different recordings by different orchestras and conductors. But the best-seller lists of records during the past two years or so in record shops throughout the country have disclosed some startling information. Sibelius sells better than Tchaikovsky; Bach better than Dvořák; Mozart better than Chopin. Many times Bach has achieved the status of a best seller—though this is largely because of the appeal of Stokowski's orchestral transcriptions. One of the best-selling albums of 1939 was Prokofiev's *Peter and the Wolf*. In 1945–1946, Prokofiev's cantata *Alexander Nevsky* was also a best seller.

Again and again record collectors have proved their eagerness to explore completely unfamiliar realms of the musical art. It is for this reason that record lists of recent years have often been more progressive than the programs of concert halls. Old music, long relegated to obscurity, now finds an eager public. The following works, rarely heard in public performances, have been steady sellers: Pergolesi's *Stabat Mater*, Scarlatti's sonatas for harpsichord, Bach's *Peasant* and *Wedding* cantatas, harpsichord fantasias of Telemann, early American music, cantatas of Buxtehude, early symphonies of Stamitz, Purcell's music for chamber orchestra, works by Grétry, Lully, Rameau. These works constitute only a small fraction of the library of unexplored musical masterpieces which appear regularly on the record lists.

Modern music also finds a great demand. The piano concerto of Jean Françaix appeared on records a year before it was given its American première in New York. The Violin Concerto of Ernest Bloch and the Second Violin Concerto of Prokofiev were familiar to record owners months before they became known to New York concertgoers. Many other compositions appeared on records almost immediately after their premières—works like Shostakovitch's Fifth Symphony, Bartók's *Mikrokosmos,* Bartók's *Contrasts,* Rachmaninoff's Third Symphony, Siegmeister's *Ozark Set,* McDonald's *My Country at War,* Copland's *Appalachian Spring,* Samuel Barber's First Symphony, and the violin concertos of Gruenberg and Bartók. The recording catalogues now boast a well-represented cross-section of the music of our time. Besides, a conscientious attempt has been made by the phonograph companies to record every major work of the leading composers. Richard Strauss, Sibelius, Rachmaninoff, Delius, Ravel, and Stravinsky are represented on discs by virtually every one of their important works.

Almost from the first, phonograph companies realized astutely what a major force phonograph records could be for developing taste in the young in the schools of America. As early as 1911 the Victor Company organized an educational department. By 1915 this department was sufficiently expanded to include special music teachers who were sent to representative schools and colleges, establishing courses in music with the aid of records and giving advice to teachers on how to supplement their lectures with recorded programs. It was estimated that in the second year of this program, thirteen teachers visited 1,283 cities and gave 4,000 demonstrations. By the end of 1916 more than 15,000 Victor machines were being used in the schools of some 5,000 cities.

Since then, recorded music has been a vital element of music education in schools throughout the country. The master-pieces of music, as conceived by the composer, now enter the classroom in place of the formerly scattered musical examples produced by the instructor on the piano. In 1933 the Carnegie Foundation of New York provided $30,000 for the distribution of special sets to colleges throughout the country; these sets in-cluded a good phonograph and records covering the entire history of music. Almost three hundred schools throughout the country have been beneficiaries of this philanthropy, thereby enriching the musical experiences of young people.

Four million phonographs are supplemented by 51 million radios in actual use throughout the country. Almost every other person in the United States can, with the turn of a switch, come into direct contact with the greatest available operatic, sym-phonic, and chamber music. What this means in terms of edu-cating the masses can only be guessed at on the basis of what already has been accomplished in some twenty years.

Twenty years of experimenting in the transmitting of pro-grams over the air was the background for the first successful broadcast. In the early 1900's, Lee De Forest—generally credited with being the inventor of the radio—broadcast from the stage of the Manhattan Opera Hause, via Marconi air waves, an aria from *Carmen* sung by Mariette Mazarin. For the first time, through squeals and roars, a human singing voice was sent over the air waves. But not even the most farsighted could have guessed that in this primitive experiment lay the embryo of an epoch-making instrument.

But experiments went on apace. On Christmas Eve, 1906, Reginald Fessenden transmitted a musical program "successfully." On March 5 of the following year De Forest took his equipment to the Telharmonic Hall in New York to broadcast the *William Tell* Overture. Somewhat later—on January 20, 1910 —De Forest was responsible for the first broadcast to take place on the stage of the Metropolitan Opera House when portions from *Cavalleria Rusticana* and *Pagliacci*, both with Caruso, were sent through the air and picked up by fifty radio amateurs, several ships in the Navy Yard in Brooklyn, and a group of invited guests in a Times Square hotel.

Not until 1920 was the first radio station to come into existence. Shortly after the close of World War I, Dr. Frank Conrad, an engineer at Westinghouse, built a transmitting set in his garage. His hobby was to send out programs of recorded music, interspersed with news and some personal comments. His programs, received by numerous amateurs over a considerable area, met with such an enthusiastic response that Westinghouse realized for the first time what a force the radio could become if given the proper direction. With the aid of Dr. Conrad, Westinghouse organized a pioneer radio station for the purpose of publicizing its electrical products. In November, 1920, it sent out its first national broadcast by reporting the presidential election. Meanwhile, on August 20, 1920, the first commercial station had begun regular broadcasting—WWJ in Detroit.

Other radio stations mushroomed up throughout the country. In 1922 WEAF in New York put on the first known commercial program, advertising a New York real-estate company. In the same year, on August 3, the first radio sound effect was produced by WGY, Schenectady, when the slamming of a door was simulated by the banging of two pieces of wood in front of the microphone. In 1926 the first major radio network came into existence, formed by the National Broadcasting Company. Already the role to be played by great music in radio was suggested when the inaugural program of the network, on November 15, featured Mary Garden, Titta Ruffo, Harold Bauer, the New York Symphony Society, and the Oratorio Society of New York. In 1927 a second radio network was created by the Columbia Broadcasting System.

Those were the days when the crystal set was giving way to the battery set. Jazz and light salon music dominated the programs. Radio executives said that great music would never take an important place in radio because radio depended for its existence on mass consumption, and who ever heard of mass consumption of great music? Many great artists considered it below their dignity to appear before a microphone. Those were the days when good music meant Victor Herbert and more Victor Herbert, or a fifteen-minute violin program by Godfrey Ludlow, or a half-hour of "slumber- music" at the hour of midnight. Those were the days when music had to be listened to through major air disturbances and static, when the musician acidly spoke of the radio as "De Forest's prime evil."

But the experiments in the laboratory continued indefatigably. Electricity replaced the battery. The superheterodyne set and the Magnavox loud-speaker became obsolete. The quality of transmission was improved with the elimination of much of the static. Reception was ultimately so faithful that programs could be heard undistorted by extraneous noises.

As reproduction over the air became more faithful, good music began to acquire a slowly increasing importance. Two early broadcasts of good music—a performance of *Aida* from the Kingsbridge Armory in New York and a concert of the New York Philharmonic from the Great Hall at the College of the City of New York—proved that there was an audience for more

serious musical efforts. Hesitantly—in spite of their so-called
better judgment—radio executives doled out bits and dribbles
of good music. In 1926 John McCormack and Lucrezia Bori
were sponsored on a joint program, and they received an
avalanche of congratulatory letters. In the same year Walter
Damrosch became associated with the National Broadcasting
Company and directed twenty weekly symphonic broadcasts
during the season—the first extensive series of symphonic concerts over the radio. It was estimated that the combined audience
for this series of concerts was 200 million.

In 1927 the first regular series of opera broadcasts was undertaken from the stage of the Chicago Civic Opera. Concerts by
the Boston Symphony and the New York Philharmonic were
also transmitted during the same year. In 1928 Mr. Damrosch
inaugurated his Music Appreciation Hour for the nation's schoolchildren, and he was sponsored by General Electric to present
symphonic concerts for adults. In 1929 Leopold Stokowski and
the Philadelphia Orchestra came to the radio, beginning a rela-
tionship which was to have a far-reaching effect on the quality
of orchestral transmission. Other great orchestras, numerous
opera stars, and virtuosos, even a few chamber-music ensembles,
joined the ever-growing parade coming before the microphone.
And, to the amazement of radio executives who had always felt
that great music was for only a limited audience, the more frequently good music was put on the air, the larger the audiences
grew and the more enthusiastic became the reception.

Even so adamant a foe of the radio as Gatti-Casazza, general
manager of the Metropolitan Opera House, was eventually won
over. For several years officials of the National Broadcasting
Company had begged for permission to broadcast opera performances directly from the stage of the Metropolitan. Gatti-
Casazza was stubborn in his refusal because, he felt, radio was

not sufficiently developed to permit an artistic transmission of good music, particularly good opera. He eventually consented to a trial broadcast, on the basis of which he would issue his final decision. He and his musical staff visited a private studio of the NBC to listen to the relay of a performance of *Madame Butterfly*. Gatti-Casazza was so impressed by the quality of the reproduction that, then and there, he realized that his fears had no basis whatever. On Christmas Day, 1931, the first broadcast of a full opera from the Metropolitan took place—Humperdinck's *Hänsel and Gretel*—inaugurating the broadcasts from the Metropolitan Opera House.

Two years before this the New York Philharmonic had begun its historic series of Sunday afternoon broadcasts. Two of America's leading musical institutions were now permanent fixtures on the radio. They were to have their audiences of several million devoted listeners. The mail to the Metropolitan following each broadcast (not only in grateful appreciation of the performance, but also to acquire information about the operas and their composers) was so great that it inspired the creation of the Metropolitan Opera Guild in 1935, drawing the bulk of its membership from radio listeners. Its publication, *Opera News*, reaches all radio subscribers with full information about each opera broadcast. A similar organization was created by the New York Philharmonic primarily for its radio audiences.

The horizon was ever expanding. More and more, great music assumed an important role in radio broadcasting. International broadcasts, inaugurated in 1931, with a performance at Covent Garden, brought the major European festivals to the American home. Chamber music, long considered the property of the élite, came to the air. In 1929 the Perolé String Quartet introduced, over WOR, the first long series of chamber-music concerts on the air. In 1934 the NBC Music Guild was founded to present chamber music four times a week. The first opera written expressly for radio—*The Willow Tree*—was created by Charles Wakefield Cadman in 1931 and was broadcast over NBC. Five years after this, the Columbia Broadcasting System launched an ambitious program for commissioning special symphonic works exclusively for radio performance, recruiting some of the foremost American composers for this purpose, including Louis Gruenberg, Aaron Copland, Roy Harris, Howard Hanson, Walter Piston, Robert Russell Bennett, Leo Sowerby, Vittorio Giannini, Quincy Porter, and many others. A large symphony orchestra became a permanent fixture of every radio network. The NBC Symphony Orchestra—now one of America's great symphonic organizations—was founded in 1937 to bring Arturo Toscanini to the radio. Leading commercial sponsors found that great music was an effective salesman for their products: Ford, General Motors, Philco, Chesterfield, Firestone, General Electric, U. S. Rubber Co., Texaco, Bell Telephone, and others reached for a large audience through broadcasts of great symphonic music.

At least one commercial station discovered that good music pays—WQXR in New York, the programs of which are, for the most part, transmissions of the greatest available recorded music. The broadcasting of recorded music did not, of course, originate with that station; the New York municipal station, WNYC, had inaugurated a Masterwork Hour many years before WQXR came into existence and later extended its programs to include many other hours of good recorded music. Other small commercial stations throughout America also devoted an hour or so a day to programs of great music through records. But WQXR was the first commercial station devoted primarily to good music; the fact that it is a profitable venture makes its experiment doubly significant. Incorporated in 1936 by John V. L. Hogan—who always worked on the assumption that the radio listener is "an intelligent and cultured person"—it increased its listening public in New York and vicinity to a million people in 1941. In 1945, the station was acquired by the New York *Times*. The average WQXR listener, according to surveys, listens to this station an average of 3½ hours a day and to all other stations only 1½ hours. Thus, WQXR has its own large, devoted public. The influence of WQXR has been a salutary one. Certain small stations, up to now run mostly by universities, have modeled themselves after it, and are proving to be a powerful agency for the spread of good music.

The growing popularity of recorded programs of good music over the air caused one of the major record companies to institute a suit to prevent such broadcasts. A decision was finally handed down by the United States Circuit Court of Appeal which stated that a broadcaster, in playing ordinary phonograph records, did not infringe upon the rights of the copyright owner. "Copyright in any form, whether statutory or at common law, is a monopoly," Judge Hand wrote in his decision. "It consists only of the power to prevent others from reproducing the copyright work." However, those stations which broadcast recorded music have "never invaded any such right." This decision is an important one for music lovers throughout the country. Radio listeners who have been keeping their dials consistently tuned to the smaller stations, which are pouring out great music through records, are not to be denied their favorite form of radio entertainment.

It now remains to speak of those significant figures who have been major influences in the growth of good music over the air. One of the earliest of these was, of course, Walter Dam-

rosch, who resigned his position with the New York Symphony
Society to devote himself exclusively to radio work. "I had always dreamt of the time when I could reach through music a
wide and limitless audience," he said. "Radio magically offered
me the means. I realized that with one performance I could
reach more people through the radio than I could previously in
five years of concert work." He was one of the first to bring concerts of great symphonic music to the radio—at a time when it
was felt that there were simply no audiences for such programs.
His broadcasts in 1926, 1927, and 1928 set the stage for all future
symphonic broadcasts. Equally important, Damrosch was the
first to realize the value of the radio as an educational medium.
In 1928 he inaugurated his famous Music Appreciation Hour for
schoolchildren. His audience grew from 1½ million to an estimated 5 million listeners, relayed to some 70,000 schools
throughout the country. He became the music teacher to a
nation—a voice known almost to every schoolboy and schoolgirl.
Once, on a visit to the West, he was invited by a public-
school principal to address his children at the assembly. Damrosch offered to come on the condition that he be allowed to
appear without an official introduction. The principal agreed,
merely announcing that he had the honor to present a man
known to all of them. Damrosch arose and quietly began: "Good
morning, my dear children"—his radio greeting. Immediately a
clamor arose among the children. "It's Papa Damrosch!" they
cried. Damrosch had required no introduction. In the fall of
1942, Damrosch's music appreciation program was discontinued.

Other musical figures have also been of consequence in radio's
musical development. On September 18, 1927, a young American conductor, Howard Barlow—who had up to that time only
a limited experience as a conductor—made his radio debut by

performing excerpts from Deems Taylor's *The King's Hench-man* over the Columbia network. He said:

I was certainly nervous before the performance began. I pictured the "mike" as a central spot from which countless wires, endless in length, stretched all over the country. I felt like a tiny fly caught in the center of a spider's web. But when the music started, and I felt the baton in my hand, I forgot everything but the music.

Barlow was soon afterward appointed conductor of the Columbia Broadcasting Symphony Orchestra, ultimately increasing its membership from its original sixteen musicians to thirty, then to sixty-seven. His regular symphony concerts over the air helped to create a new standard for orchestral programs in which modern music—particularly works by American composers, many of them especially commissioned by the network—received flattering attention. Since Barlow's resignation from CBS its orchestral concerts have been admirably directed by Bernard Herrmann, Nicolas Berezowsky and others.

Frank Black succeeded Walter Damrosch at the National Broadcasting Company in 1928. For a long time Black had urged radio officials to pay greater attention to good music. He had approached the National Broadcasting Company with the idea of directing a thirty-piece string symphony orchestra in a regular series of concerts. The idea was rejected as too highbrow. For a while Black contented himself with random assignments given him to conduct special radio concerts. His following grew until the company finally permitted him to organize his own string orchestra for regular radio performances. As a conductor of his Sinfonietta, and as musical director of the National Broadcasting Company, he has been one of the truly progressive forces for good music. To realize the lofty musical aims of its director, one need only consider one of his radio series

—devoted exclusively to the music of young and less-known American composers. A unique feature of this series was that each new composition was performed twice on the same program, before and after an explanatory commentary.

Radio found another vital influence in Alfred Wallenstein, who deserted the first cello desk of the New York Philharmonic Orchestra in 1935 to become music director of WOR (Mutual). In this capacity he served for several years, conducting many important concerts of the Sinfonietta and Symphonic Strings (both of which he founded), and successfully resurrecting numerous masterpieces of music long forgotten. Besides these orchestral concerts, he directed many series of concerts of unquestioned artistic importance, including a Sunday evening series devoted to all the church cantatas of Bach, a Saturday evening series of Mozart operas, and a midweek series of all the piano concertos of Mozart, with Nadia Reisenberg as soloist. When Wallenstein abandoned radio to become the permanent conductor of the Los Angeles Symphony, the air waves lost a major musical force.

Davidson Taylor, music director of the Columbia Broadcasting System, was responsible for bringing great chamber music to radio prominence. He also originated the plan of commissioning American composers to write music especially for radio use. Ernest La Prade, director of music research of the National Broadcasting Company, brought many important small ensembles to the microphone, particularly during the series of concerts prepared by the NBC Music Guild. Deems Taylor, for many seasons the music consultant of the Columbia Broadcasting System and commentator for the New York Philharmonic concerts on Sunday afternoons, humanized music through his informal talks.

Many statistics have been published showing the ever-increasing importance of great music as radio entertainment. The National Broadcasting Company in 1937 issued the following table to emphasize the increase of good music over the radio in the ten-year period between 1927 and 1936, according to number of broadcasts:

	1927	1936
Symphony concerts	56	420
Grand opera	26	34
Choral music	21	243
Chamber music	93	297

In the same year (1937) the Columbia Broadcasting System issued the following statement:

Even a brief analysis of the broadcasting of music on the Columbia Broadcasting System reveals the current trend in favor of serious music on the air. There is an abundance of evidence to show that more and more listeners find such broadcasts much to their liking; also that there has been a commensurate increase in the broadcasting of such programs both by the Columbia network and by its clients in response to the interest shown by the audience.

In 1939 a national survey among radio listeners revealed the fact that 62.5 per cent of the radio public listened to programs of serious music. In 1940 it was estimated that serious music over the major networks consumed nearly 2000 hours.

"All musicians must feel gratitude to the radio," said Lily Pons in an interview. "It has done so much for musical taste. Even in the ten years that I have been here I see a great difference in what people like to hear. You will be surprised at how much better selections the people ask for. They get to know concert works. I can see this in my tours."

José Iturbi has told two anecdotes in the *Pictorial Review* which eloquently demonstrate how good music over the air is continually finding a larger and more responsive audience:

I was riding on a bus between two Missouri cities. It was Sunday afternoon, and the program from Carnegie Hall was being broadcast. The bus carried a radio; the set was turned down in volume. A distinguished violinist began to play just as we reached the outskirts of a small town in a slight traffic jam. Someone turned the radio up, and finally, as we weren't getting anywhere, he remarked: "Does anyone object if we pull up to the side of the road and hear the rest of this number?" No one objected. The driver turned off the motor and twenty-three passengers listened with a great deal of pleasure.

Driving to New York after a concert in Williamstown, Mass., I stopped for coffee at a lunchwagon in the Connecticut countryside just as a Sunday evening symphonic program went over the air. What happened amused me greatly. There was a good deal of clatter and rattle among the diners. First the counterman stopped washing dishes and listened. A man rattling his cup next to me set it down carefully—and listened. The waitress, stacking dishes on a small table, stopped her activities, sat down—and also listened. The place was comparatively quiet, but the counterman wasn't satisfied. He scowled at four hamburgers sizzling on the griddle and carefully removed them one by one. We all sat there for the remainder of the program, when the waitress confirmed our verdict by remarking: "Gee, that was swell!"

These two anecdotes could be multiplied by a hundred to prove that, through the radio, good music is reaching the average man in the street.

Music and motion pictures have always been partners, even before the screen acquired a voice. In the days of the silent film, music was an indispensable ally of the shadows on the screen, emphasizing the dramatic action, heightening the suspense, bringing a touch of saccharine to the sentiment. It was obviously bad music for obviously bad theater. Stereotyped dramatic situations called for equally stereotyped musical settings: *Rustle of Spring* (bucolic scenes), *Hearts and Flowers* (moments of heartbreak), the storm from *William Tell* (climaxes), *Light Cavalry Overture* (suspense).

But from this primitive use of music to intensify drama there was to be an advance—an advance which led from an improvised thumping piano accompaniment of the "flicker" days to the full-sized symphony orchestra of the "cathedral" era. As early as 1915 the New York presentation of D. W. Griffith's *The Birth of a Nation* called for an elaborate and specially prepared musical accompaniment, written by Joseph Carl Breil, and performed by a full orchestra. One year after this, Victor Herbert was the first American composer engaged to write an original score for a motion picture, *The Fall of a Nation*. Music became more and more inextricably associated with the movies; as the years passed, the music improved. When the motion-picture "cathedral" came into being, the full symphony orchestra was used. Under the direction of such pioneers in motion-picture music as Erno Rapee, David Mendoza, and Hugo Riesenfeld, it featured as part of its entertainment first the popular overtures of Suppé, Hérold, or Rossini, and presently even movements from the more popular symphonies. The music utilized to accompany the screen play also acquired discrimination. These were a few notable examples among New York productions: D. W. Griffith's *Drums of Love* had background music from *Tristan und Isolde; Variety* with Emil Jannings borrowed incidental music from Strauss's *Salome; Michael Strogoff* (the first silent version) had music from Tchaikovsky's *Eugen Onegin*.

The success of the "talkies" was, from one point of view, a major blow to the music industry. Unemployment became a trade disease as motion-picture theaters throughout the country (except for a few scattered "cathedrals") dismissed their orchestras and replaced them with sound equipment. Musicians paraded outside theaters as pickets in protest against the new "musical robot." Once again mechanized music was derisively referred to as "canned." Yet once again what first seemed an evil force turned out to be beneficial. Another important instrument had been created to transmit music to the masses—a powerful ally to the radio and the phonograph in educating the masses to serious music.

It is quite true that it was some time before Hollywood was bold enough to avail itself of the use of good music. Popular music received first consideration: Tin Pan Alley migrated to Beverly Hills and flourished there. As for the more serious composer, he was for a long time dismissed (just as the radio had first dismissed him) as too highbrow for general consumption. When a film required atmospheric music of a comparatively serious nature, it preferred its own brand of composer—competent craftsmen who borrowed a little, imitated a little, and had the necessary technique with which to create a coherent musical score. Originality and imagination were not called for. What was wanted was skillful adaptations of the music of the masters. The story goes that a Hollywood composer was assigned to do a full score in a few days' time. "That will take an awful lot out of you," remarked a friend. "Out of *me?*" answered the candid composer. "Rather out of Tchaikovsky, Brahms, and Dvořák!"

After all, argued the Hollywood producer, why take the musical score seriously? No one ever listened to it! Indicative of the general indifference to the musical share in a screen production was the fact that, though the Academy of Motion Picture Arts and Sciences was instituted in 1928 to give awards in every field of motion-picture activity, not until 1934 did it make its first award for the musical score.

In Europe the greatest composers had been recruited to prepare original music for this new medium: composers like Honegger, Milhaud, Auric, Florent Schmitt, Satie, Ibert, Shostakovitch, Prokofiev, Rathaus, Pizzetti, Castelnuovo-Tedesco, and

Kurt Weill. Sometimes these composers wrote music for a film production which was good enough to be included on symphony programs: Prokofiev's incidental music to the film *Lieutenant Kije,* for example, was performed by the Boston Symphony Orchestra. But, for a long period at any rate, Hollywood did not have much use for good music; it preferred to ignore the serious composer. There arose instead the Hollywood brand of composer—men like Alfred Newman, Max Steiner, Herbert Stothart, Frederick Hollander—excellent musicians all, but musicians who made no pretense at artistic creation. They were adept in manufacturing *Gebrauchsmusik*—utilitarian music—which served the purposes of the screen play, but had no intrinsic distinction of its own.

These composers, and others like them, are still the principal creators of music for the American screen—since Hollywood prefers adapted music to the original score. But, in recent years, as the sound pictures have grown more mature, there has been an increasing tendency to recruit important composers to write *original* music for the purposes of the screen. One of the earliest of these composers to come to Hollywood was Erich Wolfgang Korngold, formerly one of Vienna's major composers. Since writing special music for Max Reinhardt's *A Midsummer Night's Dream,* Korngold has remained a permanent fixture in Hollywood, creating many striking scores for a variety of special films, including *Anthony Adverse, Juarez, Elizabeth and Essex,* and *Robin Hood* (the last of these won the award of the Academy of Motion Picture Arts and Sciences in 1938). Korngold's tasteful musical settings have done much to popularize the original score in Hollywood.

Other composers were also enlisted. Ernst Toch, a composer of great originality and good taste, produced sensitive and imaginative music for *Peter Ibbetson.* Unfortunately (as is too

often the case in Hollywood), Toch's talent has been abused to
a point where he is engaged almost exclusively for the produc-
tion of weird atmospheric music for mystery pictures! Other
admirable composers responsible for improving the quality of
screen music include: Dimitri Tiomkin (*Lost Horizon, The
Road Back*), Aaron Copland (*Of Mice and Men, Our Town*),
Werner Janssen (*The General Died at Dawn, Blockade*),
Richard Hagemann (*Stage Coach, The Long Voyage Home*),
Bernard Herrmann (*Citizen Kane, All That Money Can Buy,
Jane Eyre, Hangover Square, Anna and the King of Siam*),
Louis Gruenberg (*So Ends Our Night*), Hanns Eisler (*The
Spanish Main*), Castelnuovo-Tedesco (*And Then There Were
None*), Miklos Rosza (*The Lost Weekend*), and Earl Robinson
(*A Walk in the Sun*).

Some of the best original music for the screen thus far has
been written for documentary films. Vital and experimental
composers have been given greater freedom to exploit their
imagination in the preparation of musical settings for films
which were not intended for widespread commercial distribu-
tion. In this way, several scores of striking power and original
treatment have resulted. Kurt Weill has described Louis Gruenberg's music to *The Fight for Life* as "a masterwork in this
category, a completely integrated piece of film dramatic music."
The best of these were given a performance at a special concert
of the League of Composers early in 1941. Music by Douglas
Moore (*Power and the Land*), Marc Blitzstein (*Night Shift* and
Valley Town), Virgil Thomson (*The River*), Roy Harris (*One
Tenth of a Nation*), Aaron Copland (*The City*), Hanns Eisler
(*Forgotten Village*), and Marc Blitzstein (*The True Glory*)
represents some of the best scores prepared for this kind of
screen play. These documentary films suggest strongly that
the sound film is not only a powerful means for the dissemina-

tion of music culture, but is also a new medium for the composer with which to expand the horizons of his art.

The recruiting of serious and important composers for the preparation of special film music was, of course, a bold and significant step forward for Hollywood. It is quite true that the original argument of the Hollywood producer had a certain basis of truth: Your average motion-picture audience does not consciously listen to the music accompanying a film. Yet—though the audience may not listen to it *actively*—its emotional response to certain scenes in a film has been heightened because of the accompanying music. Several experiments have been made by Hollywood producers through "sneak" performances in small Hollywood motion-picture houses, and it was discovered that many scenes which were an outright success in one house "fell flat" in another house when they were deprived of their musical setting. The audience may therefore not listen consciously to the score, but it is aware of it, and its response to the screen play is sensitized because of the presence of the music. It has thus become increasingly apparent to the Hollywood producer that the composer is no negligible factor in a screen production. With this realization, Hollywood is beginning to make more frequent calls on the gifts of the serious and experienced composer.

Another important step forward by the motion-picture industry in connection with good music was in making good music good screen entertainment. The sensation scored by Grace Moore in *One Night of Love* in 1934 proved decisively, even to the most obdurate movie magnate, that good music was not followed exclusively by a limited circle, but could have enormous mass appeal. Consequently there followed an entire cycle of pictures featuring opera singers who sang the great arias of operatic literature: Lawrence Tibbett, Kirsten Flagstad, Helen

Jepson, Gladys Swarthout, Lily Pons. The success of some of these films—others were too imitative and stereotyped to have appeal—inspired an even more adventurous program which enlisted Leopold Stokowski (conducting music by Bach, Mozart, Tchaikovsky); Jascha Heifetz (once again Bach appears among the performed composers; and with him, Mendelssohn—the last movement of the violin concerto); Walter Damrosch; Lauritz Melchior; Artur Rubinstein; José Iturbi. The most striking proof of the popularity of good music in films was supplied in 1941 by Walt Disney when he presented his *Fantasia*—animated cartoons inspired by Beethoven's *Pastoral* Symphony, Stravinsky's *The Rites of Spring*, Dukas's *The Sorcerer's Apprentice*, Tchaikovsky's *Nutcracker Suite*, Bach's Toccata and Fugue in D Minor, and other works by Mussorgsky, Schubert, and Ponchielli, all performed by the Philadelphia Orchestra under the direction of Leopold Stokowski. Never before had the screen attempted such an ambitious program of musical masterpieces. And this prodigious undertaking attracted one million customers in less than a year of two-a-day performances in New York.

Biographies of great composers also came into vogue, bringing the great music of these masters to popular attention: Chopin, Gershwin, Rimsky-Korsakov. Even the biography of a great concert auditorium, Carnegie Hall, was found to be suitable dramatic material for a grandiose musical production enlisting the services of virtually an honor roll of world-famous musicians.

It was to be expected that the invasion of Hollywood by good music should give rise to many an amusing episode. There was a singular naïveté among Hollywood directors and producers where music was concerned. Great music was to them a strange and alien world with which, suddenly, they had to familiarize themselves. More than that, to satisfy their ego, they had to assume some authority in this foreign cosmos. There is the story of a Hollywood producer who, eager to inject a bit more fluff and froth into the musical score of a French film, insisted that the composer use several French horns in his orchestration. An equally fantastic assignment was given to another composer preparing a score for Deanna Durbin. "Make the music sound like Wagner—only *louder.*" When Samuel Goldwyn negotiated with Jascha Heifetz for a screen appearance and was disconcerted by the high price demanded by the celebrated violinist, he cried in desperation: "Money isn't everything, Mr. Heifetz. I can make you *famous!*" There was the time when a Hollywood director, learning that a projected film would utilize Brahms's *Wiegenlied* as a sort of leitmotiv, exclaimed grandiloquently: "This will be a super-special production. We must get Brahms himself to come to Hollywood to prepare the complete score." When Igor Stravinsky demanded $2,000 a week for his services, a startled executive cried: "For *that* kind of money I can get Al Newman!" Finally—for these anecdotes can go on indefinitely—there is the incident of the producer who shouted with joy when told that he could get Maurice Ravel to do a special score for him because he thought that Ravel was a member of that successful song-writing team of Gordon and Revel.

The association of good music and the screen is still in its early stages. Progress will yet be made. More and more will important composers devote themselves to this new medium, which should eventually result in some music of genuine significance. More and more will motion-picture audiences be brought into contact with intelligent and serious musical creation. No doubt, too, great music as screen entertainment—through the appearance of great musical figures—will increase. We should eventually have opera on the screen. In any case, the motion picture

has already proved its efficacy in spreading musical culture. It
has been commented upon that when the *Big Broadcast of 1937*
was playing in the nation's motion-picture houses (this was the
film which introduced Stokowski to motion-picture audiences)
newsboys in the streets began whistling the theme of a Bach
fugue. In its ultimate development, the film can become more
than a transmission belt for great music. It may well become the
basis for a new musical art, inspiring the composer to achieve a
new type of dramatic music.

CHAPTER ELEVEN

Government-Subsidized
Music

====

THERE WAS an increasing awareness of civic responsibility toward music throughout the country after World War I. In Europe, great music had been a responsibility of the state. Opera houses and orchestras, which could never hope to be self-supporting, were subsidized by the government, accepted as indispensable features of the annual budget. But in America, music was a luxury with which the government could not concern itself. Music was dependent on the generosity of patrons. If they supported the local opera house or symphony orchestra, there would be music for the community; otherwise, music had to be dispensed with.

But the dark years of depression following 1929 saw at least a partial reorientation. The shattered fortunes of many patrons forced the removal of their support from many musical institutions. In some instances the patron was supplanted by the public itself, which rallied to keep alive the great musical organizations of the country. In 1933 and 1934, with the Metropolitan Opera House threatened by extinction because of the withdrawal of financial support by a select few, three million dollars was raised by public subscription. No longer was opera being financed exclusively by a few generous public-spirited patrons. It had become the cooperative property of an entire country of music lovers. Once again, in 1940, the Metropolitan called for a million dollars with which to purchase its opera house. A hundred thousand music lovers answered the plea. One woman from Arkansas sent in a check for ten dollars with a note saying: "Ten-dollar bills are not plentiful in these parts, but neither is great music. We can deprive ourselves of necessities, but a winter season without hearing the opera broadcast every Saturday afternoon is unthinkable." One man walked up to the box office with a five-dollar bill, saying that he wanted to buy one brick of the building. Another from upper New York State wrote that he could not afford to send five dollars in one lump sum, but that he would like to send in a dollar a week for five weeks.

In 1934 the New York Philharmonic sent an appeal to the music lovers of the country and received a half-million dollars. A great part of this sum came in one-, five-, and ten-dollar contributions, obviously from people who were depriving themselves to send in their gifts. The manner in which music lovers everywhere in the country rushed to answer these appeals, and others like them, remains perhaps the most eloquent testimony to the indispensable place that great music had begun to occupy in the lives of Americans.

Together with public support on a cooperative basis, there came recognition on the part of local governments that music was a civic responsibility. As early as 1915 the city of Baltimore subsidized an orchestra, placing it under the supervision of the municipal department of music. A seasonal budget of $34,000 provided six adult and five children's concerts a season at moderate admission prices. Some time later, Baltimore levied a special municipal tax to support its musical institutions. In

1925 Long Beach, California, provided support for a Women's Symphony Orchestra for free concerts. But since these were isolated cases they were not of sufficient importance to create repercussions.

The tendency to support music municipally did not develop until after 1929. In 1934 a special tax was levied in San Francisco to provide the necessary funds for the maintenance of the Symphony Orchestra; two years earlier the first municipally owned opera house was opened in the same city. Civic opera, as a matter of fact, assumed ever-increasing importance. Philadelphia was the first city in America where opera received direct government support; it was soon emulated by Cleveland, Cincinnati, Detroit, Chicago, St. Louis, and Los Angeles. Orchestras also began to receive government sponsorship. Massachusetts contributed $15,000 a year for the Esplanade Concerts of the Boston Symphony Orchestra. Los Angeles provided $7,500 for the Hollywood Bowl concerts. Pasadena, Detroit, and Vermont also contributed sizable sums to keep their symphonic organizations functioning. In 1944, the city of Dallas, Texas, provided the funds for a major symphony orchestra, and has since then helped to support its ambitious artistic program. One of the most striking experiments in civic music was launched successfully in Cincinnati. There a special recreation commission, regulated by the city council, took a personal hand in the musical activity in the city. At first it sponsored choral groups, which met and rehearsed in the public schools. Then it subsidized orchestras and music classes. By 1937 it controlled the activities of fourteen orchestras, twelve choruses, and thirty-five classes in music.

But the most significant movement in the attempt to provide government support for music came through the agency of the Federal Music Project of the old Works Progress Administra-

tion. Created in 1935 to relieve unemployment among musicians, it soon became a musical influence of gigantic proportions. Its work proved a beneficial stimulus in every part of the
country.

The aims of the Federal Music Project were clearly stated
at the time of its inception:

It is the aim of the Music Program . . . through the employment
of creative and recreative musicians in the allied music fields, to
secure and to present for public use outstanding examples of music
literature of other countries and periods; through the teaching of the
music in community centres and recreational music activities to create a broader national music consciousness and to work out construc-
tive ways of using leisure time; through music services to aid various
community campaigns of social value; and through research projects
to clarify the background in the arts. The W.P.A. Music Program is
designed to work toward an integration of the arts with the daily life
of the community.

The Music Program is designed to preserve socially valuable skills
of unemployed musicians; to benefit the public through exercise of
these skills of unemployed musicians under their competent direction; to retain and reorient skills so that their possessors may find
permanent reemployment off the Government rolls; to provide needed
services for both government and non-government use in the development of an efficient, coordinated community program.

The direction of this all-embracing program was placed in
the hands of Nikolai Sokoloff, formerly conductor of the Cleveland Symphony Orchestra. Sokoloff realized that the Federal
Music Project could be something infinitely more than an employment agency for musicians; that it could become the
most important power for spreading the culture of music
throughout America that this country had ever known. He
recognized the fact that with the cooperation of the extensive
musical forces placed at his disposal he could reach a public
which did not generally attend high-priced concerts; he knew,

too, that since his was a government-financed project, not dependent for its existence on financial returns at the box office, he was able to experiment in programs, to tap musical resources which the professional organizations were afraid to exploit. With few concessions to public taste, Sokoloff launched a gigantic musical program which was no makeshift affair exclusively to provide employment for the unemployed. Every field of musical endeavor was to be touched: serious opera, comic opera, symphony, chamber music, choral music, and the dance. Experiments were to be undertaken fearlessly.

Figures tell the story of the achievements of the W.P.A. more eloquently than do descriptive phrases. Between October, 1935, and August, 1939, about 50 million dollars was expended on musical programs. This sum financed about 225,000 performances which were attended by more than 150 million people. At the height of its activity (1936), the W.P.A. music program consisted of 700 projects enlisting the services of more than 15,000 musicians. Within the first eight months of 1936, more than 10,000 performances had been given before audiences totaling over 11 million. In this way, symphony concerts, choral concerts, operas, chamber music—always maintained on the highest levels —came to the masses, sometimes free, at other times at prices they could afford to pay. The American composer, too, profited through this government agency. Between 1936 and 1938, there were performed more than 5,000 American works by over 1,000 American composers.

Through W.P.A., music education also spread throughout the country. Almost 90 million people took advantage of the educational facilities of the Music Project.

One of the most significant arms of the Federal Music Project was the Composers' Forum-Laboratory, inaugurated in the fall of 1935, and successfully carried out in New York, Boston, Philadelphia, Cleveland, Detroit, Chicago, Milwaukee, Minneapolis, Oklahoma City, and Los Angeles. The laboratory presented entire programs each devoted to the work of a living American composer. The composer himself was usually present at the concert to answer questions about his music. "The purpose of these Forums is to provide an opportunity for serious composers residing in America, both known and unknown, to hear their own compositions and to test audience-reactions." The laboratory, therefore, had two important missions: it brought modern American music to the public free of charge, and it gave the American composer a valuable opportunity of hearing his own music performed and studying the reaction of an audience to it.

American composers, known and unknown, mature and young (for these programs included the works of ninety-four student composers as well), were provided an audience. About a thousand different works were performed, the compositions of several hundred composers. The importance of this project cannot easily be overemphasized. It was commented upon by Olin Downes in the New York *Times* of January 10, 1937:

Until very recently they [American composers] had few opportunities of hearing their music, discovering their weaknesses, and profiting by their experience. But the situation is rapidly changing for the better. One of the most promising of these developments has taken place under the auspices of the music division of the W.P.A., a development which goes by the name of the Composers' Forum-Laboratory. This institution affords real laboratory work for American composers, in an eminently useful and practical way. There are sufficient musical forces available to provide any composer whose works are considered, with such performers as his score requires. He can hear his song, a piano composition, works for chamber or large orchestra, or choral works. With these resources, the Composers' Forum-Laboratory pursues its activities, which have had a decidedly stimulating effect in encouraging our young musicians to create and develop.

In an illuminating article in the January, 1940, *Musical Quarterly*, Ashley Pettis—who was founder and director of the New York Composers' Forum-Laboratory—gives the case history of the young and brilliant composer William Schuman as an example of how the American composer profited by the laboratory. The first performance of one of Schuman's serious works was given at the Composers' Forum in 1936. "As a result of hearing his *First String Quartet* and the *First Symphony* rehearsed, publicly performed, and discussed, he decided to 'shelve' them. Afterwards he said he had gained ten years by the experience." Subsequently Schuman produced a new string quartet and a new symphony which were performed by the forum. These works revealed the fruits of the lessons he had previously acquired at the forums—greater experience in the use of his resources, a surer technical grasp, a self-assurance he had never had. Since then, Schuman's works have been performed by Koussevitzky, over the radio by Howard Barlow, and by other major musical organizations. "Mr. Schuman," adds Pettis, "may well be considered a child of the Composers' Forum-Laboratory." And Mr. Schuman, it might be added, was only one of many.

But not only the composer had profited by these concerts, Mr. Pettis continues:

The audience has also learned a great deal. . . . The questions raised in the Forum periods, following performances of the music, have been taken down verbatim, and form a living record dealing with the creative processes of contemporary music, which, it is safe to say, is not equalled by the annals of any country at any time. That the audience had grown in its perceptions is attested by the improvement in the type of question asked. . . . The questions are increasingly intelligent and show a real desire to understand the composer's creative processes and underlying principles.

The curtailment of W.P.A. funds in 1939 disrupted the ambitious program of the Federal Music Project. Important organizations—like the admirable Madrigal Singers in New York, the various opera groups, most of the chamber-music ensembles, a majority of the orchestras, and the Composers' Forum-Laboratory—disbanded. Schools closed down. But the four years of the W.P.A. had far-reaching results. Great music in every possible form was brought to many people. It left behind a permanent and ineradicable influence. It also proved forcefully what significant results can be achieved through the government sponsorship of music. It pointed out a definite direction for music in America.

CHAPTER TWELVE

"I Hear America Singing"

I N 1930, RACHMANINOFF told his biographer, Oskar von Riesemann:[1]

In the course of my last eleven years of concert experiences in America, separated from my first visit by an absence of ten years, I have had ample opportunity of convincing myself of the great progress made by American audiences both in their power of assimilation and in their musical taste. Their artistic demands have grown to an astonishing extent. The man who exposes his art to public opinion notices this immediately. This opinion is not mine alone, but is shared by all other artists who have given concerts in the United States, and with whom I have discussed this subject. From this one may conclude that the remarkable efforts of American, and especially New York, society to raise the standard of musical life have not been in vain. They have used every means in their power and have not spared any money in their effort to surpass Europe in this respect. They have succeeded. No man will dare to dispute the fact.

If there were unmistakable indications to Rachmaninoff of music's "great progress" in America between 1919 and 1930,

[1] *Rachmaninoff's Recollections* (New York, 1934). Quoted by permission of the Macmillan Company.

209

how much stronger must these indications have become during the decade after 1930!

The bleak years following "blue Monday" of 1929 left music in a sorry state. There were innumerable musicians in the growing army of the unemployed, brought there (as we have seen) both by the invasion of mechanization and by the depression. But for the special efforts of the Musicians' Emergency Fund, created in 1931 as a direct result of the suicide of a needy musician, and the employment agency of the W.P.A., many professional performers would have faced despair. Others besides performers were victims of the crisis. Music teachers suffered acutely through the loss of pupils. From the normal annual sale of 400,000 pianos a year, the figure suddenly collapsed to 90,000. Music publishers, instrument makers—each and every branch of the music industry felt the pinch of depression.

And yet—this is a point well worth emphasizing!—not a single important musical institution collapsed during the economic hurricane. Not a single important school of music, or symphony orchestra, or opera house passed *permanently* out of existence —even though in other cultural fields the mortality rate was high. Where the existence of a major music organization was threatened through the evaporation of substantial subsidies, there was always found generous public support. Music had become indispensable to the general public.

Indeed, there was even visible expansion in certain branches of musical activity. In the world of the symphony orchestra, for example. Whereas only fifty-five new important orchestras had come into being between 1920 and 1930, eighty-four were started during the following decade. One half of all the major orchestras functioning in the United States in 1940 came into existence *after* 1929. What is more, most of the orchestras throughout the United States reported excellent sales of tickets, and the half-dozen or so of the most important orchestras in America were playing regularly to almost capacity houses.

Now, more than ever, do audiences demand the best in their music. The standards are consistently rising. American audiences refuse to be treated like children. Their taste has improved to a notable degree. They rarely concern themselves with superficials, but only with sound musical considerations. Once they had been hypnotized by European reputations, Continental stage manners, and foreign names. Now only the music is of importance. It may be recalled that when Artur Schnabel first came to America—it was in 1922—he was, for the most part, a failure. He looked too much like an American businessman: he was short and stocky; his hair was closely cropped; his stage behavior was unaffected. His great art passed virtually unnoticed by the general public, even though he had come to America with a formidable European career behind him. Yet so greatly had the American music public grown in astuteness that when Schnabel returned to America after a seven-year interval he was no longer considered an unromantic figure. American audiences now heard his magnificent interpretations of Beethoven and Schubert and appreciated the musicianship and scholarship infusing them.

Once audiences had made virtuosity their first consideration. The Jaschas, Toschas, Saschas of the violin who came in a seemingly endless parade after 1917, the Josefs and Ignazes of the piano, dazzled their audiences with their digital miracles. The programs they played generally consisted of standard favorites from the classics, together with a generous supply of pyrotechnical pieces to take the breath away. New and unfamiliar music bored the public, and thus was rarely introduced by recitalists. Only the more courageous and the more firmly established artists dared to give a "first performance," or even play sonatas by César Franck, Chausson, or Richard Strauss. In those days —the days following World War I—for a violinist or a pianist to include two or three concertos or two or three sonatas on one program would have been to invite box-office disaster. But today, virtuosity is no longer an end in itself. Audiences, of course, still acclaim prodigious techniques, but these techniques must be combined with sound musical judgment and taste if the artist is to succeed. What audiences demand, first, is great music— the greater the better. Today Menuhin can pack the house whenever he chooses to play three concertos at one concert; so can Adolf Busch with a program devoted exclusively to Beethoven sonatas. Today, a Heifetz, or a Szigeti, or a Milstein would not draw large houses if their programs did not avoid stereotyped patterns. The demand for novelty has become so great that many virtuosos now resort to the necessary expedient of commissioning modern composers to prepare new works expressly for their use.

Today the best chamber-music concerts draw capacity audiences—as, for example, those of the New Friends of Music in New York. On the other hand, more than one highly publicized prima donna has known the experience of performing in a halfempty hall. Once again returning to the case of Artur Schnabel: When he gave his monumental series in New York in 1935 devoted to all the Beethoven sonatas (his managers said that such a venture would have no public appeal whatsoever!) he attracted 18,000 people for the seven concerts, earning more than $23,000 in paid admissions—an unheard-of achievement for a series of piano recitals. In the opera house, Wagner outsells Verdi and Puccini and has been for many years the most frequently performed composer at the Metropolitan Opera House. In 1937, as we have already mentioned, *Tristan und*

Isolde alone grossed more than $150,000 in nine performances—
thereby becoming the greatest "hit" ever to strike Broadway.
In 1940–1941 the largest crowds to come to the Metropolitan
were those for the Wagner music dramas and for operas by
Beethoven and Mozart conducted by Bruno Walter. In 1941–
1942, Mozart became the most popular composer at the Metropolitan. Twenty years earlier it would have been an Italian
opera, with a romanticized coloratura soprano, which would
have appealed to the public.

Again and again has the general public revealed the sharpness of its tastes. Walter Gieseking was virtually unknown when
he first arrived here in 1926, but the reception given him at his
début, and subsequent concerts, proved that the audiences
recognized his genius without the benefit of publicity warnings.
Lawrence Tibbett was an obscure member of the Metropolitan
cast when he substituted for an ailing singer in *Falstaff* in 1925
and received one of the greatest ovations to have been heard at
the Metropolitan. Despite his obscurity, the audience recognized
his genius and acclaimed it. One of the most forceful evidences
of the capacity of audiences to recognized unheralded genius
was provided by Kirsten Flagstad at her début at the Metropolitan in 1935. Only a scattered few had heard the name of
Flagstad before the evening of her first American appearance.
Yet she had not been on the stage more than a few moments
when the house was electrified. At the close of the first act, the
audience rose to cheer her. She had come without any publicity, yet Americans immediately recognized her unquestion-
able greatness.

Keener musical perception resulted in an ever-increasing indifference to a musician's background and past; interest has
come to center exclusively on his gifts as an artist. What matter
if Grace Moore once sang in the *Music Box Revue*? If the man-

ager of the Metropolitan, Edward Johnson, once appeared in operettas? If Stokowski's successor, Eugene Ormandy, served his baton apprenticeship in the motion picture theater and over the radio? Twenty years earlier such questionable backgrounds would have seriously handicapped the careers of these artists.

There was a greater demand throughout the entire country by symphony audiences for adult diets of music. No longer, as we have seen, were New York, Philadelphia, Boston, and Chicago the exclusive centers of great orchestral music in America. Important first performances and concerts of major artistic importance might just as easily take place in Cleveland, Detroit, Los Angeles, Cincinnati, or San Francisco, or even in Kansas City, Rochester, Pittsburgh, or Indianapolis.

Besides this, audiences now demanded better music from their orchestras. In the early 1920's, the more famous symphonies of the masters surpassed in popularity the much preferred lighter classics of the preceding generation. Not Suppé, Liszt, Johann Strauss, or Raff drew capacity houses now, but the all-Tchaikovsky, all-Beethoven, and all-Wagner programs. And the tastes have since become increasingly sharper.

We have a more or less definite yardstick by which to measure the increasingly fastidious desires of present-day symphony audiences. Music has long had a Gallup poll of its own, a fairly accurate barometer indicating the level of the music tastes of the American public. The barometer consists in polls conducted among concertgoers by various musical organizations to determine the preferences of audiences. It is these polls, taken at periodic intervals and in different parts of the country to help arrange all-request programs, which give us a coherent picture of our musical growth. They tell us, more forcefully than all the figures compiled by statisticians, that we have now become a country of comparatively discriminating music lovers. By revealing to us the music we liked yesterday, as well as the music we prefer today, they trace the evolution of a country from musical naïveté to sophistication.

Earlier we have seen that polls taken for all-request programs at the beginning of the present century revealed a desire by audiences for music in a lighter vein, by composers like Rossini, Rubinstein, Suppé, and Johann Strauss, betraying an utter lack of interest in the great symphonies and concertos of the masters. Contrast these choices with two polls conducted in the 1930's—one of them among symphony audiences of Grand Rapids and Los Angeles combined; the other among radio listeners throughout the entire country. In the former poll, 95 per cent preferred serious music to the so-called semiclassics; in the latter (conducted by Leopold Stokowski and the Philadelphia Orchestra) a comparatively popular selection—Tchaikovsky's *Overture 1812*—did not appear until the twenty-fourth place. In both, celebrated symphonic masterpieces were selected as the favorites of the great majority. Among the Grand Rapids–Los Angeles music lovers, the César Franck Symphony received the greatest number of votes, followed by the symphonies of Beethoven, Brahms, Tchaikovsky, and (mark!) Sibelius. The Stokowski vote showed the nation's preference to be, in the order of selection: Beethoven's Fifth Symphony, Tchaikovsky's *Symphonie Pathétique,* Tchaikovsky's Fifth, Franck's D minor Symphony, Schubert's *Unfinished,* and Rimsky-Korsakov's *Scheherazade.*

More recent polls further emphasize the refinement of taste. In 1935 the New York Philharmonic conducted a nation-wide radio poll for favorite orchestral compositions. The American modern composer Roy Harris (whose music is not easily comprehended) received the greatest number of votes among living composers, only a few votes fewer than the poll for the single favorite work, the Franck D Minor Symphony. Sibelius also scored heavily—more heavily, indeed, than Tchaikovsky.

At the R.C.A.-Victor Exhibit at the New York World's Fair in 1939, visitors were asked to indicate their favorite musical works, these works to be performed through records. Over three thousand requests were tabulated and showed striking results. More than 80 per cent of these requests were for serious works, while less than 20 per cent were for swing and popular numbers. Of the more popular works, Earl Robinson's *Ballad for Americans* was asked for so frequently that it was placed on a regular performance schedule three times a day. Of the serious works, Tchaikovsky's Fifth, Rimsky-Korsakov's *Scheherazade,* and Wagner's overtures to *Tannhäuser* and *Rienzi* were most often called for. The favorite modern composer was Sibelius, while the favorite single modern work proved to be Ravel's *Bolero.*

A New York concert program conducted a poll exclusively among successful businessmen to determine their musical preferences. Once again the revelations were illuminating. Some two thousand prosperous businessmen voted *Tristan und Isolde* their favorite opera. Beethoven and Brahms were the symphonic composers most in favor. Sibelius was the best-liked modern composer.

Even polls conducted among children have shown rare discrimination. Only one of these need serve as illustration—that conducted in 1935 among the children attending the special Saturday morning concerts of the New York Philharmonic. They selected for rehearing at the final concert of the series Dukas's

Sorcerer's Apprentice, Mozart's *German Dances,* and Wagner's overture to *Tannhäuser.*

Another proof of the change in public taste is afforded by the summer concerts. Formerly they consisted almost entirely of brass-band or light classical concert music. Today they are —for the most part—on an artistic plane not much below that of the winter season of the major orchestras. At the Lewisohn Stadium in New York, summer symphony concerts by the New York Philharmonic were inaugurated in 1918. The opening program was typical of the summer orchestral concerts of the period: Elgar's *Pomp and Circumstance;* Rossini's *William Tell* Overture; Volpe's *American Reveille;* Dvořák's *Symphony from the New World;* and two Italian opera arias. During the first years of the Stadium Concerts, a symphony was heard only *one* evening a week; the rest of the programs were devoted to the more popular orchestral items.

The transformation of the Stadium Concerts from such unpretentious beginnings into events of major musical importance is, to a large degree, an epitome of a similar transformation among American concert audiences. What attracted in 1920 simply would make no impression in 1946. Record attendances at the Stadium established in recent seasons—24,000 at a single concert, an average of a little less than 300,000 per season—were made possible only through the attraction of programs of the utmost seriousness: Menuhin playing two concertos; a Mozart program that included two symphonies, a concerto, and a Sinfonie Concertante; an all-Sibelius program; opera performances of works by Wagner (during one season the entire cycle of the *Ring!*), Mussorgsky, or Richard Strauss; soloists like Heifetz, Artur Rubinstein, Hofmann, Serkin, Zimbalist, Flagstad, Casadesus; and conductors like Iturbi, Rodzinski, Golschmann, Ormandy, Monteux—the call at the Stadium in recent years has been for the best in music. And the statistics of recent seasons prove unmistakably that the better the music, the larger the audiences. The year 1941—which provided some of the best programs heard at the Stadium—surpassed the attendance record of the previous season by nearly 40,000. Almost 334,000 paid admissions to these concerts, a figure which undoubtedly would have been much greater if bad weather had not canceled several important events.

The insistent demand for good music, and good music alone, was curiously emphasized at the Robin Hood Dell in Philadelphia, where summer concerts by the Philadelphia Orchestra were inaugurated in 1930. The directors of these summer concerts hoped to increase attendance through the inauguration of a series of Sunday evening popular concerts. These concerts had the smallest attendance of the week and proved so unpopular with the audiences that, before long, it was found necessary to revise the plans—to discard the light classics in favor of serious programs. Immediately the Sunday evening attendance mounted.

Other summer symphony concerts have attracted fabuloussized audiences, but always with the best possible programs. The Sunset Symphony on the Potomac, in Washington, D.C.; the Esplanade Concerts on the Charles River, in Boston; the open-air opera performances at the St. Louis Municipal Stadium or at the Cincinnati Zoo draw each season several million music lovers. The Hollywood Bowl concerts have attracted, since their inception in 1922, more than five million. Even higher attendance figures have been recorded at Grant Park, Chicago, where free summer performances were inaugurated in 1935 through the courtesy of the American Federation of Musicians.

The Chicago Symphony Orchestra, supplemented by such soloists as Heifetz, Martinelli, Rosenthal, Flagstad, or Pons, attracted an evening attendance as high as 100,000!

It is no less interesting to study the improvement of the band
music conducted by Edwin Franko Goldman in the New York
public parks. Park band music, before 1920, consisted of little
better than marches, Italian opera potpourris, and salon numbers. It was often said that free open-air concerts for the masses
simply would have no appeal if they were ambitious in their
programs. Yet Goldman has disclosed the fallacy of such a
belief.

He first introduced his band concerts on the Green at Columbia University in 1918. In 1922 the band moved to the Mall in
Central Park, and two years after this it became financially independent through a subsidy by the Guggenheims. From this
time on, Goldman was able to improve the artistic tone of his
concerts immeasurably. Although, at first, his programs were
hardly more ambitious than those offered by competing bands,
he slowly set about to introduce to the public the masterpieces
of music. Before several seasons had passed, works by Bach,
Richard Strauss, Wagner, Beethoven, and Mussorgsky appeared
side by side with the usual band assortment of marches
and light classics. Goldman soon introduced programs half of
which were devoted to some great composers like Bach, Tchaikovsky, Beethoven, or Wagner. How far these Goldman programs had progressed artistically was partly proved in 1941
when the most frequently performed composer during the that
entire summer was—Johann Sebastian Bach, leading his closest
rival (Tchaikovsky) by almost twice as many performances!
Besides this, the Goldman Band performed during the summer of 1941 the works of thirty-one American composers. One
of these composers, Roy Harris, had created a serious work,

Cimarron, expressly for the use of the band. Since then, Goldman has habitually commissioned American composers to write new works for his concerts.

Despite the improved quality of his programs (Goldman insists that it is *because* of it; and he is no doubt correct) the Goldman Band has drawn prodigious audiences. During any one season, about a million music lovers attend his concerts. Obviously the moral is this: Great music does *not* alienate the masses.

Notable progress has been made in another phase of summer musical activity—that of the summer music festival; though it must be confessed that, in this direction at least, progress has come much more slowly. The *Anschluss* in 1938 imposed a temporary recess on the Salzburg Festival, which for so many years had been one of the great artistic events of Europe. The outbreak of war in 1939 brought the activity of other famous European festivals to an abrupt end. The death of the European music festival raised to the surface a question which for a long time had lurked somewhat timidly in the background: Why not a Salzburg in America? Why not a festival town in this country where, each year, lovers of great music can congregate for several weeks of festival performances?

While no music festival in America as yet aspires toward the ambitious goals once realized at Salzburg, the music festival idea is attaining increased importance. Certain festivals already mentioned in an earlier part of this book are still functioning—and with expanded resources: the Bach Festival in Bethlehem; the biannual festival of symphonic and choral music in Cincinnati; the Ann Arbor Festival in Michigan. To these have been added other festivals of interest which attract responsive audiences: the Modern Music Festival held each spring at the Library of Congress in Washington, D.C.; the festival of old chamber music at the historic Governor's Palace in Williamsburg, Virginia, directed by the harpsichordist Ralph Kirkpatrick; the Chautauqua Festival which, each summer, in a setting of incomparable scenic beauty, calls upon the forces of the Juilliard School to present ambitious programs of symphonic, choral, operatic, and chamber music.

But the most famous of all the summer festivals, and that which promises most for the future, is the one held at Tanglewood (of Hawthorne's *Tanglewood Tales*) in Lenox, Massachusetts. The Berkshire Symphonic Festival was inaugurated in 1934 when Henry Hadley conducted a series of symphony concerts on an estate in Stockbridge, Massachusetts. In August, 1936, the Boston Symphony Orchestra, directed by Koussevitzky, supplanted Hadley's orchestra. The success of the Boston Symphony concerts tempted the sponsors of this festival to plan a permanent institution. The estate of Tanglewood was presented to the Boston Symphony Orchestra by Mrs. Gorham Brooks. From this time on, the Berkshire Symphonic Festival had its own permanent home. An open-air shed, remarkable for its acoustics, in 1938 replaced an impromptu tent. In 1941 several grants made possible the building of a special opera house (modeled architecturally on the open-air shed) and a small concert hall for chamber music. From almost every state in the Union music lovers have come to Lenox during the three-week period in August in which the symphony festival takes place. They come in ever-increasing numbers. During the summer of 1941, the average attendance for each concert was a little less than ten thousand. After Pearl Harbor, the Festival was temporarily suspended, then revived on a curtailed program. But normal conditions were resumed in the summer of 1946.

Thus far, performances at Tanglewood have been devoted primarily to symphonic and choral masterpieces. Opera and chamber music is heard only in trial performances by the students of the Berkshire Music Centre. But there is promise that the Berkshire Festival will expand to include performances of great operas and chamber music. In the summer of 1946, one of the major events was the American première of Benjamin Britten's opera, *Peter Grimes*. In any case, it now appears that if America is to have its Salzburg, it will be found on the grounds of Tanglewood. The facilities are there; the audience, too; certainly, the talent.

It would be a mistake to ignore other potent forces in promoting our musical growth besides the radio, phonograph, motion pictures, and the Federal Music Project. I am thinking specifically of certain groups and organizations founded for the express purpose of educating America to good music. In the vanguard of such groups are the National Council of Women (music department), the National Federation of Music Clubs, and National Music Week.

The music department of the National Council of Women has been indefatigable in promoting broadcasts of the best music, in encouraging the launching of educational programs in schools, and in arranging public concerts. The National Federation of Music Clubs comprises about five thousand different clubs and a half-million members in forty-seven states. Over a period of many years it has sponsored concerts in communities many of which could not possibly afford to support serious musical activity (expending for this purpose about three million dollars a year). It has created important competitions for American concert artists and has commissioned new works from American composers. It has promoted and encouraged ambitious educational programs in the schools. Obviously an influences such as this has left its mark on our development.

National Music Week has been a significant propaganda agency for music. First launched in New York, in 1920, it has spread until today there are more than two thousand such observances each year throughout the country. In 1939 forty-five governors issued formal proclamations establishing Music Week, urging the coordination of all music forces, and encouraging the participation of the general public. In local communities, National Music Week has served to stress and fill an immediate need: the support of some local educational program, the launching of a more intensive local concert activity schedule, the fostering of neighborhood talent, and the like.

The remarkable way in which music is filtering into the everyday life of Americans is further demonstrated by the adoption of music by industry. It has been discovered that music can prove a stimulus for work; that music provides necessary diversion to workers from the monotony of certain factory tasks; further, that music proves a tonic for harassed nerves, an uplift for general morale. Particularly during World War II music proved its ability to spur production. As William Green said, even before Pearl Harbor, "music is a friend of labor—it lightens the task by refreshing the nerves and the spirit of workers."

Quite a few years ago, an ingenious building manager in Oakland, California, installed loud-speakers in the corridors of his building, to relay good music into every office during the working day. After a month, a careful checkup among his tenants convinced him of the success of his experiment. In some offices the output and efficiency of the workers had increased. In others it was said that a new spirit of cheerfulness had set in. Workers in the building attested to the beneficial results. They said that

at the end of each working day, they were as calm and as re-
freshed as if they had spent a day of rest at home.

An envelope-addressing company in New York discovered
that, when music is transmitted to the workers, there is a 25
per cent increase in production. And the workers tolerate their
boring tasks more cheerfully.

In war factories it was noted that a new spirit of cheerfulness
entered the factory with music. In 1943, careful computations
were made to determine the value of music to production: It
was disclosed that from 6 to 12 per cent increase took place in
those factories in which music was utilized.

In most factories the preferred procedure is to have special
periods in the day when work is suspended to permit the workers to relax while listening to a brief concert. At the Ware Valley
Manufacturing Company in Massachusetts, work is interrupted
at ten in the morning and at three in the afternoon for brief
concerts of recorded music. At the Westinghouse plant in New-
ark, N. J., there are periodical 40-minute concerts, also through
records, to interrupt the work routine. In both cases, the loss of
time is more than compensated for by an increase in efficiency
and production. In other factories, like the Republic Aviation
Corporation in Farmingdale, Long Island, symphonic music
during the noon-hour lunch period has proved a magic tonic
to workers' nerves. It has been noted that workers return to
their tasks with renewed freshness and energy as a result of
music's stimulation.

In many factories the procedure is to transmit music softly to
the workers during the entire working day. Generally this is
done through central loudspeakers, but in places where factory
noise makes it difficult to hear music from a central speaker,
means have been found to pipe it directly to the worker's machine, so that he can have music at his very ear. At the Curtiss-

Wright Corporation in Buffalo, 600 loudspeakers released an uninterrupted parade of classics and semi-classics. At the Roanoke classifying yards of the Norfolk & Western railroad, at the Des Moines Ordnance Plant, at the United States Munitions Depot at New Brunswick, Minn., at the Oregon Shipbuilding Corporation, and in many other war plants music has emphatically proved its power to stimulate work.

Philip C. Sales, president of the Bell Telephone Company in Philadelphia, experimented with the use of music among the clerical workers in his company. "Music," he reported, "was of real value in large groups where the work was of a routine nature not requiring any considerable amount of conversation or close mental concentration." As a result, he installed a central recording device with 23 amplifiers on three floors to provide uninterrupted music during the day to some 600 employees.

But a country to be truly musical must not only sponsor important musical organizations, attend concerts, create festivals, work to music, play to music, or even reveal increasing discrimination. To be truly musical, in the sense that the Germans and the Austrians were musical in days gone by, a people must fill the role not only of audience but of performer as well. I mean that a country must not only *listen* to music but also *make* it. When Americans become amateurs of music more extensively, producing performances of their own (however inexpertly)— then, truly, can it be said that America has become musical.

The past decade has shown an ever-growing tendency on the part of Americans to make music for themselves. Americans are studying music much more today than ever before. A few figures are illuminating. The magazine *Life* reported in 1938 that more than 10 million people in this country are students of music. As early as 1932 *Business Week* discovered that whereas four years earlier there had been only 389 municipalities with 517 teachers giving group piano instruction, in 1932 there were 2,349 teachers in 1,006 cities. These figures have swollen since that time. Another report for 1938 showed that there was then the unprecedented number of 321 music schools in the country, a figure which grows to prodigious proportions when there are added to it the many thousands of public high schools and the six hundred or so colleges and universities which also dispense music education. Millions attended the W.P.A. schools during the few years in which they functioned. Millions more were studying with private teachers.

At least one strong indication of the expansion of amateur music-making is provided by the sales of pianos. In 1938 the sales of pianos increased 300 per cent over 1933. In the month of November, 1939, 14,300 pianos were sold—a larger figure than was reported for any one month within ten years.

The young of the country are playing in school bands and orchestras, of which there are some 50,000 today in the country. The high musical caliber of these youngsters was vouched for by Leopold Stokowski when, from school orchestras all over the country, he selected the members of his All-American Youth Orchestra in the spring of 1940. Some 15,000 young musicians from all states had auditions, and from this number 560 were chosen as outstanding. Then Mr. Stokowski personally traveled from one end of the country to the other, listened to the 560 young musicians, and was amazed by the technical proficiency and musical insight of these young performers, many of whom, he said, were of professional stature.

There are several hundred baby orchestras, comprising infants of from two to six years; their success has proved how thrilled these youngsters are by cooperative music-making. There are innumerable tired businessmen's orchestras. The

White Plains Symphony is composed exclusively of non-professional musicians, yet it is a highly creditable organization. The Vermont Symphony Orchestra is composed of office-workers, housewives, clerks, salesmen, plumbers, bricklayers. Many of them have to travel many miles after a hard day's work in order to rehearse. Yet this orchestra is one of the best musical groups in Vermont, and each season gives a series of excellent subscription concerts. Members of the North Carolina Symphony are scattered over a territory 503 miles long and almost 200 miles wide. Sometimes, when the roads are sleeted, members walk several miles on the ice with their instruments to make a rehearsal. One husband and wife brought their new-born baby in a portable basket to be taken care of while they rehearsed. A locomotive engineer confessed that he took his trombone with him on his train-rides so that he might put in a few additional periods of practicing during station stops!

Choral groups are springing up throughout the country as people learn there is good fun in singing together. They may have voices that individually annoy neighbors and are the despair of friends; but collectively these same voices prove genuinely musical.

It is not generally known that two of the greatest choral groups in the country are composed for the most part of amateurs: the Oratorio Society of New York, and the Schola Cantorum, also of New York. These choruses draw amateurs from practically every walk of life, who gather regularly for long and arduous rehearsals of the choral masterpieces. A survey was recently made of the professions represented in the Oratorio Society and the result was revealing. It was discovered that that body comprised secretaries, schoolteachers, housewives, librarians, carpenters, bankers, stockbrokers, artists, writers, nurses, interior decorators, chemists, architects, accountants, insurance

men, social workers, bank clerks; also an allergy technician, a
dealer in precious stones, a dancer, a cement tester, an archae-
ologist, and a medical interne. Yet these amateurs from so many
different walks of life are sufficiently musical to be able to give
Carnegie Hall performances of such exacting works as Handel's
Messiah and the B minor Mass of Bach.

There is a wealthy lawyer in Philadelphia who organized an
amateur choral group in his home which specializes in the music
of Bach and his contemporaries. The work of rehearsal costs
sweat and tears, for the music is extraordinarily difficult even
for schooled musicians. But there is finally the joy of singing this
wonderful music which more than compensates for all the pain
that preceded the performance.

Chamber music in the home has also come into prominence
during the past decade or so. Many years ago Walter Damrosch
was asked if he ever had private chamber-music concerts at his
home. Damrosch responded: "Oh, if you only knew how hard it
is to gather four musicians to play only for the fun of playing!"
Today, it is a general practice, even for untrained musicians, to
spend leisure hours in performing trios and quartets. More reticent performers who would like to perform chamber-music
masterpieces without disturbing friends or neighbors can do so
(and are doing so in increasing numbers) with the aid of phonograph records. Columbia issues an entire library of records,
called Add-A-Part, on which a chamber-music masterpiece has
been recorded with one instrumental part missing. The amateur
violinist or cellist can therefore cooperate with three professional musicians in playing great music for small ensembles.

Recently, an antiquated instrument called the recorder has
acquired a vogue among amateurs in this country. The recorder
is the ancestor of the flute, was rediscovered in England by the
Dolmetsch Family (specialists in old music) and acquired addi-

tional popularity through the concerts of the Trapp Family. It is not hard to understand the increasing popularity of the re-corder among laymen. It is inexpensively priced; you can get a recorder for as little as $5. Learning to play it is not difficult. Finally, it comes in different pitches, so that a few friends can join in interesting ensemble performances. Many thousands of recorders were sold in 1944, 1945, and 1946—and most of them went to people who had never before played a musical instru-ment in their lives. Recorder societies are arising in various parts of the country.

America is singing and playing. . . .

CHAPTER THIRTEEN

Recognition
for American Music

———

THE AMERICAN music lover is now capable even of divorcing himself from the one-time sense of inferiority which dictated that *nothing* American could possibly be of value.

Abram Chasins, American composer and pianist, tells of the experience had by a friend of his, a young Texan with a "compositorial background, university experience in conducting, and a Doctor's degree in music." This Texan had applied for a music post in a Midwestern college. "He was interviewed by the president, and the lady patroness of music. The young man obviously impressed them with his ability. But, after a whispered consultation between the two, the lady said in just the nicest way you ever heard: 'Although your qualifications are very satisfactory, and your ability is splendid, the president and I both feel that the next man to fill this position must have a foreign accent.'"

At one time, every phase of American music was dominated by the fetish of the European name, the foreign accent, Continental manners, exotic backgrounds. Without these, an artist in America had the cards stacked against him. But with the

ripening of musical tastes in America came a new-born tolerance for, and a greater interest in, the American musician.

There were times when this newly acquired tolerance resulted
in distortions of critical values. There was, for example, the
exaggerated attention given to Marion Talley when she made
her début at the Metropolitan Opera House. Publicity, launched
weeks before her début, inflated the importance of the event to
prodigious proportions. The desire to given recognition to an
American had blurred the perspective and transformed what
should have been an ordinary début into an artistic event of
national importance. The newspapers of the country featured
the story on the front pages and heralded the arrival of a great
artist. Unfortunately Marion Talley was *not* a great artist, and
her career after that appearance was very much an anticlimax.

Exaggerated attention was also focused on the American conductor Werner Janssen when he came to the head of the New
York Philharmonic. Being the first American-born conductor
ever to direct a major American orchestra, he was treated too
kindly. There were those who permitted their sentiment to warp
their judgment and spoke of him in terms of excessive praise.
Janssen's career in New York was killed by kindness, for he
had neither the equipment nor the native gifts to live up to
the reputation built for him.

But such abuses merely proved that a new tolerance had set
in, a healthy tolerance which would yield indescribable benefits. For in the face of this new tolerance, the American musician
and American music were to flourish as never before.

No longer was it necessary for the American opera singer to
acquire an Italian name or for the American violinist to assume
a phony Russian one before he could attract notice. American
names, therefore, have come to the roster of the Metropolitan
Opera House: Grace Moore, Lawrence Tibbett, Rose Bamp-

ton, Helen Jepson, Richard Crooks, Gladys Swarthout, Eleanor Steber, and others. In 1945–1946 more than 80 per cent of the artists of the Metropolitan were American. It has been estimated that in the past decade American singers have risen to claim more than 60 per cent of the top operatic billings throughout the country. It is illustrative of the trend of the times that Leonard Warren, who as a student at the Greenwich Music School had changed his name to Warrenoff, should have reverted to the use of his original name when he became a member of the Metropolitan.

An American-born violinist like Yehudi Menuhin could become the greatest box-office attraction our concert halls has known—without the benefit of European glamour. An American-trained conductor like Eugene Ormandy could step into the shoes of the most adulated conductor in America, Leopold Stokowski, without any ill effects on the box office. An American-born conductor like Leonard Bernstein could make important guest appearances with virtually every great American orchestra.

Organizations for the purpose of discovering latent musical talent among young Americans brought American-born soloists to the platform of the major symphony orchestras and American virtuosos into the recital halls. And wherever there was exceptional talent, there was acclaim. We have already mentioned the National Federation of Music Clubs, one of the purposes of which is to offer an outlet to young deserving recitalists. Another important organization for sponsoring native musical talent is the Naumburg Foundation created in 1925 to finance the débuts in New York of talent recitalists previously selected by a distinguished jury in a competition. In 1928 another significant group arose, the Schubert Memorial, which aims to discover young and worthy virtuosos and to provide them with appearances with the major orchestras, or else with public recitals in the principal cities. In 1945, still another group was formed to discover worthy young pianists, the Rachmaninoff Memorial Foundation. The Metropolitan Auditions of the Air have provided young American singers throughout the country with the opportunity of competing for the privilege of singing at the Metropolitan Opera House.

The American composer, too, has come into new prominence. In the earlier years of the present century, the American composer was the bête noire of the concert hall. American audiences would have none of him. Talented composers like Griffes, Gilbert, Loeffler, and MacDowell never received that homage which was their due. Any attempt on the part of courageous musicians to produce the works of Americans extensively was frowned upon. There were simply no audiences for the experimental all-American programs launched by Frank Van der Stucken, Leopold Stokowski, or Josef Hofmann. Occasionally, of course, an American work was heard on symphony programs in Boston, Chicago, New York, or Philadelphia. But the apathy which greeted such performances discouraged repetitions. The American composed languished in obscurity, forced to create his music with the realization that there was no public for it.

After the 1920's, interest in the work of American composers was awakened. The American composer began to invade the symphony programs with a certain measure of regularity, first brought there by the stubborn efforts of such conductors as Stock, Stokowski, and Koussevitzky (who were among the first important conductors in America to espouse the cause of American music *persistently* and with determination) and later made more familiar by other conductors such as Sokoloff, Reiner, and Ganz. Whereas, before 1920, the performance of an American work was a comparative rarity, between 1925 and 1930 forty-two American works were performed by Stock in Chicago, thirty-three by Koussevitzky in Boston, and ten by the New York Philharmonic-Symphony under various conductors. The vogue of the European guest conductors in the 1920's somewhat hampered this development. The European conductor, arriving here on a flying visit for a four-week session with one orchestra and a two-week session with another, could not be expected to be familiar with the works of American composers. Yet even these foreign conductors, sensing the awakened interest of the American public in the music of their own country, were prepared to pay homage to the American composer: Bruno Walter, Mengelberg, Fritz Busch, and Toscanini played, at intervals, works by Randall Thompson, Daniel Gregory Mason, Lazare Saminsky, Ernest Schelling, Abram Chasins, and others.

In the 1930's the American composer succeeded in acquiring increasing importance. No major orchestra would permit a season to pass without presenting at least a few major American works. In a survey I made about a decade ago among ten of the major orchestras of the country, I discovered that about 6 per cent of their programs had been allocated to the modern American composer; fifteen years earlier, 2 per cent would have been an extravagant figure.

Today, of course, the American composer need have no cause to complain of neglect. He is heard—and heard often. Every orchestra of any importance plays a considerable amount of American music; and this goes not only for our greatest organizations, but for the secondary orchestras as well, such as the Indianapolis Symphony (which for a long time made it a practice to include at least one American work on each of its programs), and the Dallas Symphony (which, in the first year of its revival, introduced the music of William Schuman, Morton

Gould, Copland, and George Antheil to Texan music audiences).

When Eugene Goossens returned to America from a European vacation, in 1939, he confessed to an interviewer that his trunk contained not a single European novelty for performance that coming season by the Cincinnati Symphony, but that it did have twelve new scores by Americans.

In Rochester, Dr. Howard Hanson has been conducting an annual festival devoted exclusively to American composers: over 700 works by living Americans have been performed in seventeen years of these festivals. Originally devoted exclusively to orchestral music, this program was expanded by Dr. Hanson in 1941 to include chamber music as well. Frequently broadcast over a nation-wide network of stations, these festivals have done much to acquaint America with the music of its composers. Festivals of modern American music—with particular emphasis on the work of newer and less-known composers—have also been conducted regularly over the municipal radio station in New York City (WNYC) and at Yaddo, in Saratoga Springs, New York.

The New York Philharmonic, for a long time notorious for its neglect of the American composer, responded to this trend by performing in 1939–1940, more American works than it had performed during the five-year period of 1925–1930. The centennial season of 1941–1942 placed emphasis on American music by including one modern work on virtually every program. Since Artur Rodzinski has been appointed music director of this organization, the New York Philharmonic ranks with the Boston Symphony and the Philadelphia Orchestra as a passionate sponsor of American music.

Even Arturo Toscanini, so long apathetic to the work of our composers, has become receptive. In recent years, the appearance of an American work on one of his programs with the

NBC Orchestra—which had once been "news"—has become a frequent occurrence. Toscanini has not only given brilliant performances of works by Samuel Barber (whose cause he has cordially espoused), Morton Gould, Paul Creston, Elie Siegmeister, George Gershwin, Ferde Grofé, and many others, but he has even directed programs devoted exclusively to American music.

The National Music Council has conducted extensive surveys of the performance of American music by American composers. In 1939–1940, 126 native works were performed by 16 principal orchestras in America. In 1940–1941 there was a slight decline, but in 1941–1942 and 1942–1943 there were appreciable gains. About 11 per cent of the symphony programs of the leading American orchestras are today devoted to the works of our native composers.

A rather ingenious innovation was inaugurated by the conductor Artur Rodzinski in Cleveland, and was continued by him in New York. To every new score by an American that reaches him—whether Rodzinski likes the work or not—he gives a "reading" during rehearsals. A special committee is called upon to pass verdict on the work, which is presented anonymously. If the committee is impressed by the new work, the music is then officially introduced at a regular subscription concert. Once several members of a committee were particularly vituperative over one of the new works heard. One member, asked why he remained silent in the face of such bad music, replied: "Because I wrote it!"

When there is talent and originality, there are performances. William Schuman was virtually unknown not many years ago, but his Third Symphony was such a powerfully creative work that it was performed by most of the major orchestras in the country, and was singled out by the New York Music Critics'

Circle as the best new American work of the year. Schuman since then has been performed widely. A few seasons ago, another new work won a place on the programs of practically every major American orchestra: the *Jeremiah* Symphony. The composer was a young unknown, Leonard Bernstein. Composers of more established character—Roy Harris, Copland, Thompson, Samuel Barber, Gould, Piston, Quincy Porter (to mention only a few) surely have no reason to lament any lack of performances for their best work.

We have already seen how American music is encouraged over the radio. Not only are original works written expressly for radio use, but innumerable other works are here given their première performances. We have already noticed that modern American music is now widely distributed on phonograph records—music by Aaron Copland, Roy Harris, Samuel Barber, Paul White, Walter Piston, John Alden Carpenter, Deems Taylor, Colin McPhee, Bernard Rogers, Howard Hanson, Harl McDonald, Elie Siegmeister, and others too numerous to mention here. About one hundred modern American composers are generously represented by major works in the catalogues of both Victor and Columbia. Indeed, as this is being written, a new recording company, the Concert Hall Society, has come into being, which will place a great deal of emphasis on modern American music.

The American composer is further spurred on by prizes, scholarships, and commissions which rain down upon him in never-ceasing abundance like blessed manna. The Guggenheim, the Pulitzer, the American Academy in Rome scholarships have given many composers the necessary leisure in which to study and compose. A few years ago, Serge Koussevitzky put aside a sizable sum of money for a Koussevitzky Foundation which has commissioned numerous of our talented composers to write new works and the Ditson Fund has been established at Columbia University to finance new compositions.

Commissions also come to our composers from orchestras (the Boston Symphony, the Chicago Orchestra, the Dallas Symphony), from individual conductors (André Kostelanetz, Paul Whiteman), from artists (Jascha Heifetz, Bartlett and Robertson, Sigurd Rascher, etc.), as well as from organizations (League of Composers) and opera houses. Cash honorariums for distinctive musical works or for meritorious composers come from the American Academy of Arts and Letters, the Paderewski Foundation, the Elizabeth Sprague Coolidge Foundation, the Bearns Award, and the Gershwin Memorial Fund. Music of merit is published through funds established by the Juilliard and the Eastman School of Music.

The flattery of attention has, therefore, once and for all supplanted our former frigid indifference to the work of our composers. And under this attention the American composer is uniquely productive.

The financial interests of the American composer, so long neglected, have been furthered by one all-powerful organization. In 1913 Victor Herbert was eating at Shanley's Restaurant in New York when he heard the restaurant orchestra performing selections from his operetta *Sweethearts*. The realization that his works, as well as the works of so many other American composers less affluent than he, were being performed extensively without compensation spurred him to action. He took the matter to the courts, with the performance of *Sweethearts* music at Shanley's as his test case. For four years the litigation dragged on. Finally, from the United States Supreme Court came a decision in favor of Herbert. That decision might be said to have been the Emancipation Proclamation for the American Composer.

This fight convinced Herbert that the composers of America were in sad need of uniting into an organization which would fight for their interests. In 1914, together with Sousa, Witmark, Gene Buck, and a few others, Herbert organized the American Society of Composers, Authors, and Publishers (ASCAP) for the express purpose of protecting the copyright interests of everyone connected with music. A procedure was evolved (it is not necessary to describe here the many struggles, legal and other, which took place before it *was* evolved) whereby those organizations which used music were licensed to perform the work of ASCAP composers for a stipulated fee. The procedure was also followed in the case of the radio; a fixed annual sum was paid to ASCAP by each individual radio station (*not* by the networks) for the privilege of using ASCAP music.

Since ASCAP soon numbered among its membership every important composer of popular music, and many significant serious composers, those who needed the use of music were compelled to deal with this organization or be deprived of the use of the bulk of the repertoire of American popular and serious music. Of course, the largest representation in ASCAP is among composers of jazz. Of the thousand composers listed by ASCAP, some sixty-odd are serious composers, including such figures as Ernest Bloch, Howard Hanson, Roy Harris, Daniel Gregory Mason, Deems Taylor, Walter Damrosch, and Charles Wakefield Cadman. These serious composers are given a yearly stipend varying with their importance and the frequency with which their music is performed. A powerful agency was thus created to protect the financial interests of the composer, with branch offices in more than thirty American cities, and affiliations (until 1939) with similar organizations in twenty different countries of Europe.

In the fall of 1940, a bitter struggle between ASCAP and the

radio networks brought ASCAP to the attention of the entire
country. The five-year contract between ASCAP and the radio
stations of the country was expiring in 1940. Under that license
ASCAP had collected in 1939 $4,300,000 (about two-thirds of
its revenue) from radio. To renew the contract with radio,
ASCAP demanded an increase of fee which would bring the
income of ASCAP up to about $9,000,000. The networks re-
belled, cried that the fee was exorbitant, and—as a gesture of
defiance—created a rival organization of composers, Broadcast
Music, Incorporated (BMI), for the production of music to be
used over the air. In 1941 ASCAP music was removed from the
major networks and was replaced by the works of young and
unknown popular composers who affiliated themselves with
BMI, or by composers long dead whose works belonged in the
public domain.

In this bitter war of music, both sides stated their cases forcefully. Neville Miller, president of BMI, announced:

The current controversy between the broadcasting industry and
ASCAP has its origin in the $9,000,000 fees demanded by ASCAP for
1941. Broadcasters feel that the new terms, which represent an increase of more than 100% over the 1939 fees, are excessive and
unjust in that they charge programs which play no note of ASCAP
music. Accordingly the industry set up Broadcast Music Incorporated
as an independent source of music supply and made plans to do
without ASCAP music in 1941.

The official ASCAP rebuttal came from its general manager,
John G. Paine:

Their [the chains'] favorite wail is that ASCAP wants too much
money. As a matter of fact, the chains have never paid us a cent for
music, despite the fact that they make more money than the stations
do from broadcasting. They have let the individual stations pay the
entire cost—and they want the stations to keep doing it. Now, as far
as money is concerned, ASCAP doesn't get any unless the other fel-

lows get it first. Our license calls for payment on a percentage basis. In the established tradition of the show business we are willing to gamble with the station operators. When business is good, we share it. When business is bad, we take less—even though the stations use much more music to fill the greater amount of sustaining time. Let us next look at how much ASCAP actually gets for its music. Under our new license the biggest group of stations, about 350, will pay only $1 a month for all the music they use on sustaining programs—even if they use ten, twelve or more hours of such music a day—and 3% of their net receipts on sponsored shows. That means if a station has net time sales of $300 a day, ASCAP gets $9. And this $9 must be divided among more than 43,000 composers, authors, and publishers, here and abroad. For that $9 a day, the station has nearly all of the world's best composers working for it. All their works—past, present, and future—are included in the license agreement. How can a station get its music requirements any cheaper than that?

The fight was long and bitter. Finally, on October 30, 1941, ASCAP yielded ground. An agreement was reached which was a total victory for the radio forces. The new contract, which ran for five years, and was then renewed, brought ASCAP a smaller income than it earned in 1940. It is estimated that under the new terms ASCAP earned only $3,000,000 a year, which is a little more than half of what it earned in 1940, and about a third of its original demand for 1941. Worse still, from the ASCAP point of view, a formidable rival organization had been set up, BMI. However, though there is no question that the ASCAP defeat was decisive, it was still a major force in American music, and one which continues to work for the financial interests of the American composer.

Since ASCAP did not cover performances by symphony orchestras, opera houses, or choral societies (having its major interest in popular music, it concerns itself with radio, theaters, restaurants, and hotels) a new organization was evolved in 1938 to protect serious American composers. The American

Composers Alliance grouped under its banner virtually every major American composer. Its primary aim was to supplement the work of ASCAP by drawing up the composer's contracts, collecting his royalties from performances by leading serious-music organizations, and in general keeping a vigilant eye on his business interests. But the alliance is even more than a business organization. It is also a force for the furtherance of American music by sponsoring competitions among composers, encouraging the performance of new music, and publicizing the more gifted composers.

It is not our aim to discuss the evolution of the American composer; this has been done frequently and thoroughly. But to give our story completeness we must at least look at the recent development of American music as a creative force. After World War I, the American composer came into his own as a creative artist. He had greater self-assurance, a greater command of his technical equipment. Above everything else, he was less inclined to imitate styles and idioms in fashion in Europe.

There were talented composers in America before 1920, and some of them aspired to the writing of American music. However, an entire school—or, more accurately, several schools—of composers, writing in different styles and with different materials but achieving authentic native musical expression, is virtually a present-day realization. If our composers are no longer afraid to use forms handed down by tradition, they are also ready to pour into these forms the spirit and soul of America. There is more than one way to speak of America in music. Before 1920 composers tried to do this by employing the Negro Spiritual as an idiom, or by borrowing Indian themes. This was good as far as it went, but, unfortunately, it did not go far enough. America was much more than the aboriginal Indian, or the Negro. American music, to be truly expressive of the country at large, required a larger canvas than this. After 1920 many different styles entered into the music of American composers. Some composers wrote music of the utmost objectiveness and purity, while others preferred programmatic music. Some composers were experimental and modern, others were ultraconservative. Some composers were strictly classical, others dabbled in jazz, while still others drew their melodic material from native folk-music. Though, at first, these many styles seemed to suggest confusion, we realize today that actually there is a unity in this chaos. American music is as many-colored, as many-sided, as America's population. American music is the Jewish music of a Bloch, the jazz music of a Gershwin, the futuristic music of a Charles Ives, the romantic music of a Howard Hanson, the proletarian music of a Marc Blitzstein, the folk music of a Copland.

There can be no denying the American character of most of the music produced by the more gifted composers in our country today. It differs sharply in spirit and context from anything that has been imported from Europe during the past decade. Whether it is a symphony by Roy Harris, an opera by Louis Gruenberg, a chamber-music work by Quincy Porter or Walter Piston, a concerto by Samuel Barber, a song by George Gershwin, or a choral work by Vladimir Dukelsky, it is an American product, easily recognizable as such. Thus, a vigorous music has arisen in America, and at its best this music can stand with dignity and self-respect beside the most important works produced by other composers elsewhere.

American opera has also achieved greater significance. During the early years of the Gatti-Casazza régime, his encouragement of American opera produced several works in an Indian idiom: *Natoma* by Victor Herbert (1911), *Mona* by Horatio T. Parker (1911), *Shanewis* by Charles Wakefield Cadman (1918).

Together with these there were heard a variety of other operas, not particularly American either in the subject of the libretto or in the idiom of the music, such as Walter Damrosch's *Cyrano de Bergerac* (1913); Hadley's *Cleopatra's Night* (1918), and Reginald de Koven's *The Canterbury Pilgrims* (1917).

Beginning with the 1920's there was a mounting interest in operas by American composers. The world première of Deems Taylor's *The King's Henchman* at the Metropolitan in 1927 was a brilliant event; and there were many critics who regarded this as the most artistically satisfying opera to have been written by an American. *The King's Henchman* was followed by performances throughout America of other operas, some of them utilizing an American background and an American musical style successfully for the first time. Principal among these were Deems Taylor's *Peter Ibbetson* (1930), Louis Gruenberg's *The Emperor Jones* (1932), Howard Hanson's *Merry Mount* (1934), Virgil Thomson's *Four Saints in Three Acts* (1934), George Antheil's *Helen Retires* (1934), Robert Russell Bennett's *Malibran* (1935), George Gershwin's *Porgy and Bess* (1936), Douglas Moore's *The Devil and Daniel Webster* (1939), Walter Damrosch's *The Man Without a Country* (1939), Vittorio Giannini's *Blennerhasset* (1940), Gian-Carlo Menotti's *Amelia Goes to the Ball* (1937), *The Old Maid and the Thief* (1938)—written on a commission by the National Broadcasting Company—*The Island God* (1942), and *The Medium* (1946), Ernst Bacon's *A Tree on the Plains* (1942), and Bernard Rogers's *The Warrior* (1946).

These operas made certain conclusions about American opera self-evident. American opera is most satisfying as an artistic product, and it is most warmly welcomed by audiences, when it is entirely American—in other words, when libretto and music are both intimately allied with American experiences. The most artistically satisfying American opera to have been written so far, at least in the opinion of many discriminating critics, is Gruenberg's *The Emperor Jones.* And the works which, for all their structural or artistic shortcomings, most strongly suggest what the nature and character of the great American opera will be when it finally bursts upon us are George Gershwin's *Porgy and Bess* and Virgil Thomson's *Four Saints in Three Acts.*

Gershwin's *Porgy and Bess* brings to mind another important artistic trend in America since the 1920's—the serious consideration given to American popular music. Previously, the American who visited the concert hall looked rather contemptuously on the popular idiom of ragtime or jazz. But some farsighted critics and writers recognized, even before 1920, that jazz had musical value, that if properly exploited it could become the basis for a powerful and original native musical expression. "I like to think," wrote Hiram Motherwell in 1917, "that ragtime is the perfect expression of the American city, with its bustle and motion, its multitude of unrelated details, and its underlying rhythmic progress towards a vague somewhere. . . . This is American. Ragtime, I believe, expresses it. It is today the one true American music."

The pioneer American-music concert launched by Paul Whiteman at Aeolian Hall in 1924 was the first significant gesture to bring artistic respectability to jazz. George Gershwin's *Rhapsody in Blue,* which was introduced at that concert, was the first successful attempt by an American composer to use jazz in a large symphonic form, thereby suggesting the artistic possibilities of the popular idiom. The ground was broken. One year later, jazz entered a serious symphonic program when the New York Symphony under Walter Damrosch introduced

Gershwin's jazz *Concerto in F*, with the composer as soloist. At the time of the presentation of the Gershwin concerto, Damrosch commented:

Various composers have been walking around jazz like a cat around a plate of hot soup, waiting for it to cool off so that they could enjoy it without burning their tongues, hitherto accustomed only to the more tepid liquid distilled by cooks of the classical school. Lady Jazz, adorned with her intriguing rhythms, has danced her way around the world. . . . But for all her travels and her sweeping popularity she has encountered no knight who could lift her to a level that would enable her to be received as a respectable member in musical circles. George Gershwin seems to have accomplished this miracle. He has done it boldly by dressing this extremely independent and up-to-date young lady in the classic garb of a concerto. Yet he has not detracted one whit from her fascinating personality. He is the Prince who has taken Cinderella by the hand and openly proclaimed her a princess to the astonished world, no doubt to the fury of her envious sisters.

Thereafter jazz ceased to be an ugly stepchild of music. Serious composers borrowed the vitality and voluptuousness of its idiom for the expression of American rhythm: Aaron Copland, Werner Janssen, Robert Russell Bennett, John Alden Carpenter in America; Stravinsky, Ravel, Křenek, Kurt Weill in Europe. The American music lover began to listen to it seriously and to recognize its aesthetic value. Jazz not only entered the symphony hall but the opera house as well: *Skyscrapers*, a ballet, came to the Metropolitan Opera House, while Gershwin's *Porgy and Bess* was produced by the Theatre Guild. Not only jazz worked into the larger forms but good jazz itself acquired respect; for the first time interest was aroused in the rhythmic ingenuity, melodic freshness, and dynamic drive of the best popular works. Jazz was adopted by many lovers of serious music as an expression worthy of respect and cultivation. The

American popular song, at its best—and it has reached its best with Irving Berlin, Jerome Kern, Richard Rodgers, George Gershwin, Cole Porter, etc.—is artistically significant. And the American musical-comedy, when it achieves the distinction of Jerome Kern's *Show Boat* or Richard Rodgers's· *Oklahoma,* is a distinguished example of our native art.

And, to my way of thinking, all this is an important step forward, too.

Still another manifestation of our musical growth is our increased consciousness of and interest in our own folk music. About two decades ago, American folk music was an esoteric subject for the scholar and sociologist—for people like John A. Lomax, Cecil Sharp, Franz Rickaby, E. Lincott, P. E. Barry, Dorothy Scarborough, and Jean Thomas, who poked into every corner of our country taking down melodies or recording them on phonograph discs. The enjoyment of this music was confined exclusively to the aesthete, the intellectual élite.

Today, however, folk music is more and more becoming entertainment for the masses. It is heard in the night clubs of New York, interpreted by Josh White, Tom Scott, Susan Reed. It is found in the theater (in the Theatre Guild production of *Sing Out, Sweet Land*), and even in moving pictures, in *Smoky,* with Burl Ives as the central figure. It is found in book form; indeed, a pocket edition of American folk-songs was distributed in drugstores and newsstands by the hundreds of thousands. It is heard on phonograph records, which are bought in fabulous numbers, and over the radio.

Obviously there is a vast audience for American folk music and American folk singers. Obviously, the everyday man has discovered that in this music there is variety of mood and sentiment, subtlety of nuance, and intensity of feeling, as well as originality, which make it stand with dignity alongside the best folk music of the rest of the world.

Though much of our folk music has outside origin—imported from other lands by immigrants from the Old World—it has become, by a subtle chemistry, intrinsically American, often transformed in intangible qualities by American experiences. Not only the mood and emotional quality of the songs changed, but even the melodic and rhythmic elements have been transformed—making new songs out of old, bringing to these age-old melodies an altogether new personality.

American folk music travels over a wide territory, as wide as the geography of America itself, as broad as its history. It is the songs of the Appalachian and Cumberland mountains—poignant, homespun ballads. It is the tunes the shantymen sang as they brought down the timber, and the tunes of sailors at their tasks on the sea. It is the windswept music that expresses the migration to and the opening of the West, the building of the railroad, the quest for gold in '49. It is the song of the cowboy, rallying his herd from Texas to the shipping point at Fort Dodge with nostalgic sentiments for home, a girl, peace, or his favorite horse. It is the plangent voice of the exploited coal miner. It is the fabulous folk-art of the Negro. It is, in short, an inextricable part of Americana, a treasure out of our historic past which is as much a record of the growth of our democracy as are history books and chronicles.

Our folk music has influenced our popular art immeasurably. There is no longer any question that jazz, blues, ragtime, Swing, boogie-woogie all have definitive roots in the Negro folk-song. Surely, too, there can be no question of the way in which the balladry of the Appalachian mountains inspired songs like Frank Loesser's *The Ballad of Roger Young,* or the eloquent background commentary which Earl Robinson composed for the motion-picture, *A Walk in the Sun*. Surely, too, the song of the cowboy can easily be identified in popular songs like *The Last Round-Up* or Cole Porter's *Don't Fence Me In*.

But our folk music has influenced serious music as well. More and more, our native composers recognize that they can project American atmospheres and backgrounds in their large works with authenticity and flavor through association with folk-lore elements. The mountain music of the Appalachians is echoed in Aaron Copland's highly successful and brilliant *An Appalachian Spring*, and that of the Ozarks gave Elie Siegmeister the source material for his admirable *Ozark Set*. Negro folk music—as well as "white" Spirituals—is the basis for Morton Gould's *Spirituals*, one of his best works, while another Gould composition owes its origin to cowboy music, the *Cowboy Rhapsody*. Our sailor chanteys helped Paul White write his *Sea Chantey*. Roy Harris—himself the composer of a major work based on folk-music idioms, *The Folk-Song Symphony*—put it well when he said: "If . . . folk songs stimulate him [the composer] to his best creative ingenuities, he may put the folk tune into a new form, serviceable to his people. He may find the material an esthetic chart which leads him to new riches. He may even enhance the beauty and scope of natural folk tunes, and in so doing learn to sense the inherent values of musical materials, follow the natural flow of creative form, to gather his creative thoughts into a homogeneous stream of musical continuity. For this is the basic creative process which all folk-song singers have achieved in short simple forms, and which all composers must master in more extended complex forms."

CHAPTER FOURTEEN

The Great Invasion

BEGINNING WITH 1933 and throughout World War II, an uninterrupted stream of great musicians flowed from harassed Europe to this country. Probably never before did such a formidable invasion of musical genius take place within little more than a decade. It began when the Nazis came to power in Germany and eliminated from its cultural (as well as political) life all influences which they judged to be undesirable to the "new order." A wholesale *Säuberung*— "cleansing"—took place. Germany's principal orchestras, opera houses, and conservatories were "Aryanized." Even the greatest of Germany's musicians were not exempt from this general purge. Bruno Walter's racial, Fritz Busch's political, and Hindemith's aesthetic backgrounds made these musicians (and hundreds of others like them) equally intolerable to the new masters. From Germany, therefore, fled the noblest of its musical spirits, not only those who were exiled but also many others who, though acceptable to the Nazi leaders, could not stomach the new regime. Composers, performers, scholars, teachers, critics escaped from their native land in hordes. And most of them came to America to find a new home.

From that time on, historical events in Europe kept mobile this flow of musical genius westward, across the ocean. Revolution broke out in Spain, spreading havoc and devastation. Nazi troops marched into Austria, and under their marching boots was trampled what had once been the greatest musical civilization in the world. Relentlessly, the Nazis set about their task of purging Austria of its undesirable musical influences. The bust of Mahler in the vestibule of the Opera House was destroyed. Jews and anti-Nazis were eliminated from every phase of Austrian musical activity. Once again a great exodus of musical genius took place: artists like Lotte Lehmann, Elisabeth Schumann, Erich Korngold, and Alexander von Zemlinsky severed their ties with Vienna once and for all and sought a new home in America.

Then the Nazis took Czechoslovakia. Italy, drawing closer to Germany, launched its own anti-Semitic program. Disturbances brought minor convulsions to the small Balkan countries, warnings of the volcanic eruption soon to come. Finally, the long-threatened, long-expected world war burst upon Europe and again set it aflame.

And so, musicians from every part of Europe—some of them leaders in their fields—poured into this country in ever-increasing numbers. Like the refugee émigrés of former periods, they came prepared to divorce themselves permanently from their former associations and allegiances. They wanted to become a part of us, to learn from us, to contribute the wealth of their genius to our cultural life. Most of them have applied for American citizenship.

This recent infiltration of foreign genius has been felt in every phase of our musical existence; and wherever it has been felt there has been enrichment, expansion, and growth.

Particularly in the fields of musical scholarship and musical education have we profited by this invasion of genius; America can well be said to harbor today the greatest musical minds of our time. Hardly a leading university or conservatory in this country is now without some distinguished European theoretician or teacher who is passing on his experience and wisdom to young and talented Americans. Hugo Leichtentritt, one of the finest musical scholars of Germany, was in the music department of Harvard University from 1933 to 1940, when he was retired on a pension. Leichtentritt has already produced in this country and in English several admirable scholarly works on music. Nadia Boulanger, one of the most trenchant musical minds of our time, was a member of the Wellesley College faculty; Karl Geiringer is at Boston College; Curt Sachs and Hans T. David are at New York University; Alfred Einstein is at Smith College. Besides these distinguished scholars, some of Europe's outstanding composers found a haven in our colleges and universities. Academic seats have been held in this country by Igor Stravinsky (Harvard University), Béla Bartók (Columbia University), Arnold Schönberg (U.S.C., Los Angeles, California), Ernst Křenek (Vassar College and Hamlin University), Darius Milhaud (Mills College), and Paul Hindemith (Yale University).

Some of the most gifted of Europe's modern composers are also permanently established in this country, writing works for our musical organizations, our theaters, the radio, and motion pictures. A few have been mentioned in the preceding paragraph. To these might be added Ernst Toch, Martinů, Jaromir Weinberger, Kurt Weill, and Castelnuovo-Tedesco. Undoubtedly these composers were influenced by the new life about them; undoubtedly, also, they have done a great deal of influencing in their own right. Their presence here has been strongly felt.

It is not necessary to mention all the great conductors, singers, and virtuosos, who have been transferred from their native countries to this one in recent years. Too numerous to be catalogued here, they include such eminent artists as Toscanini, Bruno Walter, Désiré Defauw, Fritz Busch, Lotte Lehmann, Rudolf Serkin, Adolf Busch, Elisabeth Schumann, Alexander Kipnis, George Szell, Wanda Landowska, Robert Casadesus, and many, many others. Our orchestras and opera houses have profited immeasurably by these artists. And our concert halls have become more active than ever before.

Through this transplantation of European musical genius to this country, we have taken one more prodigious step in our development as a musical country. Who knows?—perhaps it may even prove to be the most important step of all. Fascism sucked Europe dry of its genius and, by doing so, has rendered us a service for which we can never be sufficiently grateful. It is not beyond the realm of possibility that the musical historian of tomorrow—in surveying our present turbulent era—will point to this recent influx of musical genius into this country as the final stage in the transformation of America into the musical capital of the world.

CHAPTER FIFTEEN

A Final Word or Two

I HAVE THUS FAR stressed the brighter colors of our picture. A concatenation of forces during the past few decades—not the least of which were two global wars—has made ours the greatest musical country in the world, whatever point of view one may adopt. It is certain that we shall maintain that position for a long time to come.

Yet our picture would not be complete if, in conclusion, I did not bring to light some of the less agreeable colors. We have gone far—and in an astonishingly brief period. But (let us make no mistake about it!) we have still much farther to go.

We could, for example, practice a greater generosity toward American composers. I have pointed out that American composers are achieving recognition with an unprecedented number of performances of their works. But it is still impossible for even the best of our serious composers to acquire a livelihood exclusively from their compositions. Public performances of American works frequently pay nothing (recitalists, chamber-music groups, smaller orchestral and choral societies never pay for the right to play an American work). When payment *is* made—by the leading orchestras and opera houses—the fee is niggardly. An orchestral budget of approximately $600,000 will allot about ½ per cent as royalties to modern composers. Translated into other figures, this means that the performance of an orchestral work by a major symphony orchestra brings the composer between $20 and $50; if this work has previously been published, this sum must be divided between publisher and composer. A major opera house will pay about $100 for each performance of a work by an American, frequently less than that.

A friend of mine, for example, wrote a large symphonic work which took him three years to prepare. It was accepted for performance by the New York Philharmonic—which, from the point of view of recognition, is possibly the equivalent of a Broadway production of a play by a young dramatist. His work, since it was performed on a Sunday afternoon, was also broadcast throughout the country over the Columbia network. His total earning from this work was $75. But he had expended about $250 for the copying out of the parts for the orchestra and for other incidental expenses connected with the performance. Thus the success of having one of the great orchestras of the world play his large work netted the composer a loss of $175.

This, unfortunately, is by no means an isolated example. Daniel Gregory Mason has told in his autobiography what extraordinary success was enjoyed by his Second Symphony. Within a short period it was performed by many of the leading orchestras in America—including the Chicago Symphony under Stock, the Cincinnati Symphony under Reiner, and the New York Philharmonic under Bruno Walter. His total earnings from royalties were $175. His expenses were $395. The net result of an unusually successful American work was, therefore, a loss of $220.

What greater recognition can come to an American composer than to have an opera of his performed by the Metropolitan

Opera House? Louis Gruenberg was such a successful composer, and his opera, *The Emperor Jones,* was sufficiently appealing to warrant eleven performances. From these eleven performances Gruenberg earned about $1,000 in royalties.

Such a situation makes it physically impossible for a composer, however brilliant or successful he may be, to devote all his time to creation. Most composers earn their living by teaching—either privately or in music schools or colleges. In this class are such outstanding composers as Roy Harris, Ernest Bloch, Carl Ruggles, Walter Piston, Quincy Porter, Ernst Bacon, Douglas Moore, and numerous others. Aaron Copland, besides teaching, also writes and lectures. Virgil Thomson is a music critic. Deems Taylor holds a post with an important advertising firm, and fills radio contracts. Morton Gould and Robert Russell Bennett also work for the radio. Vladimir Dukelsky and Meredith Willson write popular songs. Louis Gruenberg, Werner Janssen, and Richard Hagemann work for the movies. Lazare Saminsky is a choirmaster. Charles Ives was an insurance man.

In no other field of artistic endeavor is this situation duplicated. The successful and gifted novelist, dramatist, critic, sculptor, painter can expect a sizable income from his most serious endeavors once he has achieved the necessary recognition. But the serious composer must through necessity scatter his energy and diffuse his efforts by spending innumerable hours in teaching, lecturing, hack work, and other such occupations in order to acquire the sheer necessities of comfortable living. Creation he must relegate to hours stolen from his many other activities. It is a luxury in which he can indulge once he has done the other things that earn him his bread. Such a situation is not likely to elicit the best results, either in quality or in quantity, from any composer. There can be no question that American music has suffered in consequence.

We do not make the best possible use of the enormous supply of musical talent at our disposal. We are, for the most part, as ungenerous to the talented musical performer as we are to the great composer—though in this direction there are notable exceptions. The hallowed great of the concert hall—the Toscaninis, Heifetzes, Horowitzes, Kreislers, Menuhins—are, of course, paid fabulously for their performances. Each of these artists can gross from a quarter to a half million dollars a year from his concert and radio activities. But for most musicians of lesser stature—and splendid musicians!—the concert world is a losing battle. We may have wonderful agencies for educating our musically talented young people and giving them a comprehensive preparation for a professional career. But once we have trained them, we seem to remain sublimely indifferent to their art if they are not in the very front rank. Our concert life seems to have room only for immortals.

The truth is that failure on the concert platform is not always the result of incompetence. Even if a musician is a fine artist, with sensibility, taste, and culture, it is questionable if he can make a living through his art. Albert Spalding once said it took him almost twenty years of supposedly successful concert work before he could derive a profit from his concerts; and Spalding, during most of those years, was recognized everywhere as America's greatest violinist. It is a well-known fact that there are artists of world-wide reputation—artists who have repeatedly received the acclaim of critics—who draw little or no profit from their concerts. A friend of mine, a remarkably gifted pianist—often praised cordially by the critics—once said that he would trade his gifts and his reputation for the income of a successful bookkeeper!

With the concert stage unprofitable for the young artist who is not in the front rank, there remains the chance of a desirable post in a leading orchestra. The demand for musicians among symphony orchestras is, however, limited and fails to absorb even a fraction of the prodigies who enter the professional class. At the beginning of the 1945–1946 symphony season there were fewer than fifty openings among all of the important symphony orchestras in this country.

To play in a symphony orchestra is not quite so desirable a goal as might appear at first glance. Artistically it promises small satisfaction. The young musician becomes a cog of a machine, losing his individuality and creative urge. But even financially there is small reward. Except for the first-desk men— and these positions are few and far between—the orchestra men barely earn a respectable salary. A violinist in one of our major orchestras draws about $125 a week. This is very good, indeed. But there is one drawback. Since the symphony season consists of no more than twenty-four weeks or so, his salary for the year is really $60 a week unless he plays in summer concerts.

But, as I have said, posts with sympony orchestras are limited in number. Where else can the young musician turn for a livelihood? The radio, of course, is in the market for musicians—but it is not a particularly rich market. The average network seldom has more than one full-sized orchestra to fulfill all its musical needs. Radio positions are few and far between.

To what, then, can the young musician turn? The final answer, I suppose, is teaching. But even here the opportunities are scarce. The leading conservatories which can afford to pay excellent salaries employ mostly famous concert artists. With a position at a conservatory denied him, the talented young musician is left with only one avenue: he opens a studio in his neighborhood, charges three dollars a lesson, and hopes that enough pupils will study under him to enable him to earn a respectable living. But a respectable living is not the usual lot of the private music teacher. There are, it is estimated, no fewer than eighty thousand music teachers in the country who have an average of ten pupils each and more than a hundred thousand teachers who have fewer than that number of pupils. Ten pupils or fewer must spell, for the music teacher, continued struggle.

Music may be a billion-dollar industry in this country, but the paradox is that in this billion-dollar industry the one who makes the music is the one who, generally, derives the smallest profit. Still another paradox exists: While there is an abundance of excellent artists who find it difficult to make their way, there are also innumerable communities and universities that are starved for good concerts. These communities, which cannot afford the price for a Heifetz or a Horowitz, could use the services of concert artists of lesser stature who nevertheless come bringing with them great music in intelligent and sensitive performances. What is needed in this country is an agency that will promote concerts of good music in smaller and less affluent communities. America is much more than New York, Chicago, and San Francisco. By creating an active concert life in small towns and cities—and at prices of admission that everyone can afford—we shall not only effect a limitless expansion of our concert horizon, but we shall also provide work and a decent livelihood for every good artist.

Perhaps the most practical solution of this problem can be provided by the Government. Government sponsorship of music is a sadly needed development if America is to expand musically to its fullest potentialities. It is well known that no great orches-

tra or opera house can be self-supporting. Why should great
music be dependent on public charity, or on the beneficence of
a few public-spirited millionaires? The Federal Music Project,
when it functioned with full force, proved how powerful Gov-
ernment-sponsored music projects could be in the spreading of
good music. When music was made accessible to the masses at
reasonable prices, the public did not ask for great performers or
world-famous conductors; it was satisfied with good renditions
of musical masterpieces. Never before in the history of concert
music had there been such prodigious audiences as those that
attended the performances of the Federal Music Project
throughout the country. And never before had so many musicians found permanent employment for their talent.

From time to time there has been talk of the creation of a
Federal Bureau of Fine Arts which would sponsor performances of great music everywhere. Thus far this ideal has not
been realized. But it *should* come. We shall then have opera
houses not only in two or three key cities but in most of the
smaller cities as well. We shall have not a hundred but a thousand large symphony orchestras. We shall have an active concert
life—recitals, chamber-music concerts, choral performances—
wherever there is an audience for it. We shall, in short, have a
place and a function for every talented musician.

Government subsidy was long ago accepted in Europe as a
civic necessity. The time should come when it will also be accepted in this country. We shall then not only have solved the
problem of the artist, but we shall also have done ourselves a
permanent service. Then, truly, will America be a country of
music lovers and music making—perhaps the greatest of its kind
the world has ever known.

"I cannot be too optimistic about anything concerning

America, and particularly about its music." So wrote the ex-Czech composer Jaromir Weinberger in a personal communication to me. No doubt the future belongs to us. We shall grow musically in more and more directions as time passes.

I should like to see development in a few other directions than those discussed in the preceding pages. I should like, for example, to see the emergence of a more dynamic form of music criticism in this country. Our music criticism has, thus far, been too much in the nature of newspaper reporting. It should be more creative than that. It should fill a much more vital need than the mere recording of the essential facts about each concert. Music criticism should fulfill its highest role, that of serving as a link between composer and performer and their audiences. It should educate audiences to a finer and more sensitive understanding of great music. At the same time it should serve as the guide for the artist, as his teacher and counselor. Our critics—the best of them at any rate—have the equipment and gifts to fulfill such a function; what they lack most is the proper facilities. They should not be made to attend a concert every day, sometimes two a day; that task should be relegated to well-equipped subordinates. Our principal critics should be concerned only with a few important performances a week—particularly those of new works. More than this, I should like to see each critic have the time in which to study each new score (or attend several rehearsals) before he attempts to discuss a new work performed for the first time.

What is probably the first important step in making music criticism in America a more dynamic and cogent force was taken in the formation of the Music Critics' Circle, headed by Virgil Thomson. The leading New York music critics are thus banded together to select each season the leading new American works.

I should like to see opera performed in the English language throughout the country. But before this is attempted, I should like to see opera librettos rewritten in English by qualified dramatists and poets, retaining the original text but bringing to it modernity and freshness of diction and viewpoint. Opera will become a more personal experience to the everyday music lover when it is presented to him in a language he understands. Experiments have been made in this direction, principally by smaller opera groups. In an informal survey conducted by Mrs. John DeWitt Peltz for the National Committee for American Opera, it was disclosed that while the major organizations prefer to present an opera in its original language, there were in one year (1940) seventy-two different operas produced in English throughout the country. The most significant and successful experiment in this direction was the presentation of Smetana's *The Bartered Bride* at the Metropolitan Opera House, which proved once and for all how zestfully audiences react to opera when they understand what is being said and done. In its revival of *The Magic Flute* for the 1941–1942 season, the Metropolitan Opera decided to present it in English—incidentally, at the express wish of the conductor, Bruno Walter, who wished the audiences to be aware of the amusing proceedings on the stage. Beethoven's *Fidelio* and Mozart's *The Abduction from the Seraglio* have also been presented in English. These are the beginnings of a movement that should spread throughout our opera world. Opera, after all, has been performed in French in France; and in German in Germany. There is no reason why in this country it should not be presented more generally in our own language.

I should like to see the birth of a music festival in this country that would truly approximate to Salzburg's. Thus far not even the Berkshire Festival is a realization in this country of what Salzburg once was in Europe. In one respect, and in one respect alone, it will not be possible to duplicate Salzburg in America. It is obvious that a setting so imbued with musical associations, so drenched with historic glamour as Salzburg is, is not to be found in this country. Except for this, America could easily duplicate—and possibly surpass—anything that has been done in Salzburg. Never before was there in one single country such an assemblage of musical genius as there is in America today. Why not gather together some of these wonderful elements— singers, conductors, performers, stage directors, scenic design- ers, orchestras, choruses, chamber-music ensembles—into the coherent and integrated pattern of a summer festival which could easily become the artistic center of the world?

The idea of an American Salzburg suggests succulent possi- bilities. Imagine a music festival in which the orchestra is not the Vienna Philharmonic but a magnificent organization like the Boston Symphony, the New York Philharmonic, or the Phila- delphia Orchestra. Imagine an orchestra such as this conducted not by any one man continuously but by a series of major con- ductors including Toscanini, Koussevitzky, Stokowski, Bruno Walter, Rodzinski—performing great symphonic music, and ac- companying our great opera stars in cycles of operas by Wagner, Mozart, Verdi, or Richard Strauss. Imagine choral performances of music by Palestrina, Bach, Mozart, Handel in which the voices of the Schola Cantorum or Robert Shaw's Collegiate Chorale are joined with the rich orchestral texture of the New York Philharmonic conducted by Toscanini. Imagine programs of modern music directed by Stokowski, Koussevitzky, or Rodzinski. Imagine cycles of chamber music (perhaps in the open air) by an organization like the Budapest String Quartet.

Imagine these things, and you have but a suggestion of what could be accomplished in America with the proper organization and initiative.

The musical lights in this country are burning brighter than ever. The frank admission that they *can* be made still more brilliant is no proof of failure to appreciate their present brightness. If the future of music rests in our hands, we must be true to our responsibility by displaying courage and imagination, wisdom and resourcefulness. What we have already accomplished should be merely the inspiration for further and more ambitious achievements. After all, to be the musical capital of the world carries with it not only a blessing but an obligation.

Bibliography

MOST OF the material for this book was acquired from magazines and newspapers. American music magazines such as *Dwight's Journal of Music, Music, Musical America, Musical Courier,* and *The Musical World and New York Musical Times* were indispensable sources of information about America's musical yesterday. Equally valuable were the files of the New York *Times,* and *The Literary Digest.* Other American music magazines, such as *Etude, Modern Music, Musical Standard, Musical Quarterly,* and *Musician,* were combed for articles of American interest and provided some useful data. Occasionally, though not very often, significant material was furnished by general American publications such as *Pictorial Review, Readers' Digest, Time,* and *The Saturday Evening Post.*

Books about American music are not plentiful and—except for those published within the past two decades—not very useful. Among the books consulted were the following:

Aldrich, Richard. *Concert Life in New York,* 1902–1923. Charles Scribner's. 1941.
Arditi, Luigi. *My Reminiscences.* Dodd, Mead. 1896.
Barnabee, Henry Clay. *Reminiscences.* Chapple Company. 1913.

Bowen, Catherine Drinker. *Free Artist: The Story of Anton Rubinstein and his Brother.* Random House. 1939.

Clemens, Clara. *My Husband Gabrilowitsch.* Harper. 1938.

Damrosch, Walter. *My Musical Life.* Charles Scribner's. 1923.

Da Ponte, Lorenzo. *Memoirs.* Houghton Mifflin. 1929.

Elson, Louis. *The History of American Music.* Macmillan. 1904.

Farwell, Arthur. *Music in America.* The National Society of Music. 1915.

Finck, Henry T. *My Adventures in the Golden Age of Music.* Funk & Wagnalls. 1926 .

Franko, Sam. *Chords and Discords.* Viking Press. 1938.

Gaisberg, Frederick William. *The Music Goes Round.* Macmillan, 1942.

Gatti-Casazza, G. *Memories of the Opera.* Charles Scribner's. 1941.

Gipson, Richard M. *The Life of Emma Thursby.* New York Historical Society. 1940.

Gottschalk, L. M. *Notes of a Pianist.* J. B. Lippincott. 1881.

Grant, Margaret, and Hettinger, Herman S. *America's Symphony Orchestras.* W. W. Norton. 1940.

Heylbut, Rose, and Gerber, Aimé. *Backstage at the Opera.* Thomas Y. Crowell. 1937.

Howard, John Tasker. *Our American Music* (third edition). Thomas Y. Crowell. 1946.

—— *Our Contemporary Composers.* Thomas Y. Crowell. 1941.

Hubbard, W. L. *History of American Music.* Irving Squire. 1908.

Huneker, James G. *Steeplejack.* Charles Scribner's. 1921.

Kaufman, Helen L. *From Jehovah to Jazz.* Dodd, Mead. 1937.

Kaye, Joseph. *Victor Herbert.* G. Howard Watt. 1931.

Key, Pierre V. R. (with Bruno Zirato). *Enrico Caruso.* Little, Brown. 1922.

Kellogg, Clara L. *Memoirs of an American Prima Donna.* G. P. Putnam. 1913.

Kinscella, H. G. *Music in the Air.* Viking Press. 1934.

Klein, Herman. *Musicians and Mummers.* Cassell. 1925.

—— *The Reign of Patti.* Century. 1920.

—— *Unmusical New York.* John Lane & Co. 1910.

Kolodin, Irving. *The Metropolitan Opera House.* Oxford University Press. 1936.

Krehbiel, Henry E. *Chapters of Opera.* Henry Holt. 1908.

—— *More Chapters of Opera.* Henry Holt. 1919.

—— *The Philharmonic Society of New York.* Novello, Ewer & Co. 1892.

Lehmann, Lilli. *My Path Through Life.* G. P. Putnam's. 1914.

Leiser, Clara. *Jean de Reszke.* Minton, Balch. 1934.

Madeira, L. C. *Annals of Music in Philadelphia.* J. B. Lippincott. 1896.

Maretzek, Max. *Crotchets and Quavers.* 1855.

Mason, Daniel G. *The Dilemma of American Music.* Macmillan. 1928.

—— *Music in My Time.* Macmillan. 1938.

—— *Tune in America.* Alfred A. Knopf. 1931.

Mason, William. *Memories of a Musical Life.* Century. 1901.

Matthews, W. B. *A Hundred Years of Music in America.* G. L. Howe. 1889.

Milinowski, M. *Teresa Carreño.* Yale University Press. 1940.

Moore, Elizabeth C. *An Almanac for Music-Lovers.* Henry Holt. 1940.

Moore, Edward C. *Forty Years of Opera in Chicago.* Horace Liveright. 1930.

Moses, Montrose J. *Heinrich Conried.* Thomas Y. Crowell. 1916.

Paderewski, Ignace J. (with Mary Lawton). *The Paderewski Memoirs.* Charles Scribner's. 1938.

Perry, Bliss. *Life and Letters of Higginson.* Atlantic Monthly Press. 1921.

Phillips, Charles. *Paderewski.* Macmillan. 1934.

Riesemann, Oskar von. *Rachmaninoff's Recollections.* Macmillan. 1934.

Ritter, Frederic C. *Music in America.* Charles Scribner's. 1884.

Russell, Charles E. *Theodore Thomas and the American Orchestra.* Doubleday, Page. 1927.

Russell, Henry. *The Passing Show.* Little, Brown. 1926.

Samaroff-Stokowski, Olga. *An American Musician's Story.* W. W. Norton. 1939.

Slonimsky, Nicolas. *Music Since 1900.* W. W. Norton. 1937.

Sousa, John Philip. *Marching Along.* Hale, Cushman & Flint. 1928.
Upton, George P. *Musical Memories.* A. C. McClurg. 1908.
—— *Theodore Thomas: An Autobiography.* A. C. McClurg. 1905.
Van de Wall, William. *The Music of the People.* American Association for Adult Education. 1938.
Wagner, Charles L. *Seeing Stars.* G. P. Putnam's. 1940.
Who Is Who in Music. Lee Stern Press. 1940.

Index

Hatton (pianist), 5

Hauk, Minnie, 53

Hawthorne, Nathaniel, 221

Haydn, Joseph, 18, 23, 33–
34, 36, 43, 86, 162
The Creation, 18

Haywood, Frederick H., 163

Heifetz, Jascha, 172, 178,
198–99, 212, 217, 219, 238

Hempel, Frieda, 126

Henderson, W. J., 79, 105

Henschel, Georg, 159

Herbert, Victor, 70–71, 84,
86, 183, 193, 238–39,
243
Natoma, 243
Sweethearts, 238

Hérold, Louis, 193

Herrmann, Bernard, 189, 196

Hertz, Alfred, 109–10, 144

Herz, Henri, 6

Hickenlooper, Olga, *see* Samaroff-Stokowski

Higginson, Henry Lee, 30, 87,
127–31

High School of Music and
Art, New York 166–67

Hill, Edward Burlingame, 96

Hill, Ureli Corelli, 19–21

Hiller, Ferdinand, 15

Hindemith, Paul, 162, 250,
252

Hirschman, I. A., 157

Hob-in-the-Well, 48

Hofmann, Josef, 160, 217, 233

Hogan, V. L., 187

Hollander, Frederick, 195

Hollywood, Calif., 194–99,
203, 218
Bowl concerts, 213,
218

Home, Sweet Home, 12

Homer, Louise, 103, 109, 120,
171

Honegger, Arthur, 76, 194

House, Colonel, 125

Howard, John Tasker, 91

Hugo Kortschak Quartet, 155

Huguenots, Les (Meyer-
beer), 79

Humperdinck, Engelbert, 109,
118, 185
Hänsel und Gretel,
109, 185
Die Königskinder, 118

Huneker, James Gibbons, 46

Hutcheson, Ernest, 159

Ibert, Jacques, 194

Indianapolis, Ind., 214, 234
Symphony Orchestra,
234

Indy, Vincent d', 15, 90